Female
EXECUTIONS

FEMALE EXECUTIONS: Martyrs, Murderesses and Madwomen

This edition published in 2013 by Summersdale Publishers Ltd.

First published as LIPSTICK ON THE NOOSE by Summersdale Publishers in 2003.

Photo work by Chris Holmes Photography, Kendal, Cumbria

Summersdale Publishers Ltd
46 West Street
Chichester
West Sussex
PO19 1RP
UK

www.summersdale.com

Printed and bound in Great Britain

ISBN: 978-1-84953-493-2

Substantial discounts on bulk quantities of Summersdale books are available to corporations, professional associations and other organisations. For details contact Nicky Douglas by telephone: +44 (0) 1243 756902, fax: +44 (0) 1243 786300 or email: nicky@summersdale.com.

Female EXECUTIONS

Martyrs, Murderesses and Madwomen

GEOFFREY ABBOTT

summersdale

OTHER BOOKS BY THE AUTHOR

The Executioner Always Chops Twice: Ghastly Blunders on the Scaffold, Summersdale, 2002

A Beefeater's Grisly Guide to the Tower of London, Hendon, 2003

Ghosts of the Tower of London, Hendon, 1989

Great Escapes from the Tower of London, Hendon, 1998

Beefeaters of the Tower of London, Hendon, 1985

Tortures of the Tower of London, David & Charles, 1986

The Tower of London As It Was, Hendon, 1988

Lords of the Scaffold, Hale 1991/Dobby, 2001

Rack, Rope and Red-Hot Pincers, Headline, 1993 / Dobby, 2002

The Book of Execution, Headline, 1994

Family of Death: Six Generations of Executioners, Hale, 1995

Mysteries of the Tower of London, Hendon, 1998

The Who's Who of British Beheadings, Deutsch, 2000

Crowning Disasters: Mishaps at Coronations, Capall Bann, 2001

Regalia, Robbers and Royal Corpses, Capall Bann, 2002

Grave Disturbances: The Story of the Bodysnatchers, Capall Bann, 2003

William Calcraft, Executioner Extraordinaire!, Dobby, 2003

Grave Disturbances, the Story of the Body-Snatchers, Capall Bann, 2003

A Macabre Miscellany, Virgin, 2004

William Calcraft, Executioner Extraordinaire!, Eric Dobby, 2004

More Macabre Miscellany, Virgin, 2005

It's a Weird World, Virgin, 2006

Who's Buried Under Your Floor?, Eric Dobby, 2007

The Gruesome History of Old London Bridge, Eric Dobby, 2008

Plots and Punishments, Willow Bank, 2010

Crowning Disasters and Royal Corpses, Eric Dobby, 2011

Execution, Summersdale, 2012

ABOUT THE AUTHOR

Geoffrey Abbott served in the RAF for 35 years then became a 'Beefeater' at the Tower of London. He has written more than 24 books on torture and execution, has appeared in numerous TV documentaries as consultant or executioner and, by invitation, has written entries on torture and execution for the *Encyclopedia Britannica*. He once stood on the 'drop' trapdoors in the execution chamber of Barlinnie Prison, Glasgow (as a fact-finding author, not a convicted criminal!) and has also experienced having a noose placed around his neck by a professional hangman – the late Sydney Dernley, a man endowed with a great, if macabre, sense of humour! He lives in the Lake District and keeps his adrenaline flowing by piloting small, temperamental helicopters.

FOREWORD

Geoffrey Abbott is an enthusiast, a natural storyteller with a gift for resuscitating dead trifles. With inside information and access to the worst, he revels in shocking and enlightening.

He is an actor on a paperback stage relishing the role of narrator, star and epilogist. He defies you to leave his theatre until you have the player's last words haunting your mind.

As a visitor to all of Geoffrey's previous productions I heartily invite you to another triumph. Let the show begin!

Jeremy Beadle (1948–2008)

Jeremy Beadle was a keen student of true crime for many years. Before television beckoned he was a hugely successful tourist guide specialising in blood, sex and death. He won Celebrity Mastermind, *specialist subject London Capital Murder 1900–1940, was the host of international Jack the Ripper Conferences and amassed one of the finest true-crime libraries in Britain.*

To Michelle with thanks for her continued active encouragement, without which my pen is completely non-productive!

CONTENTS

INTRODUCTION

The Law, in its wisdom, did not differentiate between men and women when it came to passing sentence of death on those found guilty of capital offences, and so in these pages you will read how, in some countries, many women were first tortured on the rack, in the boots, by the bridle, the water torture or the thumbscrews. They were whipped and exposed to public humiliation in the pillory; they died by the rope, axe, and sword; by the electric chair, the gas chamber, the firing squad; by being pressed beneath heavy weights or boiled to death, by lethal injection or burned at the stake; by being drowned, or beheaded by the guillotine or Scottish Maiden. Nor, afterwards, were they all given a decent burial; some were dissected, others skinned to provide bizarre souvenirs.

A few, such as Margaret Clitheroe and Alice Lisle, were martyrs; some, such as Marie Brinvilliers and Mary Ann Cotton, were serial murderesses; others, like Elizabeth Barton and Mary MacLauchlan, were mentally unbalanced and, in more civilised times, would instead have been given the necessary psychiatric treatment.

Some executions were botched either by the executioners or by the equipment involved, yet despite the appalling ordeal they faced, some women were incredibly brave, some resigned to their fate; a few fought with the executioner, others were hysterical or in a state of collapse; some indeed were totally innocent, yet nevertheless were put to death.

But even the Law with all its sombre overtones has its lighter side, and so the cases are interspersed with quirky quotes.

MARTYRS, MURDERESSES AND MADWOMEN

A

Antoinette, Marie (France)

Nine long agonising months had passed since her husband King Louis XVI was beheaded by the guillotine, his execution ecstatically applauded by the revolutionary mob, and it was not until the dreaded day arrived, 16 October 1793, that the executioner Charles-Henri Sanson and his son Henri reported to the Conciergerie, the Paris prison, to collect Queen Marie Antoinette and convey her to the scaffold. In the vast room known as the 'Hall of the Dead' Marie awaited, guarded by two gendarmes. Nearby stood Bault, the turnkey, whose wife had provided their distinguished prisoner with a cup of chocolate and a bread roll.

FEMALE EXECUTIONS

As the two executioners entered, the Queen stood up. The Vicomte Charles Desfosses, who was present, later wrote: 'I had time to observe the details of the Queen's appearance and of her dress. She wore a white skirt with a black petticoat under it, a kind of white dressing-jacket, some narrow silk ribbon tied at the wrists, a plain white muslin fichu [a shawl or scarf] and a cap with a bit of black ribbon on it. Her hair was quite white; her face was pale, but there was a touch of red on the cheekbones; her eyes were bloodshot, and the lashes motionless and stiff.'

Charles-Henri and his son respectfully removed their hats. 'Gentlemen, I am ready,' she exclaimed, as the former started to explain the need to prepare her for the ordeal, and she turned slightly to display the back of her neck from where her hair had been cut away. 'That will do, I think?' she continued, and then held out her hands for him to secure.

Under strong guard the entourage was then escorted out of the building to where the tumbril, the horse-drawn cart, stood. Her hands being tied, the Queen allowed herself to be assisted into the vehicle, where she sat down facing forward on the plank that served as a bench. Charles-Henri, a man totally averse to the task of decapitating the aristocratic victims of the Revolution but realising that refusal would simply result in his being replaced by someone who would doubtless not hesitate to treat them with savage brutality, gently persuaded her to turn and sit facing the other way so that she would not see the guillotine until the very last moment.

The courtyard gates swung open, those on duty forcing the tumultuous, jeering crowd to give way as the cart lumbered out on the street. To prevent any attempt at a rescue, the route was lined with 30,000 armed soldiers, cannons also being positioned at all intersections, squares and bridges. Marie Antoinette ignored the screams of abuse from the massed spectators; instead she studied the numbers on the houses as the cart trundled along the Rue St Honoré, looking for a cleric, the Abbé du Puget, who had agreed to stand near a certain house and give her absolution *in extremis* as she passed. On seeing the prearranged sign from him as he stood on a pile of stones, she bent her head and prayed.

As the vehicle approached the scaffold site it halted near the Tuileries, the palace in which her two children had been imprisoned. For a moment she swayed, and Sanson heard her murmur 'My daughter! My children!' before the cart advanced, finally to halt by the scaffold. Once again she had to be assisted by Charles-Henri in order to dismount, and she looked round in surprise on hearing him whisper, 'Have courage, Madame!' She paused for a moment, then replied, 'Thank you, sir, thank you.'

As she approached the scaffold escorted by the two men, the younger executioner attempted to take her arm, but he desisted on hearing her exclaim, 'No; I am, thank Heaven, strong enough to walk that short distance.'

By that time the noise from the immense crowd had reached a crescendo, the tumult intensified by the drummers' successful

The execution of Marie Antoinette

efforts to drown any last words that might be spoken by the victim. Wasting no time, young Henri led the Queen forward and swiftly bound her to the upright hinged plank of the guillotine, the bascule. As he did so, she exclaimed: 'Farewell, my children, I am going to join your father.' Next moment the executioner swung the plank into the horizontal position so that she lay immediately beneath the pendant blade. The iron lunette dropped with a resounding clang, its half-moon shape pinning her neck immovable, and Charles-Henri operated the lever, causing the weighted blade to fall and sever the Queen's head instantly.

The sound of the blade's impact had scarcely ceased reverberating around the square before wild cheers, intermingled with cries of *'Vive la République!'* broke from the multitude of spectators, the roar increasing as one of the executioners complied with tradition by lifting the severed head from the basket into which it had fallen, holding it high for all to see. The gory trophy was then placed in the nearby coffin together with the body and carried to the cemetery of La Madeleine. There all the Queen's clothing was removed and taken away for disposal; her remains were covered with quicklime, the coffin then being buried next to that of her husband.

Following Marie Antoinette's execution, revolutionary Jacques Hebert exultantly wrote: 'All of you who have been oppressed by our former tyrants, you who mourn a father, a son, or a husband who has died for the Republic, take comfort, for you are avenged. I saw the head of the female fall into the sack. I could describe to you the satisfaction of the Sans-Culottes [his fellow agitators] when the rich tigress drove across Paris in the carriage with thirty-six doors [referring to the intervals between the staves that formed the sides of the tumbril]. She was not drawn by her beautiful white horses with their fine feathers and their grand harness, but a couple of nags were harnessed to Master Sanson's barouche [carriage] and apparently they were so glad to contribute to the deliverance of the Republic that they seemed anxious to gallop in order to reach the fatal spot more quickly. The jade, however, remained bold and insolent to the end. But her legs failed her as she got upon the see-saw [the bascule] to play hot cockles [the choking sound made by a victim as the lunette pressed their head down], in the fear, no doubt, of finding a more terrible punishment before her, after death, than the one she was about to endure. Her accursed head was at last separated from her crane-like neck, and the air was filled with cheers of victory for the Revolution!'

It may, perhaps, give readers some satisfaction to know that less than six months later, Hebert himself, his legs failing him, had to be lifted out of the tumbril, half-fainting with horror at the fate awaiting him; bound to the bascule, he too cried hot cockles before the blade descended!

Antonio, Anna (USA)

Sometimes the condemned person had to wait an unconscionable length of time before being executed, and one wonders whether it was due merely to a laborious judicial process or, more disquietingly, to a society which deliberately meted out retribution in that fashion. On occasion the delays were further exacerbated by the issue of a temporary reprieve or two; if so, Anna Antonio's crimes must surely have been the most horrific ever, for she was granted no fewer than three reprieves, with all the accompanying mental suffering and suspense – and then she was electrocuted.

She had been found guilty of conspiring with two men, Sam Faraci and Vincent Saetta, to kill her husband, who had been found murdered on Easter morning 1932, the court being convinced that her motive was to claim his life insurance money. All three were sentenced to death by electrocution, and although her lawyers submitted an appeal, it was rejected by a higher court.

Her execution was scheduled to take place in Sing Sing Prison at 11 p.m. on 28 June 1934. The executioner, Robert G. Elliott, a man renowned for his expertise, arrived, and after examining the electric chair and its associated circuitry, waited for the all-important official witnesses to arrive and take their places in the death chamber. But time passed and it was not until 1.15 a.m. that he was informed that just before 11 p.m., Saetta, also awaiting execution, had stated to the prison's warden that he and his accomplice Faraci had committed the murder, and Anna Antonio had had no part in it. On being notified of this, the State Governor had granted a 24-hour delay. When Anna was given this information, she was so overcome with relief at having escaped the death penalty that she fainted.

On reporting to the prison 24 hours later, the executioner was told that the postponement had been extended to a week.

Then further complications arose, another respite being granted in order to examine some recently discovered evidence. At that stage the mental state of the condemned woman can only be imagined; suffice it to say that her wardresses reported their prisoner's condition alternated between bouts of hysteria and collapsing into a semi-coma. Eventually the decision was issued that the executions would take place on 9 August and all hopes were dashed.

The decision to execute Mrs Antonio aroused much controversy nationally, many declaring it to be a grave miscarriage of justice in view of Saetta's statement exonerating her from involvement;

even Robert G. Elliott expected her sentence of death to be commuted to one of nominal imprisonment, but it was not to be.

On the fatal day the prison warden visited Anna in the condemned cell to hear her deny once more the charges against her, she pointing out that her husband was a drug dealer with guns in the house, giving her the opportunity to kill any time she had wished to. The two men, she went on, had told her they intended to kill her husband (probably for reneging on a drug deal) but all she had wanted to do was to safeguard her children. Then, utterly resigned to her fate, she walked calmly to the death chamber, rejecting all offers of assistance from her escort.

Seating herself in the electric chair, she trembled slightly as the straps were tightened about her, her voice shaking as she prayed with her priest, Father McCaffrey. Upon the cleric moving away, executioner Elliott positioned the electrodes on her head and leg and, returning to the control panel, immediately operated the switch. The official witnesses watched with mounting revulsion as the powerful current surged through her, causing her to jerk convulsively, faint tendrils of smoke rising from behind the mask which covered her face, the pungent smell of burning flesh filling the close confines of the room. Then, as her body slumped in the restraining straps and the hum of the current ceased, the doctor, stethoscope in hand, moved forward and confirmed her demise. And it was of little or no consolation to anyone that the executions of the actual murderers, Faraci and Saetta, then followed.

As it was considered that no reports of executions could possibly be complete without a description of how victims were dressed at the time of their deaths, the New York Times *satisfied their readers' insatiable*

curiosity by including the vital information that Anna Antonio 'wore a pink dress trimmed with a white collar, which she had made while in prison'.

Askew, Anne (England)

A third Tudor head, in addition to those of Anne Boleyn and Katherine Howard, could well have rolled across the scaffold boards on Tower Green; as it was, the one who actually died an appalling death was a commoner, Anne Askew.

That lady was a vehement Protestant, one of a group of friends who met and discussed religious matters with Queen Katherine Parr, Henry VIII's sixth wife. Such get-togethers were dangerous activities in a royal court riven with opposing factions, and the Queen's enemies were not slow in seeing such discussions as evidence of Katherine's heretical leanings towards Protestantism. This was reported to the authorities and a warrant for her arrest was drawn up, one which could have led to her being tried and executed, had it not been for negligence on the part of Chancellor Wriothesley who, en route to deliver the warrant to the King, dropped it in a corridor of Westminster Palace. Luck must have smiled on Katherine that day, for the missive was found by one of her servants, who handed it to her mistress. Aghast at its contents, she sought an audience with her husband and, by a show of affection, won him into such a forgiving mood that when Wriothesley reappeared with another warrant, he was greeted with an outburst of royal wrath and ordered out of the royal presence.

But any such luck had forsaken Anne Askew. The warrant for her arrest had reached its destination only too safely, and Anne was lodged first in Newgate Prison, and then, in June 1546, in the Tower of London, for, reasoned the plotters, the Queen could still be disposed of if evidence of her heretical leanings could be obtained from Anne Askew – and the Tower's inventory included a device guaranteed to extract the desired confession – the rack!

Anne was taken to the torture chamber in the White Tower. There, half underground, illuminated only by the flickering brands in wall sockets, she was first shown the persuasive instrument. At her obvious refusal to be frightened, Chancellor Wriothesley ordered that she should be secured to the device. Under the supervision of the rackmaster, the Yeoman Warders bound her wrists and ankles to the rollers at each end of the bed-like device, and as the levers were operated and the ropes creaked under tension, the questions were put – but not answered. Anne, strong-willed and stubborn, was determined to remain silent, despite the relentlessly increasing strain imposed on her leg joints, hips, shoulders and arms, but Wriothesley, thwarted in his initial attempt to bring about the downfall of Katherine Parr, was equally determined to wrest the secrets from his helpless prey. Furiously he urged the warders to continue turning the levers to increase the agonising pressure on the woman's limbs.

However, also present was the Lieutenant of the Tower, Sir Anthony Knivett. Aghast at the suffering being inflicted – for few, if any women had ever been racked before – he ordered his warders to release Anne, but on their obeying, Wriothesley and his cohort, Sir Richard Rich, seized the levers and started to apply even greater pressure. According to her later account quoted in *Foxe's Book of Martyrs* 'They did put me on the rack because I confessed to no ladies or gentlemen to be of my opinion [Protestantism] and therefore kept me a long time on it and because I lay still and did not cry out, my Lord Chancellor and Master Rich took pains to rack me with their own hands till I was nigh dead.' Her ordeal was also described by the historian Bale: 'So quietly and patiently praying to the Lord, she endured their tyranny till her bones and joints were almost plucked asunder.'

Although outranked by the two officers of the law, Sir Anthony exclaimed that he would go to Westminster immediately and report their brutal actions to the King; at that, Wriothesley, determined that he would get his explanation in first, left the chamber and, mounting his horse, set off at speed. But the Lieutenant had a trick up his sleeve for his official barge was moored on Tower Wharf – and travel via the river was infinitely quicker than through London's narrow huddled streets! Arriving at Westminster, Sir Anthony gained audience with Henry who, although he had not hesitated to have two of his wives beheaded, nevertheless was outraged at the idea of a woman being tortured in the manner described by the Tower officer, and he promptly ordered that it should cease forthwith.

Triumphantly Sir Anthony returned to the Tower and instructed his warders to release Anne from the machine, then summoned the Tower's surgeon to revive the half-fainting and semi-crippled victim.

Regardless of all the heroics and brave initiatives shown, however, there was no happy ending for Anne Askew. She was still a heretic and, charged with high treason by refusing to acknowledge the supremacy of the King as head of the church, and also declaring that if any fugitive priest asked her for sanctuary she would have granted the wish, she was sentenced to the punishment prescribed for those crimes. On 16 July 1546, unable to walk, she was carried to Smithfield strapped in a chair, where she was burned at the stake before a large crowd, hours passing before her remains were finally reduced to ashes.

 On execution days in London thousands of spectators would pack the streets around Smithfield, Tyburn or Tower Hill, many arriving the night before in order to get

the best positions near the scaffold or stake. Refreshment vendors would do a roaring trade, much ale being quaffed and many pies devoured. Broadsheets describing the crime and its perpetrator were peddled among the onlookers, and clerics exhorted the crowd to join in with hymns appropriate to the occasion.

In Texas on 3 February 1998, hundreds of spectators and scores of reporters from all over the world gathering outside a prison there, in which Karla Fay Tucker was executed for murder. The excitement was intense, snack bars did a roaring trade, pictures of the condemned person were displayed, prayers were said, hymns sung, and protesters raised their voices in condemnation of the verdict. Those who were unable to attend listened to the non-stop radio commentaries or watched the pictures unfolding live on their television screens. It seems that human nature doesn't change all that much.

Aurhaltin, Elizabeth (Germany)

Pretending to possess magical powers, one-legged Elizabeth Aurhaltin of Vielseck would visit houses and once inside would then collapse, professing to be ill or in convulsions. She would explain that she had a wise vein in her leg by which she could prophesy the future and even discover hidden treasure. Moreover, the pain in the vein would not cease until she had informed the inhabitants of the house of what she knew – for which she would expect to be suitably rewarded, of course. If they doubted her ability, she offered to prove it by being allowed to stay the night 'so that she could speak to the spirit of the treasure'. Once alone, she would then whisper questions and answers as if she was speaking to someone else; next morning she would explain that she had been conversing with a poor lost spirit who could not rest until the residents had dug for the buried gold. During the excavating, Fraulein Aurhaltin would 'discover' a jar of coals in the ground and promptly advise her hosts to lock it up securely in a chest for three weeks, after which they would find that it had turned into gold.

Time and again she repeated this fraud until the authorities finally arrested her. Investigation revealed that she had 4,000 florins in her possession. She was sentenced to be executed by the sword on 9 February 1598. Having only one leg, she had to be carried to the scaffold and secured in a chair to make sure she did not move as Master Franz Schmidt, the Public Executioner of Nuremburg, wielding the heavy double-handed sword, decapitated her.

Franz Schmidt's diary includes an entry for 6 August 1579, which describes how one Michael Dieterich of Pernetswin and two other robbers were taken to the scaffold to be beheaded. 'When they were being led out,' the diary reveals, 'Frau Dieterich wanted to see the poor sinners as they passed her house, and saw her own husband among them, whom she embraced and kissed, for she had not known her husband had been arrested, nor that he was a fellow of that sort.'

B

Balfour, Alison (Scotland)

In the sixteenth and seventeenth centuries torture was illegal in England – except by royal prerogative – but lawful in Scotland, much to the regret of those accused of heinous crimes. One of these was Alison Balfour 'a witch of repute' who, at the instigation of John Stewart, Master of Orkney, was, together with her servant Thomas Papley, charged with conspiring to poison the Master's brother, Patrick, Earl of Orkney.

In June 1596 she was subjected to the cashilaws, a version of the dreaded boots, iron footwear which were slowly heated up; these she had to keep on for 48 hours, while watching her 90-year-old husband undergoing *peine forte et dure*, being pressed under 700 lb of weights. So determined were the authorities to force her to confess to consorting with the Devil that her son was given 57 lashes of the whip and her seven-year-old daughter was subjected to the agonies of the thumbscrews.

Understandably Alison, undergoing such torture and having to watch her family suffering so appallingly, gave in and admitted the charge, but on being released from the cashilaws, promptly recanted her confession. It didn't help her though, for on 16 December 1596 they took her away and burned her as a witch.

It is recorded that on seeing the hangman waiting for her, Sarah Pledge, mentioned elsewhere, showed her distaste for him and swore that she'd rather go naked to the gallows than have him claim his perquisites and have her clothes. 'But,' quoth a contemporary chronicler, 'Jack Ketch soon deprived her of her life – and her clothes!'

Barfield, Margie Velma (USA)

Many women in all walks of life seek to achieve records of one kind or another, be they for long-distance running, climbing mountains,

Female prisoners taken to be tortured

or even numbers of years lived. But Margie Velma Barfield's achievement was one that, given the choice, she could well have done without; it certainly was not for longevity, on the contrary: she was the first woman to be executed by lethal injection.

Her misfortune was that, following a nervous breakdown, she became hooked on drugs, sleeping pills, tranquillisers, Librium and similar prescription pills, so dependent that she forged some of her husband's cheques to pay for her obsession and then, fearing that he would report her to the authorities, she poisoned him by adding rat-poison to his beer. Such was the solicitude she showed towards him during his last few doomed hours that his family not only acceded to her wish to have his gold wedding ring but also gave her four hundred dollars – which she promptly spent on more drugs to feed her addiction.

However, the symptoms of her husband's death alerted the authorities, the inevitable autopsy revealing the manner of death. Velma was arrested, and although at first she pleaded insanity, she later confessed not only to dispatching her husband, but also her own mother and an elderly couple she had once nursed, all for the same reason: drugs.

She spent six years in prison while lawyers fought her case on the grounds that she had been abused as a child and beaten by her husband. During that time she turned to the Bible for solace, but all pleas by religious leaders and others came to naught. Given the choice of death in the gas chamber or by lethal injection, she opted for the latter, and on 2 November 1984 this 52-year-old grandmother lay on the trolley in the execution chamber. Three syringes were attached to intravenous tubes, one carrying a saltwater solution. While the prison chaplain prayed with her, the other two syringes were pressed, only one of them passing the toxic contents into her body (the other was a dummy so that the operators would never know which of them had executed her). Within minutes she was dead.

In an attempt to compensate society for her guilt, Velma had donated her kidneys for transplant purposes, but severe difficulties then arose, for such organs could only be removed while the donor's blood was still circulating, and the only way to achieve that would be to inject a heart stimulant – but what if the victim then came back to life? She had already been declared dead, so could they legally execute her again? Finally it was decided to attempt removal of her organs in a hospital some distance away, and once in the ambulance doctors desperately tried to revive her by forcing oxygen into her lungs, and although at one time during the journey her cheeks showed a pinkish tinge, her heart failed to resume beating. But Velma's wish came partially true, for at the hospital her eyes were transplanted, giving blessed sight to another.

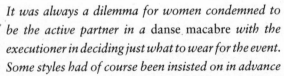

It was always a dilemma for women condemned to be the active partner in a danse macabre with the executioner in deciding just what to wear for the event. Some styles had of course been insisted on in advance by the relevant authorities: off-the-shoulder blouses were de rigeur for the guillotine, short-sleeved dresses mandatory for lethal injection, and an upswept hairstyle essential for the axe or the sword. Only minimal jewellery was permitted: if being hanged, necklaces were forbidden (other than the one provided and positioned by the hangman), as were pendant earrings, on the left ear lobe at least (the knot of the noose was always on the left); heavy bangles and sequinned frocks played havoc with the flow of the current in the electric chair, and there was little point in applying perfume prior to taking one's place in the gas chamber. So the choice was limited. Nevertheless, pink floral pyjamas worn with fuzzy pink slippers? That was what Margie Velma Barfield wore, after a last meal of Cheez

Doodles and a Coke, when, as described above, she was executed by lethal injection in the USA in 1984.

Barton, Elizabeth (England)

It was not unknown in the sixteenth century for people to have visions of the future, usually religious ones, and when the news spread that this 19-year-old maidservant had the ability to see into the future while in trance-like states, even such famous men of the day as Sir Thomas More and the Bishop of Rochester, William Fisher, took notice; indeed, so great was the latter's approbation that in 1527 he arranged for the 'Holy Maid of Kent', as she became known, to be admitted into the Benedictine Nunnery at Canterbury.

All would have been well and Elizabeth could have spent a cloistered life revered as one possessing second sight, but, imbued with religious fervour and inflamed by Henry VIII's action in divorcing Catherine of Aragon, she overstepped the mark by prophesying that the King would 'die a villain's death' within a month of marrying Anne Boleyn.

To Henry, renowned for reacting violently at such prognostications, this was not just the immature outburst of a hysterical woman – this was High Treason. And so it was that in June 1553 Elizabeth Barton was escorted under heavy guard to the Tower of London, and, after being subjected to some minor torture, was carried to St Paul's Cross where she performed public penance by having to repudiate her treasonable statements.

However, Catholic support for her continued to run high in the country, so high indeed that only by applying the proven Tudor recipe could the situation be resolved – by eliminating the source.

And so, on 20 April 1534, the Holy Maid of Kent was drawn to Tyburn and there hanged in front of the inevitably vast crowd. Unusually – and doubtless in order to publicise more widely the fate of such traitorous prophets – hanging was not considered sufficient; on the scaffold she was decapitated by the axe, her head then displayed on London Bridge, the only woman believed to have been so exhibited: 'its long black locks falling over its pallid features as a terrible warning to all.'

In 1643 at the Manorial Court in Bridlington, Yorkshire, the Lord of the Manor enquired why a certain Jane Key had not been brought before him. The constable explained that the sentence passed on her at the last sitting was that she should be whipped by him the full length of the High Street, but that before he could carry out the sentence the woman had met with an accident and had broken her neck. On hearing that an offender he had sentenced had not, for whatever reason, received the punishment handed down by the Court, the Lord started to rebuke the constable but desisted when the officer hastily pointed out that despite her accident he had not failed in his duties, adding, 'Every morning I rubbed her neck with neatsfoot oil, and then I whipped her as ordered!'

Bateman, Mary (England)

Starting her working life as a housemaid, Mary Bateman became ambitious and left her job to become a fortune-teller in Leeds, waxing prosperous on the fees and valuables she extorted from her more gullible clients and by providing young women with nostrums with which to bring about abortions. Obsessed by greed, the 41-year-old 'Yorkshire Witch' sold some 'magical' potions to a Mrs Perigo as a health cure, but they had the opposite effect and brought about the woman's death.

At her trial Mary Bateman was found guilty of murder, but when she was sentenced to be hanged, she 'pleaded her belly', i.e., claimed that she was pregnant. On hearing her say that, many women in the public gallery tried to leave the courtroom in order to avoid being inducted as a jury of matrons who would have to examine the prisoner and ascertain the truth or otherwise of her claim – much rested on such a verdict, for the law of the day stated that 'if the claimant be four and a half months advanced in that state, she shall not be executed until after giving birth'. But the judge ordered that the courtroom doors be locked, Mary then being escorted to another room where twelve women eventually pronounced that her claim was unfounded (although obviously she could have been in the earlier stages of pregnancy).

Her well-attended execution took place at York on 20 March 1809, many of the credulous spectators believing that she would employ her supernatural powers to vanish into thin air when the noose tightened; however, when it did, she didn't! Meanwhile, 23 miles away in Leeds, 2,500 residents had paid three pence each in admission charges to view the corpse on its return to the town; the crowds, entertained by jugglers and balladeers, supplied with food and drink by itinerant purveyors of pies and ale, waited more or less patiently.

At midnight the hearse finally arrived, the queues then lining up to file past the cadaver, after which it was taken to Leeds General Hospital for dissection. Not only did that medical institution benefit surgically by the invasive examination of her anatomy, but also financially, its coffers being enhanced by the proceeds from those who had viewed her external torso. As was customary, following dissection her corpse was skinned and after being scraped and tanned, was sold in small pieces as souvenirs to ghoulish-minded collectors.

In 1949 a case was brought in a London Court against a horse's owner and its trainer, alleging their negligence in that, on the horse leaving the unsaddling enclosure, it kicked the plaintiff on the head, she thereby sustaining a fractured skull. Some legal argument then arose regarding the correct way in which a horse should be led in order to prevent such an incident. The matter was resolved by the counsel for the defence who proceeded to borrow the stuffed head of a horse from a London shop, which dealt in harnesses, outside which the head was usually displayed.

Then followed the strange and doubtless unprecedented sight within the hallowed precincts of the court, of the counsel and the usher parading the stuffed head around the chamber, one carrying the head, the other controlling the steed as they demonstrated to the jury the manner in which it should have been done. This evidence, straight from the horse's mouth, proved conclusive, the case being settled in favour of the plaintiff.

Becherin, Ursula (Germany)

On 17 July 1582 Ursula Becherin of Hessdorf, an arsonist, burnt down a stall belonging to her master, a farmer, because people there were harsh to her. Later in the year she did the same to her new employer, and also stole clothing belonging to him and one of his workers, because, she said, in their opinion she could do nothing right. On the scaffold she stood upright while Franz Schmidt, the Nuremberg executioner, beheaded her with the sword, her body afterwards being burnt.

Barbara Ludtwigin, a barber's wife of Nuremberg, must have had a vocabulary to be envied, for she was charged with 'having blasphemed so horribly against the Almighty that a galley and two small ships besides could have been filled with her profanities.' A picturesque description indeed, and one that resulted in her being pilloried in the town square, a target for all, and then whipped out of town.

Benwell, Eliza (Australia)

There is a marked difference between 'seeing' and 'keeping watch', and this distinction was never more crucial than when Eliza Benwell was on trial for murder. Regrettably in her case, that difference, literally a matter of life or death, was fatally blurred.

In the days when English convicts were transported in prison ships to penal colonies on the other side of the world, many were then put to work on farms and large estates, some as house servants or members of hotel staff. On the arrival of one such ship in Hobart, Tasmania, four convicts, Thomas Gomm, Isaac Lockwood, William Taylor and Eliza Benwell, were employed in that city's Derwent Hotel, their various tasks being to attend to the general welfare of the guests. Among the visitors accommodated there in 1845 was a wealthy couple who had brought their own maid, Jane Saunders, with them. One evening, on being told to go to the hotel larder for some food for her employers, she went – but never returned. The entire premises were searched but no trace of the young woman was found until a few days later when a body, identified as hers, was discovered floating in the nearby River Derwent, stab wounds to the head and neck being indicative of a brutal murder.

Among the hotel staff on duty on the night of her disappearance were Taylor, Gomm, Lockwood and Eliza Benwell. The three men were charged with murder, Eliza Benwell with aiding and abetting them. At their trial, damning evidence against the accused was given by Keo-Moi Tiki, a native of the Sandwich Islands, through an interpreter. He swore that he had witnessed the attack being carried out by the three men and that the maid had also been there, keeping watch for them. After a day's deliberations the jury found the men guilty of murder, and all three were subsequently hanged, protesting their innocence to the last.

When Eliza faced the court the same evidence was presented, following which the jury retired. After due consideration, they came to the conclusion that because the murder had not been planned but had resulted when Jane Saunders resisted the men's advances, they declared the defendant to be innocent. But Eliza had hardly time to breathe a sigh of relief before the judge ordered them to reconsider their verdict on the grounds that the accused was just as blameworthy for keeping watch while a rape was attempted. Again the jury retired, again failing to reach a conclusion; sent back for a further hour's deliberation they returned to pronounce the prisoner at the bar guilty, whereupon she was sentenced to death.

In the condemned cell she swore she was innocent, that she had not been 'keeping watch' as stated in court, but purely by accident had happened to see Lockwood dragging the murdered maid's body from the building; moreover, she declared, she had seen neither Gomm nor Taylor at the scene. But despite her statements no attempt was made to reopen the case. To do so might well have been disastrous for the judiciary, forcing it to admit that a gross miscarriage of justice had been committed. Gomm, Lockwood and Taylor were already dead, and the Benwell execution would perforce have to go ahead. And so Eliza mounted the scaffold, her calm demeanour evoking nothing but sympathy and admiration from the large crowd as hangman Solomon Blay, himself an exiled convict, having placed the noose around her slim neck, pulled the lever – and the body of Eliza Benwell dropped the length of the short rope, a seeming eternity elapsing before her lifeless body hung inert and motionless.

One day in 1744 London housewife Lydia Adler attacked her meek and henpecked husband, knocking him down and kicking him so severely that he later died. At her trial at the Old Bailey she was charged with murder, but this was changed to one of manslaughter when medical evidence was produced testifying that her husband was already suffering from a rupture at the time of his death that was the material cause of his death. She was sentenced to be 'burned in the hand', and as the court officials were heating the branding iron, Lydia, as bad-tempered and impatient as ever, exclaimed, 'Come on, hurry it up, can't you? I've got my linen to do!'

Bevan, Catherine (USA)

In England the penalty of being burned at the stake was usually inflicted on those unfortunates who happened to have a different religion to the one more generally practised at the time. Two differing reasons for such a horrific death were that it prepared the heretical victim for the ever-burning fires that surely awaited him or her below, and that only by fire could the victim's soul be cleansed of his or her heretical thoughts.

The English colonists brought many of their quaint customs with them into America, including the home-grown methods of execution. Hanging needed no introduction, but strangely enough being burned at the stake rarely occurred except in the notable case of Catherine Bevan, not for being a heretic but a murderer.

In 1731 she, together with her servant lover, planned the death of her husband. Unable to kill him by herself, it was agreed that the young man would knock him unconscious and she would then strangle him. Having carried out their plan, they reported to the coroner that he had died while having a fit and that the funeral had been arranged. However, the official insisted on inspecting the body and on opening up the coffin discovered the bruised and battered corpse.

After being sentenced to death, Catherine, her hands bound behind her, was taken to the market square and there tied to a stake by means of a rope around her neck. Kindling was heaped around her and while the local residents either cheered or watched appalled, the tinder was ignited. As the flames leapt upwards the executioner attempted to reach forward and pull the rope with the intention of ending her life quickly by strangling her but, ironically, considering the method by which she had murdered her husband, the rope, singed by the mounting flames, had burnt away and Catherine collapsed, to be slowly incinerated in the roaring inferno.

Unlike in Catherine's case, a rope did Hannah Dagoe a favour. Sentenced to death for robbery in 1763, this strongly built Irishwoman had no intention of

going quietly as the cart stopped beneath the Tyburn gallows. Somehow she got her hands free and attacked the hangman, nearly stunning him. Then, turning to the crowds surrounding the scaffold, she tore off her hat and cloak and tossed them as souvenirs to the many outstretched hands. As she was doing so the hangman gathered his wits again and managed to drop the noose over her head – but rather than submitting to be slowly strangled (as usually happened at Tyburn), she threw herself over the side of the cart with such violence that her neck was broken, and she died instantly.

Bockin, Margaret (Germany)

When, in 1580, a neighbour asked Margaret Bockin to look for lice in her hair, Margaret struck her from behind with an axe. Needless to say she was found guilty of murder and was led out in the tumbril to the scaffold in the market square. There, naked to the waist, she was nipped three times with red-hot pincers, then beheaded, standing, with the sword. Finally, as a deterrent to all, her head was fixed on a pole above the gallows and her body buried beneath it.

On 29 August 1587, in Nuremberg, Elizabeth Rossnerin smothered her companion and stole her money. For that crime, Master Franz Schmidt executed her with the sword as a favour, instead of hanging her, because, as he wrote in his diary, she was a poor creature and had a wry neck.

Bowe, Alice atte (England)

A thirteenth-century story that had everything: love, lust, murder, sacrilege, faked suicide, imprisonment in the Tower of London, and ending in death by the rope and the flames – and it all revolved around a reputedly attractive woman named Alice atte Bowe. In 1284 she was the mistress of a man named Ralph Crepin, but Laurence Ducket, a goldsmith who lived nearby, cast covetous and no doubt lecherous eyes on her and made repeated advances for her favours, all of which she spurned. At length, frustrated and vengeful, he broke into their house one night while the couple were asleep and stabbed Crepin to death. At the commotion Alice woke up and recognised the assailant; rushing to the window she saw him cross the street and enter the nearby Bow Church, so, summoning some of her friends and neighbours, they gave chase. In the church they found their quarry cowering beneath a pile of old sacks; dragging him out, they proceeded to put a rope around his neck and hang him before one of the church windows, making it appear that he had committed suicide.

At the subsequent inquest it was decided that Ducket had indeed taken his own life and so, that being a crime in the eyes of the Law, the corpse was denied a Christian burial but was thrown into the City Ditch, the church being closed and its doors barred with thorns pending a spiritual cleansing.

But, as related by Alfred Marks in his *History and Annals of Tyburn*, 1908, 'shortly after, as related by a boy who had been asleep under the sacks, the truth of the matter was disclosed'. Alice and sixteen of her accomplices were arrested, Tower records showing that they were incarcerated therein. Dire punishment, that of being drawn and hanged, was administered to seven of the men; Alice was burned at the stake.

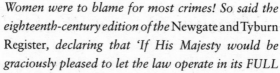

Women were to blame for most crimes! So said the eighteenth-century edition of the Newgate and Tyburn Register, declaring that 'If His Majesty would be graciously pleased to let the law operate in its FULL force against women convicts, it would indisputably produce very happy results. It is to the low and abandoned women that hundreds of young fellows owe their destruction. They rob, they plunder, to support these wretches. Let it not seem cruel that we make one remark, of which we are convinced, experience would justify the propriety. The execution of ten women would do more public service than that of a hundred men; for exclusive of the force of example, it would perhaps tend to the preservation of more than a hundred.'

Branch, Elizabeth and Mary (England)

Elizabeth, aged 67, and her daughter Mary, 24, were both charged with the cruel murder of their maid, Jane Butterworth. A transcript of their trial, which took place at Taunton, Somerset, in March 1740, reported that:

It was obvious, judging by the suspicions of their neighbours, that both the accused had also committed other murders in the past. Mrs Branch's husband died under circumstances that led others who lived nearby to believe she had poisoned him and they were convinced that she had hanged her mother, after murdering her, to avoid an investigation into the cause of the death. Human bones were also discovered in a well near her [Elizabeth's] farm, which were believed to be those of one of her servant girls who disappeared and was never heard from again. With such a reputation Mrs Branch found it difficult to get female staff in the locality and when she was in need of one she went further afield and brought Jane Butterfield from Bristol.

The young girl was hardly in the house before the two women subjected her to a brutal regime, and eventually beat her so savagely that she died. The older woman had Jane's corpse buried secretly in the graveyard and might have escaped blame, in spite of the complaint of her other maid, who had witnessed the murder and had been forced to lie next to her in bed, if a strange light had not been seen over the girl's grave, by several persons. This unearthly manifestation confirmed the neighbours' suspicions, and when the body was secretly removed at night, it was found by Mr Salmon, a surgeon, to be covered with wounds and other marks of violence.

Elizabeth Branch and her daughter beating their victim

When the case was first called, it was discovered that Mrs Branch had bribed some of the jurors, and there was some delay before they could be replaced. The trial lasted over six hours, and after a short consultation the jury brought in a verdict of guilty. It was noticed that Mrs Branch's expression remained unchanged at their findings, but several times kicked Mary Vigor, one of the prosecution witnesses, as she stood by her at the bar while she was giving evidence. When sentence was passed the next day, the condemned elder woman complained bitterly to the court about the illegality of changing the jury, exclaiming that if she and her daughter had been tried by the first jury, they would not have been convicted.

Some time after they had both been removed from the court, Mary Branch, realising what was to happen to her, fainted, and when she was revived by a wardress her mother cried, 'Zounds, what are you going to do? Hadn't she better die like this than be hanged?'

During their imprisonment Mrs Branch behaved sullenly and seemed more concerned by the conditions under which they were confined rather than the welfare of her soul, but her daughter told the gaoler, with whom, before the trial, she had been allowed to take a walk past Ilchester churchyard, that she would like to be buried there.

The women were sentenced to die on 3 May 1740, Mrs Branch expressing a wish to be hanged early in the morning before the expectedly large crowd of spectators could assemble. She got up early, called her daughter and told her to get ready, 'because if they didn't make haste, the mob would be in on them and they should not be hanged in peace'. On being escorted from the gaol, Mrs Branch called out to a passer-by: 'I have forgotten my cloak and clogs; pray fetch them, lest I should catch cold.'

When they reached the execution site at about 6 a.m. it was found that one of the gallows' uprights and the crosspiece had been cut down, probably by vandals rather than by anyone who might have been in sympathy with the two women. In order to get the ordeal over, Mrs Branch said she would be prepared to be hanged from a nearby tree instead (as befitted her name!) but a carpenter was sent for and a new gallows quickly constructed and erected.

Giving her cloak and purse to a friend, Elizabeth then helped the hangman to position the noose around her daughter's neck, afterwards asking him for a dram of strong drink, but he refused, saying that she had already had a couple of drinks earlier in the prison. After brief speeches, in which Mrs Branch swore that she had never intended to kill the deceased and begged for forgiveness, and her daughter Mary beseeched the crowd to pray for her, the halters around their necks tightened as the drop was operated. The bodies were allowed to hang for three-quarters of an hour before being cut down and taken away to be interred in Ilchester churchyard.

Horace Walpole, the renowned eighteenth-century author, reported an appalling breach of the law committed by those whose job was to uphold it! In 1742 he wrote:

There has lately been the most shocking scene of murder imaginable; a parcel of drunken constables took it into their heads to put the law into execution against disorderly persons and so took up every woman they met, till they had collected five- or six-and-twenty, all of whom they thrust into St Martin's lock-up [a small, temporary gaol] where they kept them all night, with doors and windows closed. The poor creatures, who could not stir or breathe, screamed as long as they had any breath left, begging at least for water; one poor wretch said she had eighteen pence on her and would gladly give it for a draught of water, but in vain!

So well did they keep them there, that in the morning four were found stifled to death, two died soon after, and a dozen more are in a shocking way. Several of them were beggars who, from having no lodging, were necessarily found in the street, and others were honest labouring women. One of the dead was a poor washerwoman, big with child, who was returning home late from washing.

One of the constables has been arrested and others absconded, but I question if any of them will suffer death; there is no tyranny the police do not exercise, no villainy they do not partake. These same men broke into a bagnio [a house of ill-repute] in Covent Garden and arrested a number of men, among them Lord George Graham, and would have also thrust them into the lock-up with the poor women, if they had not had more than eighteen pence on them!

Brinvillers, Marie Madelaine de (France)

If you want someone's money, poison them! If you don't like someone, poison them! If you simply want to ascertain whether certain poison works, try it out on anyone! That principle governed Marie's whole life. Having an aristocratic background – her father, Dreux d'Aubray, was a wealthy State Councillor – in 1615 she married the Baron Antoine de Brinvilliers, an Army officer, but neither of them wasted much time in gambling away the immense dowry that was settled on her at the time of her marriage. At the gaming tables Marie happened to meet Gaudin de St-Croix, a man with a roving eye for pretty women, and they started a liaison. The Baron, no slouch himself when it came to extra-marital affairs, turned a blind eye, but the couple were so blatant in their behaviour that word reached Marie's father, who used his influence with the Paris authorities to have St-Croix confined in the Bastille. It was an event which was ultimately to result in the deaths of scores of innocent people, for one of St-Croix's fellow prisoners was an expert on poisoning and taught his companion virtually all he knew about the craft. When released, St-Croix passed on to his lover, Marie, all that he had learned. Both were short of money; he had little love for her father, who had had him gaoled, she would inherit her father's wealth if he died, and they both knew lots about poisons – so what were they waiting for?

Marie set to work, making acquaintance with a chemist from whom she cajoled some poison but, not wanting to take the risk of it being detected in her father's body during an autopsy, set out to confirm that, despite the chemist's assurances, it would leave no trace in the body. The obvious place to try it out was the Hotel Dieu, the public hospital in Paris, and so under the pretext of being a gracious, upper-class do-gooder sympathetic to the sick and infirm, she visited the patients, bearing gifts of fruit and delicacies to which she had added varying proportions of the poison. Time went by, and by 1666 many of her 'guinea pig' patients had died (some estimates put the number at as many as fifty). Autopsies were of course carried out, but the finger of blame failed to point at anyone. Marie was now ready to go into action.

First her father became ill and so, as a devoted daughter, she nursed him – until he died. But there was even more wealth in the family simply begging to enrich her lifestyle even further, but unfortunately it belonged to her two brothers. Needing help, she enlisted the aid of another poisoner, La Chausee, and their combined efforts resulted in the tragic deaths of her siblings, the autopsies finding nothing suspicious.

MARTYRS, MURDERESSES AND MADWOMEN

Despite her increased wealth, Marie still needed every franc she could lay her hands on, for she was being blackmailed not only by her confederate La Chausee, but also by her lover, St-Croix, who had several incriminating letters that she had written to him in the past. Despite his attitude towards her, she still longed to marry him, but in order to do so she had to dispose of her husband the Baron. St-Croix, however, perhaps wisely, had no intention of joining her in holy matrimony, and as fast as she administered poison to her husband, he, St-Croix, administered the antidote! But when, in 1672, Gaudin de St-Croix died – of genuine natural causes – his widow, whom he had deserted decades earlier, found the damning letters among his effects and handed them over to the authorities. For Marie and La Chausee, the game was up.

Her accomplice was apprehended, and, after being tortured, was executed by being broken on the wheel, limb after limb being shattered. Marie sought refuge in England but when the French started extradition proceedings she returned to the Continent and entered a convent in Liège, which at that time was in neutral territory. However, in March 1676 a French detective, Desgrez, disguised himself as a trendy young abbé, and obtained an introduction to her in the convent. Always susceptible to flattery, she succumbed to his flirtatious approaches and did not demur when later he suggested a stroll by the river, nor did she pay much attention to a coach which had stopped nearby – until she was suddenly seized and dragged inside: she had been caught at last.

In police custody she attempted to commit suicide, once by swallowing a pin, another time by smashing a tumbler and trying to swallow the fragments. Put on trial, so overwhelming was the evidence produced against her that she was found guilty. Her sentence was read out to her; 'Marie Madelaine d'Aubray, wife of the Marquis de Brinvilliers, is declared duly accused and convicted of having poisoned Maître Dreux d'Aubray, her father;

Antoine d'Aubray, master of requests and civil lieutenant of the county of Paris; and Monsieur d'Aubray, councillor of the court, these being her two brothers; and also attempting the life of the late Thérèse d'Aubray, her sister. In reparation she is condemned to make the *amende honorable* before the principal door of the cathedral church in Paris, where she will be taken in a tumbril, with naked feet, a rope around her neck and holding in her hands a lighted torch weighing two pounds. There, being on her knees, she will declare that wickedly, and from motives of vengeance, and in order to possess their property, she has poisoned her father and her two brothers and attempted the life of her sister. From thence she will be conducted to the Place de Grève, to have her head cut off upon the scaffold. Her body will then be burnt and the ashes thrown to the wind. Before execution she will be applied to the Question Ordinary and Extraordinary [tortured], in order to compel her to reveal the names of her accomplices.'

It was reported that she was then taken to the torture chamber and for seven hours put to the Question. Having been tied hand and foot to a wooden frame, a trestle about two and a half feet high was placed under the small of her back so that her body was strained into an arch. A leather funnel with a metal ring at its narrow end was strapped to her mouth (the water torture) and the Question began. Four jars of water, each containing two pints, were poured into the funnel at intervals and between each the clerk interrogated her. When she had first entered the room she had smiled at the array of jars. 'Do you wish to drown me?' she had asked. 'I am too small to swallow all that.' But by now her face was mottled and her hands and feet bruised where the ropes had constricted them. She refused to say anything, so the trestle was removed and replaced by another which was three and a half feet high, so that her body was distended so tightly that the cords cut into her limbs. 'You are tearing me to pieces!' she cried. 'Good

Lord have mercy on me!' Four more jars were then administered, causing her to sink into unconsciousness.

She was placed on a mattress in front of a large fire and revived with eggs and wine, and after a little while she was clothed in a white gown and hood for the *amende honorable*. Accompanied by the executioner, his assistant and her confessor, she was taken by tumbril from the Conciergerie Prison to the porch of the Notre Dame, a dense crowd swarming about the vehicle screaming abuse. Through swollen lips she uttered the words of the *amende*: 'I admit that wickedly and for vengeance I poisoned my father and my brothers, and attempted to poison my sister-in-law, in order to possess myself of their property. For which I ask pardon of God, of the King and of Justice.'

She was then taken to the execution site, the Place de Grève where she had to kneel for half an hour amid the execrations of the crowd, while the executioner, with deliberate and inhumane slowness, cut away the thick swathes of her hair. While her confessor intoned the *Salve Regina*, her eyes were bandaged; the abbé's voice fell silent – and the last sound she heard was the terrifying hiss of the headsman's sword.

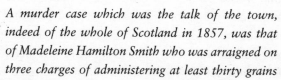

A murder case which was the talk of the town, indeed of the whole of Scotland in 1857, was that of Madeleine Hamilton Smith who was arraigned on three charges of administering at least thirty grains of arsenic to her erstwhile lover Pierre Emile L'Angelier. A member of Glasgow's upper classes, Madeleine, according to a journalist who was present in court, 'entered the dock with the air of a belle entering the ballroom or a box at the opera. Her steps were buoyant and she carried a silver-topped bottle of smelling salts. She was stylishly dressed and wore a pair of lavender gloves.'

As the lengthy trial went on, the young lady remained calm and composed, showing little reaction when the jury brought in the verdicts on the three charges: 'not guilty' on the first charge and 'not proven' on the other two, so Madeleine went free. Some years later it was reported that a member of her family, dining with them on the day of Pierre's death, noticed that although Madeleine usually made no effort to hide her long and slender hands, she seemed to be keeping them out of sight as much as possible on this occasion. However, he happened to catch a glimpse of them and casually noticed that they were stained a bluish colour. And it was not until the trial ended that he discovered the rat poison used to kill Pierre L'Angelier was impregnated with a bluish compound to signify its toxicity and he realised the truth – too late.

Britland, Mary Ann (England)

In his book *My Experiences as an Executioner*, published shortly before his resignation in 1892, James Berry expressed the opinion that those murderers who are most brutal and cold-blooded while committing the act for which they had been condemned to death, were the most cowardly when they had to face the consequences. This was most certainly the case with Mary Ann Britland, whom he hanged at Strangeways Prison, Manchester, on 9 August 1886.

Mary Ann, her husband and daughter lived in Ashton-under-Lyne, Lancashire, in the house of a Mr and Mrs Dixon. It might have been that Mary Ann feared her daughter had discovered the fixation she had for Mr Dixon which impelled her to poison the girl, and then remove, by the same means, the next obstacle to her desires – her husband. But not until Mrs Mary Dixon had also been removed would the way be clear, and so out came the poison bottle again.

At the trial, no evidence whatsoever was produced to show that Mr Dixon ever responded to any of Mary Ann's approaches, and he was acquitted. But she was found guilty, and when asked whether she had anything to say regarding why sentence should not be passed, not only did she burst into a flood of tears, but also continued to scream for mercy when the death sentence was pronounced. While being taken down to the cells, her cries still reverberated around the crowded courtroom and were even heard by those outside the building.

In the condemned cell Mary Ann maintained that she was innocent and expected a sudden reprieve, but it was not to be, and as the customary three weeks dragged by she was reduced to a shadow of her former self, hardly eating or sleeping. On the morning of her execution hangman James Berry entered the cell to find her almost in a state of collapse, the two female warders having to support her while he pinioned her, ready for the ordeal. As he did so she continued to moan, the only coherent words from her being 'I must have been mad!'

As the procession made its way to the scaffold, the wardresses almost having to carry her, Mary Ann sobbed piteously, a reporter describing how, when Berry pulled the white hood over her head, 'she uttered cries such as one might expect at the very separation of body and spirit through mortal terror'. Holding the woman on the drop while the hangman placed the noose in position about her neck, the two wardresses were then replaced by two male warders, who watched Berry intently for the signal. On him giving it, they instantly released their hold on their prisoner and stepped off the drop – simultaneously the hangman operated the lever and before Mary Ann could even buckle at the knees, the trapdoors opened and down she went into the pit.

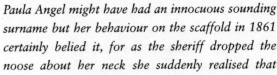

Paula Angel might have had an innocuous sounding surname but her behaviour on the scaffold in 1861 certainly belied it, for as the sheriff dropped the noose about her neck she suddenly realised that he had neglected to bind her wrists, so she reached up and grabbed the rope above her. Instinctively the officer seized her around the waist and added his weight to hers in order to tighten the noose and render her at least unconscious, but somehow she wriggled free from his grasp. In the frantic struggle that ensued, the sheriff managed to secure her arms and ankles, and then continued with the execution. By now the crowd, horrified at the woman's desperate efforts to stay alive, threatened to rush the makeshift scaffold and it was not until the officer had threatened to shoot the first person who tried to rescue her that the noose finally tightened around Paula Angel's neck, plunging her into eternity.

Broadingham, Elizabeth (England)

Taking advantage of her husband John's temporary imprisonment in York Castle, Elizabeth enjoyed an intimate relationship with a younger man, Thomas Aikney, and when John was released, she, having tasted the fruits of illicit love, left him and went off to set up house with Thomas. Why she did not just leave matters as they were is not known; perhaps she wanted marriage, rather than just cohabitation with Thomas. Whatever the reason, over the next few weeks she slyly suggested to Thomas that John be removed – permanently. The man vehemently refused to have anything to do with the idea, but Elizabeth was nothing if not determined to get her way, and one night she plied her lover with liquor before turning on the pressure again. Intoxicated both with the drink and her, he finally agreed to help her.

Elizabeth's next move was to ingratiate herself with her husband, a simple and decent man who longed for his wife to return to their family home. Within days she had moved back in with him, and then contacted Thomas. He tried to persuade her to abandon the murderous scheme, to elope with him, but without success, and on the night of 8 February 1776 she woke her husband up and told him that someone was knocking at the door. Half asleep, John made his way downstairs and opened the door – to be attacked by Thomas, who proceeded to stab him in the thighs and body, finally leaving the knife inserted in the husband's stomach before fleeing. The badly wounded man staggered out into the street, calling for help, and the neighbours who rushed out 'found him holding the bloody knife in one hand and the other supporting his bowels, which were dropping to the ground'. He died the next day.

Thomas was captured, Elizabeth arrested, both confessing their guilt. On 20 March 1776 Thomas Aikney was hanged at York, his body subsequently being sent to the Leeds Infirmary as a surgical specimen to be used in the training of students. Petit treason having been committed by Elizabeth by instigating the murder of her husband, she was tied to the stake, and after the executioner had strangled her she was burned, her ashes being collected by some of the onlookers as souvenirs (in egg-timers, perhaps?).

John Howard, the famous prison reformer, visited gaols across the Continent in the 1770s. In his report on prisons in Stockholm, he noted that Swedish executions are by the axe, and that women are decapitated on a scaffold, that structure afterwards being set alight at its four corners and consumed by the flames, together with the victim's body.

Brownrigg, Elizabeth (England)

Hangman Thomas Turlis had a rewarding task, and the vast crowd were in full agreement with his actions, for once not abusing him too obscenely, when, on 14 September 1767, he executed Elizabeth Brownrigg, a lady assuredly receiving everything she deserved!

Originally a servant, Elizabeth had married James Brownrigg and they lived in Fetter Lane, near Fleet Street in London. Elizabeth became a midwife and, needing to have assistance in the house, contacted the local Foundling Hospital for some apprentices. Two of the girls were thus employed as servants, Mary Mitchell and Mary Jones, but soon found that they had left the frying pan only to end up in the fire, for Mrs Brownrigg was a cruel and violent woman who did not hesitate to beat them. Mary Mitchell endured the hardships for a year and then managed to escape, only to be captured by the son of the family, who brought her back to his mother's tender mercies.

Not long afterwards, the Marys were joined by yet another Mary, 14-year-old Mary Clifford, who was particularly ill-treated by her mistress. For the most trifling offence she would be tied up naked and beaten with a cane, a horsewhip, a broom handle or anything else that came to hand; made to lie in the cold, damp cellar on sacking; and was fed only on bread and water. Later she was confined in the yard, a chain around her neck securing her to the door, her hands being tied behind her.

Mrs Brownrigg's cruelty knew no bounds, but retribution was in sight when, on 13 July 1767, she stripped Mary Clifford naked and hung her up by her arms to a staple in the ceiling, then whipped her already severely scarred body until the blood flowed across the kitchen floor. But the brutal treatment was

Elizabeth Brownrigg flogging Mary Clifford

witnessed by a neighbour, who sent for the police. On arrival, although they released Mary Clifford from her bonds, 'her body being one continual ulcer, ready to mortify', Elizabeth Brownrigg and her son had escaped. The badly injured Mary Clifford died in St Bartholomew's Hospital a few days later; the Brownriggs, mother and son, were now wanted on murder charges.

The couple had rented rooms in Wandsworth in a house owned by a Mr Dunbar, and he happened to see a wanted poster that included a detailed description of his two lodgers. He promptly informed the police and both were arrested. On 12 September they appeared in the Old Bailey; Master Brownrigg received a prison sentence but, after a trial lasting eleven hours, during which every lurid detail of the injuries sustained by the victim was described, Elizabeth Brownrigg was sentenced to death.

FEMALE EXECUTIONS

On 14 September, en route to Tyburn scaffold, she was accompanied in the horse-drawn cart by the Ordinary, the Reverend Mr James, and a prison missionary, Silas Told, who afterwards described how the two men sat, one each side of her, continuing:

> When we had fixed ourselves, I perceived that the whole powers of darkness were ready to give us a reception. Beckoning to the multitude, I desired them to pray for her, at which they were rather silent, until the cart began to move. Then they triumphed over her with three huzzas; this was followed by a combination of hellish curses. When we had passed through the gates [of Newgate Gaol], carts had been placed each side of the street, filled principally with women. Here I may say, with the greatest truth, nothing could have equalled them but the damned spirits let loose from the infernal pit. Some of the common cries from the thoughtless concourse were 'Pull her hat off, pull her hat off, that we may see the b*****s face!', accompanied by the most dreadful imprecations.

As they neared the execution site Elizabeth joined in prayers with the Ordinary and acknowledged the justice of her sentence, but on arrival, so great was the uproar that she was held firmly while hangman Thomas Turlis noosed her, tied the rope to the overhead beam of the gallows, then, hastily dismounting, gave the horse a smart slap on the flanks. At that the cart moved away, leaving Mrs Brownrigg to swing in the same manner as she had

MRS BROWNRIGG.

Elizabeth Brownrigg

suspended poor Mary Clifford from the staple – although not by the wrists, but by the neck!

Her body was subsequently taken to Surgeons' Hall and handed over to be anatomised. After that 'her skeleton was exposed in the niche opposite the first door in the Surgeons' Theatre, so that the heinousness of her cruelty may make the more lasting impression on the minds of the spectators attending the dissection sessions.'

As a perquisite, English executioners would sell small lengths of the rope with which they had hanged particularly notorious criminals as souvenirs or for allegedly curative purposes. But this facility was not available across the Channel during the French Revolution, and so French women, desperately requiring such bizarre artefacts to bring them luck at the card table, would contact the appropriate government department in London, pleading to be given the address of the possible supplier!

C

Calvert, Louise (England)

Mrs Lily Waterhouse lived in Leeds and in March 1925 her husband died. Although so desirous of making contact with the spirit of her dear departed that she attended seances, she did not neglect her physical desires, the police being aware that a large number of men frequently visited her house, to the detriment of the neighbourhood. A year following her husband's death she took in a lodger, Louise Calvert, but no doubt regretted it, for within weeks she went to the police to complain that her lodger had stolen some of her belongings. She was told to come back the next day and make a formal statement, but when she did not reappear there an officer was sent round, only to find her dead. Her hands had been bound and she had been strangled.

A witness, another lodger, testified that she had seen Louise leave the house and when she questioned her and mentioned noises she had heard, Louise told her that Mrs Waterhouse was upset because Louise had announced that she was not staying any longer. Upon being later arrested, Louise explained that she had not stolen anything but that Mrs Waterhouse had asked her to pawn some of her property, but a search of her own house situated some distance away from that of Mrs Waterhouse's revealed not only some items belonging to the murdered woman, but she was even wearing Mrs Waterhouse's boots! Such incriminating evidence disposed of the alternative theory that Mrs Waterhouse had been murdered by one of her many male visitors, and Louise Calvert was put on trial.

Little could be said in her defence, and the judge did not hesitate to sentence her to death. However, a complication then arose, for Louise claimed a stay of execution on the grounds that she was pregnant. Such factors had of course been taken into consideration by those responsible for drafting laws governing executions, and so the judge selected a jury of mature women, accompanied by the prison doctor, to adjourn to an anteroom and carry out the necessary examination. On their return the doctor stated that although the prisoner was not pregnant, she could well be in the very early stages of that condition, and this was confirmed by the spokeswoman, adding that in the opinion of the matrons, the execution of the prisoner would not involve the death of any person other than Louise herself (at the time the law stipulated that a condemned woman could not be classified as pregnant unless such condition had existed for a length of 140 days or more).

Understandably the trial was given a great deal of attention in the local newspapers, one investigative journalist discovering an earlier murder tenuously linked with Louise Calvert, the victim being a John Frobisher for whom Louise had acted as housekeeper. He mysteriously disappeared in 1922 and when his body was retrieved from the Liverpool–Leeds Canal he was found fully dressed – except for his boots!

Her final plea not having been upheld, Louise Calvert was taken to Strangeways Gaol, Manchester, and despite many pleas by the public on her behalf, she was hanged within the prison walls.

Condemned women occasionally 'pleaded their belly' (claimed to be pregnant in order to avoid being hanged), but in 1848 Charlotte Harris, guilty of murdering her husband, actually was pregnant and so she was informed that she would be allowed to have the baby – and then be hanged. At that, petitions for clemency were raised, signatures obtained across the country, public protest meetings held, and eventually, after no fewer than 40,000 women from all walks of life had appealed to Queen Victoria, a reprieve was granted.

Clitheroe, Margaret (England)

This lady, the first of her sex to suffer martyrdom in the reign of Queen Elizabeth I, sacrificed herself for her deeply held religious principles. Imprisoned for failing to attend services in

The martyr Margaret Clitheroe

*Margaret Clitheroe suffering
peine fort et dure*

the established Protestant churches, she suffered several terms of imprisonment, and in 1586, when she was about 35 years of age, a gang of pursuivants, professional priest-hunters, raided her house and discovered not only a hidden priest hole, but also a large number of vestments and other religious items necessary for Catholic worship.

The existence of such incriminating evidence resulted in Margaret's immediate arrest, and she was eventually charged with the heinous crime of being a Papist and for harbouring Jesuits and Catholic priests, and was committed to imprisonment in York Castle. At her trial the vestments and religious artefacts were then paraded before the court by 'two lewd fellows', who donned the vestments and masqueraded with altar bread in their hands, saying: 'Behold thy gods in whom thou believest!'

When asked whether she pleaded guilty or not guilty, she refused to do so, saying: 'Having made no offence, I need no trial.'

Judge Clinch, losing his patience with her, told her plainly that if she refused to plead, there was no more room for mercy, and she must have the law provided in such cases. He then pronounced that she was to be subjected to *peine forte et dure*, severe and hard pain, saying:

> *You must return from whence you came, and there, in the lowest part of the prison, be stripped naked, laid down, your back upon the ground, and as much weight laid on you as you are able to bear, and so continue three days without meat or drink, except for a little barley bread on the day you do not drink, and puddle water on the day you do not eat, and on the third day be pressed to death, your hands and feet be bound to posts, and a sharp stone under your back.*

Before the 'persuasive' torture started, various attempts to save her were made while she was confined in prison; some begged her to go to a Protestant church and abide by the statutes, but she refused outright.

On 23 March 1586, Good Friday, she was walked barefoot to the Tollbooth in York, carrying over one arm a long linen gown she had made. In the cell she was stripped by the women and donned the gown she had brought. Upon lying down, a sharp stone about the size of a man's fist was placed beneath her and her arms were stretched out wide and bound to posts set in the ground. Her face was covered with a handkerchief and a heavy door laid upon her. So stubborn was her refusal to answer the questions then put to her that it appears the preliminary two days were dispensed with, because men were then ordered to pile stones upon the door, the total weight being estimated at in excess of 800 lb. From beneath the handkerchief came an agonised prayer for help and strength, those gathered round hearing her exclaim: 'Jesu! Jesu! Have mercy on me!'

After about fifteen minutes of excruciating pain, her bones being crushed, her blood vessels being burst, she passed away. The press was left in position until the afternoon, when her body, as was the custom, was thrown into a hole beside a filthy dunghill near the city's walls. However, six weeks afterwards, after a diligent search, her corpse was found by a pious Catholic who declared that 'it was whole, without putrefaction, without corruption or evil savour.'

Her final burial place, where she was interred 'unbowelled, before necessary preservatives could be gotten' is unknown, but the Convent of the Institute of Mary, near Micklegate Bar in York, reportedly the oldest existing foundation in England, possesses what is affirmed by constant oral tradition to be the severed hand of the 'Pearl of York'. Originally it was preserved in a silken bag enclosed in a box and kept under the altar in the chapel until 1840, when Bishop Briggs, concerned by the absence of any authentication of its identity, ordered it to be removed. Thirty-four years later, Mr Charles Weld of Chideock defrayed the cost of a handsome reliquary in which the hand was to be kept. Of turret shape, from

The hand of Margaret Clitheroe

its base spring palm leaves supporting a jewelled cross; the metal work is of silver gilt. Within the glass globe, the hand, pointing heavenwards, is small and well-shaped, brown and dry with age. The flesh and sinews still remain, and the fingers are contracted, the curvature showing all the agony suffered during the ordeal of the *peine forte et dure*. The hand lacks one finger, severed at the joint, it having been presented to the donor of the reliquary. The vessel itself bears the inscription in Latin: 'The hand of the valiant woman Margaret Clitheroe née Middleton, who suffered at York with the greatest constancy for the faith and love of Christ, on the 25th day of March, 1586. She has deserved to be called the proto-martyr of her sex, under the tyrant Elizabeth. Charles Weld, of Chideock, and Mary, his wife, devoutly and humbly offer this shrine in honour of the Martyrs of England, AD 1874.'

It is only 150 years or so since women prisoners, being taken from York Gaol to the Assizes Courts, were led through the streets handcuffed and chained by the neck.

Coghlan, Margaret (Australia)

It could hardly be expected that nineteenth-century Antipodean hangmen would be any more skilful or use longer ropes than their fellow tradesmen back home, and this was certainly the case where Solomon Blay, chief executioner in Tasmania from the 1840s to the 1890s was concerned, although it is believed that his performance did improve somewhat towards the end of his career. Having been found guilty in England of counterfeiting, he had been transported in a prison ship to that distant colony, no doubt volunteering to fill the scaffold vacancy rather than labour in the quarries or build roads in the penal settlements.

One of his victims was Margaret Coghlan who, although she would not have been aware of it, was the last woman to be executed in Tasmania. During a drunken row with her husband, he, not known for his chivalry towards the fairer sex, picked up an iron bar and threw it at her. It would seem that the projectile missed her, for she then proceeded to beat him about the head with it. And to ensure that he would not revive and retaliate, she cut his throat with his own razor, after which she placed it in his hand, curling his fingers around it to simulate suicide.

The investigating authorities might have been expected to believe that he had intended to end his own life, but hardly that he would have given himself several severe head wounds before getting the razor from the bathroom, so Margaret was arrested and ultimately found guilty of murder.

On that fateful day in 1862 Margaret was escorted from Melbourne Prison's condemned cell, her condition bordering on total hysteria. To prevent her from collapsing completely, the officers with her blindfolded her eyes so that she would not see the noose suspended in readiness from the gallows beam. She had to be supported as she mounted the scaffold and one of the wardresses found the ordeal so distressing that she fainted and had to be carried back to the prison building. Not so Solomon Blay; tightening the noose, he operated the drop and Margaret Coghlan, whether justified in retaliating for her husband's brutal attack or not, paid the terrible price demanded by the law.

 Eliza Fenning was accused of attempting to poison the family for whom she worked and in 1815 was sentenced to death. On the scaffold she wore a white muslin gown with a satin ribbon tied around

her waist, a white muslin cap, and a pair of high-laced lilac boots; this was her bridal outfit, for she was to have been married the day before. Because of her cap, hangman John Langley could not pull the regulation hood over her head so had to use a soiled pocket handkerchief instead. Just before the trapdoors opened she exclaimed in a muffled voice: 'I am innocent.' Her father had to pay the executioner his fee of fourteen shillings and sixpence before he could retrieve his daughter's body for burial.

Coo, Eva (USA)

One day in 1935 Mr Lawes, Warden of Sing Sing Prison, authorised the dispatch of invitations for Eva Coo's execution to the official guests, observers, medical specialists, newspaper journalists, and to those of the victim's relatives who wished to attend. The printed forms read:

In accordance with Section 507 of the Code of Criminal Procedure you are hereby invited to be present as a witness at the execution by electricity of Eva Coo which will occur at this prison on 27 June 1935. The hour of 11 p.m. has been designated by me for such execution and you will arrange to be at my office in this prison not later than 10 p.m.

I would thank you to treat this communication as confidential and advise me immediately upon its receipt of your acceptance or otherwise, so that I can make arrangements accordingly. Under no circumstances is this invitation transferable.

Very respectfully, Lewis E. Lawes, Warden

Following any horrendous and consequently well-publicised crime, there were always hundreds, sometimes thousands of applications from those who wished to watch the condemned criminal die, and there is no reason to think that the auditorium was anything other than full when Eva, deservedly or not, went to meet her Maker.

Born in Canada, Eva moved south and lived in the States where she became a prostitute before running her own brothel, the notorious 'Little Eva's Place', in a town on the outskirts of New York. There she prospered, but trade suffered badly when Prohibition ceased, and she became desperate for money. She had a close friend, Martha Clift, who acted as a hostess in Eva's establishment, and from all accounts the two women discussed different ways of overcoming their financial difficulties. Which lady suggested murdering Harry Wright, the brothel's handyman, and claiming his life insurance of several thousand dollars, is not clear, but one night in June 1934 Harry, having been plied with drink, was lured out of the building and killed. Which of the women struck him and with what type of implement is unclear; it depended on which local paper one read.

One of the murderous conspirators hit him with a claw hammer or a mallet; the other then got into the car and ran over him several times. One thing that was clear, however, was that no matter how close a friend Martha had been to Eva, it ended abruptly when the pair were arrested. Martha, to save her own skin, turned state's witness and gave damning evidence, admitting that she had driven the car over the handyman, having been promised a considerable part of the insurance money, but that it was Eva who had actually struck the fatal blows. Acting on her statement the police exhumed Wright's body on no fewer than two occasions but could not substantiate Martha's accusations.

Eva was sent for trial, journalists reporting how the judge had encouraged the all-male jury to play their part in the proceedings by saying, in a somewhat unorthodox way: 'Don't think we are locking *you* up; enjoy yourselves, laugh and talk among yourselves, get lots of exercise. You are good sports and citizens, and I appreciate what you are doing.'

When Eva entered the crowded courtroom she must have realised with horror that she would face the death sentence on learning that her 'friend', in order to face a lesser charge of second-degree murder, was prepared to testify against her. And so it proved, for after a short deliberation, the jury brought in a verdict of guilty. Eva Coo was sentenced to death; Martha Clift to twenty years' imprisonment.

In Sing Sing's condemned cell, Eva complained bitterly that all her personal belongings, expensive clothes and other valuables had been sold to defray the lawyers' expenses. The Warden, noted for his humane treatment of his prisoners, deplored the fact that one of her attorneys had even applied for four invitations so that he and colleagues could come and watch the death of the client he had defended. Mr Lawes did not justify Eva's crime in any way, but praised her fortitude and equable behaviour as appeal after appeal was dismissed. Albert R. Beatty, the executioner, described in his memoirs how the Warden visited Eva prior to the designated hour, just as one of the wardresses was attaching the electrode to one of the victim's legs. Still insisting that she was innocent, nevertheless she walked calmly and composedly into the execution chamber where she seated herself in the chair. Looking around, she bade farewell to the wardresses, saying, 'Goodbye, darlings!', then allowed the guards to strap her arms and legs securely. Her only reaction, an instinctive gasp, came when Beatty put the head electrode in position and threw the switch, sending the current surging through her body, her life ending in a matter of seconds.

Any prize for sheer composure prior to being executed would surely have been won by serial killer Louise Peete, sentenced to death in the gas chamber in 1947. When informed that she was prepared to be interviewed by the press, the reporters who expected to see a broken-spirited or possibly panic-stricken woman, were taken aback at the charm offensive which greeted them, for Louise not only flattered them outrageously but even opened a gold-wrapped box of chocolates and, as if at a party, invited them all to partake of the delicacies!

Corday, Charlotte (France)

Her full name was Marie-Anne Charlotte de Corday d'Aumont, but she was generally known as Charlotte. On 9 July 1793 she left her home in Caen with the firm intention of killing Jean-Paul Marat, a revolutionary leader who believed that only by the use of force could the necessary changes be brought about in France's fortunes. Far from being a royalist, Charlotte supported the Girondists, a political group dedicated to a more moderate approach to the country's dire problems, and she was filled with Republican fervour so intense that she regarded the assassination of Marat as the only solution.

She walked the two hundred miles to Paris, and, on arriving there, stayed at the Inn de la Providence on the Rue des Vieux Augustins. There she wrote a note and sent it to her quarry, requesting an interview. While awaiting a reply, she went to a cutler's shop on the Palais Royal where, for two francs, she bought a large sheath knife with an ebony handle. No reply having arrived, she dressed in her finest clothes, a pink silk scarf draped over her muslin gown, and an elegant hat adorned with a cockade and green ribbons, and visited Marat's house, 20 Rue des Cordeliéres, but was turned away. Determined to carry out her self-imposed mission, she returned to the hotel from where she posted a message to Marat in which she stated that she knew the names of those in Caen who were plotting against the Revolution and was prepared to reveal them to him.

A few hours later she returned, and although Marat's mistress Simone attempted to refuse her admittance, Marat heard the voices and bade Charlotte to enter. The famous revolutionary had been ill for some time. During his earlier revolutionary days he had twice had to flee to London, and once even had to take refuge from the French authorities by hiding in the Paris sewers. In those noisome and pestilential tunnels he had contracted a virulent and incurable disease which covered his body in a rash so devastating that only almost continual immersion in a sulphur bath brought him any relief. Accordingly he spent most of his time in a slipper bath, decency being preserved by having a cloth draped over it, and with the aid of a board placed across it he was able to write his notes and keep up with his correspondence. He also suffered excruciating headaches, which he sought to relieve by wrapping his head in a bandanna soaked in vinegar.

Charlotte Corday entered the room and approached her prey. As he started to query the reason for her visit, without warning she suddenly leant over and plunged the knife into his body with all the force she could muster. So violent was the blow that according to the post-mortem the blade entered his chest between the first and second ribs, piercing the upper part of the right lung and aorta, and penetrated the heart, blood gushing copiously into the bath water.

Having achieved her purpose, the young girl made no attempt to escape but stood calmly by the window where, attracted by

Marat's dying screams, she was found by an assistant, Laurent Bas who, together with Simone and her sister Catherine, had rushed into the room. Faced with the spectacle of his employer submerged in a bath of blood, Bas promptly picked up a chair and knocked Charlotte to the ground; as she attempted to get to her feet, he felled her again, holding her there until members of the national guard and a surgeon arrived. The body of the murdered man was lifted out and placed on a bed. Charlotte, calm and dignified, her hands tied behind her, was taken to the Prison de l'Abbaye for interrogation and subsequent trial before the Revolutionary Council. In court she admitted everything, calling Marat a monster who had hypnotised the French peasants. 'I killed one man in order to save a hundred thousand,' she proclaimed vehemently. The verdict and sentence were foregone conclusions, death by the guillotine being the only possible penalty.

In her cell in the Conciergerie Prison a painter, Hauer, was working on a sketch of her when, on 17 July 1793, the executioner Charles-Henri Sanson arrived to prepare and collect his victim. On entering the room he found her seemingly cool and entirely composed, sitting on a chair in the middle of the cell and guarded by a gendarme. As he approached she looked up and, removing her cap, sat still while he cropped her luxurious black hair. When he had finished she picked up a lock or two of the hair and gave some of it to the artist and the rest to the gaoler, asking that it be given to his wife who had befriended her.

Charles-Henri, marvelling at her serenity, handed her the red chemise she was to wear and turned away while she obediently put it on. He then started to bind her hands, whereupon she asked whether she might keep her gloves on because, she declared, her previous captors had bound her wrists so tightly that the cords had chafed her tender flesh. With kind reassurance the executioner agreed to her request, adding that even if she did not don them, he would make sure the cords did not cause her any discomfort. Charlotte smiled at him, 'To be sure, you ought to know how to do it,' she exclaimed and held out her bare hands for him to secure her.

He then led her out to where their conveyance waited. When she declined the offer to sit down in the tumbril, Sanson agreed, pointing out that the jolting of the cart over the rough cobbles was less trying when standing, and the procession set off through the already crowded streets.

Charles-Henri later admitted to being unable to take his eyes off his prisoner. He wrote:

> *The more I saw of her, the more I wished to see. It was not on account of her personal beauty, great as that was, but I thought that it was impossible that she could remain as calm and courageous as I saw her; yet what I had hitherto considered as beyond the strength of human nerve actually happened. During the two hours I spent in her company I could detect no sign of anger or indignation on her face. She did not speak; she looked not at those who insulted her, but at the citizens who were at the windows of their houses. The crowd was so dense that our cart advanced very slowly. As I heard her sigh, I said, 'You find the way very long, I fear?' She replied, 'No matter; we are sure to reach the scaffold sooner or later.'*

On arrival Sanson dismounted. On doing so, he noticed that some of the spectators had mingled with his assistants and as he and the gendarmes were clearing the area, Charlotte left the tumbril and unhesitatingly mounted the scaffold steps. As she reached the platform, Fermin, one of Charles-Henri's assistants, removed her scarf and, without any prompting, she approached the guillotine and positioned herself in front of the bascule, the hinged plank. The executioner, not wanting to prolong the girl's ordeal longer than absolutely necessary, quickly bound her to it, then swung the board horizontal; instantly he signalled to Fermin to pull the rope. The weighted blade descended and, as the executioner confessed afterwards, the waiting basket received the head of one of the bravest women he had ever met.

Even as he stood there, a carpenter named Francois le Gros picked up the severed head and showed it to the crowd. Sanson admitted afterwards that 'although I was used to that occurrence, this time I could not help turning my head away. It was then, by the murmurs of the crowd, that I became aware that the rascal had also slapped the cheeks, the face turning red as if insulted. I struck the man and ordered him off the scaffold, the police taking him away. He was later arrested by the Tribunal and severely punished.'

Throughout history there have been many accounts of life apparently continuing after decapitation, and during the execution of Charlotte Corday, scores of spectators swore that when le Gros smacked her cheek, the other cheek also blushed, as if with annoyance. Could there really be sufficient blood flowing within the brain to sustain consciousness for a certain number of seconds after decapitation? After all, organs transplanted for surgical purposes remain 'alive' after being removed from the donor, and as the brain is an organ...

Charlotte's headless body was buried with others in the Madeleine Cemetery. Her skull reportedly passed into the ownership of the Princess Marie Bonaparte and was described as 'being of dirty yellow, glistening, shiny and smooth, evidence that it was never interred'.

Cotton, Mary Ann (England)

Mary Ann Cotton was no ordinary, spur-of-the-moment killer; her murderous instincts were alleged to have resulted in the deaths of fifteen, perhaps even twenty people, including four husbands and eight children, and she gained the evil reputation of being the greatest mass murderess of all time.

By the age of forty she had married three times. Her first husband, whom she had married in 1852, was a young miner named William Mowbray, by whom she had four children. All of them just happened to die young, reportedly from gastric fever. William Mowbray also succumbed to illness, experiencing severe sickness and diarrhoea, and died in agony.

Mary, now seemingly grief-stricken at the loss of her husband and children, drew solace from her friends and cash from the insurance company. Realising that hospital work as a nurse would be the source not only of supplies of the poison she needed, but also of meeting further vulnerable and susceptible victims, she joined the staff of Sunderland Infirmary where, among others, she tended a patient named George Ward. So devoted were her ministrations that when he recovered he proposed marriage, her subsequent promise 'in sickness and in health' only applying to half the phrase, for fourteen months later, in 1866, he too shuffled off this mortal coil, but not before he had endowed all his worldly goods to her.

Not long afterwards, still in her widow's weeds, she met James Robinson, a widower with three children. They were married in May 1867, and by December of that year regrettable coincidences also overwhelmed that family. Not only did James' two young sons and daughter, plus William Mowbray's nineyear-old daughter fall victim to gastric fever, but a later baby born to Mary and James joined its stepbrothers and sisters in the local cemetery. James himself had cause to thank his guardian angel when Mary incensed him so much by selling some of his possessions that he ejected her from the house.

The fact that her husband was still alive did not deter Mary from starting an intimate liaison with her next prey, Frederick Cotton, a man who already had two young sons from a former marriage. When he proposed to her, she bigamously married him, and, being a prudent wife who had to take care of her future, she took out three insurance policies, just in case. The number of children in their family became three when she had a little boy by Frederick, called Robert, the number of policies thereby increasing accordingly. Early in 1872 a James Nattrass attracted her attention. This complicated matters, Frederick Cotton immediately becoming surplus to requirements – but not for long. Almost without warning he fell seriously ill, but by the time a doctor had arrived he was past all medical aid. Frederick's 10-year-old son was not long in following his father to the grave, and Mary's child, Robert, never reached puberty.

James now became her lover, but affection wasn't everything, and eventually Mary decided that £30, the sum for which he had been insured, was preferable to the man himself, and so another coffin received an occupant and another grave was dug.

Mary could have continued in this manner, unchecked and unsuspected, until her stock of arsenic, a poison little recognised or diagnosed at the time, ran out, but for some unaccountable reason, perhaps a rare, charitable thought, she spared the life of Charles Edward, the eight-year-old Cotton boy; instead she decided to hand him over to the workhouse. When told that such was not possible without the parents also being admitted, she retorted, 'I could have married again but for the child. But there, he won't live long, he'll go the way of all the Cotton family.' Nor did he. Dispensing with mercy, she dispensed arsenic instead, gastric fever again being diagnosed as the cause of death. But news of the child's demise reached the ears of the workhouse master and, remembering the woman's ominous rejoinder, he notified the authorities of his suspicions. The child's body was exhumed and the amount of arsenic found within the viscera was unmistakable. And when the corpses of her other victims were disinterred and their post-mortems produced similar results, the game was up.

In March 1873 Mary Ann Cotton was charged at Durham with one murder, that of the young Charles Edward; so overwhelming was the evidence in that particular case that one charge was considered sufficient, and so it proved. Throughout the trial the woman in the dock remained composed and utterly self-assured; having borne a charmed life so far, she probably saw no reason why it should not continue. She pleaded not guilty and coolly explained that the arsenic in her possession was used to kill bedbugs in the house, but when the judge pronounced her guilty and sentenced her to be hanged, she fainted in the dock and had to be carried down to the cells.

If she had thought that because she was pregnant – she had wasted no time in taking a new lover, a local customs officer, following James' funeral – she would escape the gallows, she was sadly mistaken: there was, of course, no question of executing her while heavy with child, but once the child was born, the law would take its course. After giving birth in gaol, she was deprived of her baby and arrangements were made for her to be deprived of her life in five days' time.

The night before her execution she was heard by her warders to pray for salvation, a prayer which included James Robinson, her third husband and the only one to escape her homicidal proclivities. The customs man might also have congratulated himself on his lucky escape!

FEMALE EXECUTIONS

Feminine fashion at that time dictated that women wore dresses with long sleeves, plus a veil and gloves, and Mary Ann Cotton's apparel on her execution day reflected this, for her veil was the white cap William Calcraft slipped over her head – nor did he omit the matching accessory, a hempen necklace. None of the watching officials saw him hesitate as he prepared his victim, nor did he waste a moment in operating the bolt. However, as usual, nearly three minutes elapsed before the twitching figure ceased rotating and finally hung deathly still.

Following removal from the scaffold, Mary's body was taken back into the prison building where, in order to take a cast of her head to be studied by members of the West Hartlepool Phrenological Society, all her luxurious tresses were cut off close to her skull. It was later stated that, far from being kept as gruesome souvenirs, every severed strand of hair was deposited in the coffin with her body.

Such was the publicity surrounding the case that shock waves of disbelief and horror spread across the country when the prosecuting lawyer described the ghastly deaths of her other victims, and with the minimum of delay a wax model of her joined the macabre company already occupying Mme Tussaud's Chamber of Horrors, the museum publishing an updated catalogue which endorsed her execution as expiation 'for crimes for which no punishment in history could atone. The child she rocked on her knee today was poisoned tomorrow. Most of her murders were committed for petty gains; and she killed off husbands and children with the unconcern of a farm-girl killing poultry'.

Murderous though eternally feminine, Mary Ann was determined to look her best even for William Calcraft. When the wardresses went to escort her from the condemned cell to the scaffold, they found her brushing

*her long black hair in front of the mirror. As they approached
her she turned and said brightly, 'Right – now I am ready!'*

Creighton, Mary Frances (USA)

Mary's problem was that she just could not accept that having
got away with murder twice, she could not get away with it a
third time! In 1933, short of money, Mary hit on the bright idea
of poisoning her brother Raymond as a means of inheriting his
legacy and claiming his life insurance as well. And although it
became known to the court during her subsequent trial that she
had indeed purchased arsenic, no one actually saw her administer
it to Raymond, so the jury acquitted her.

Mary was obviously overwhelmed by her success, for within a
short space of time her father- and mother-in-law both died, the
post-mortems revealing traces of arsenic – but this time, because
the quantity in her mother-in-law's body was not considered by
the jury to be sufficiently lethal, the case was thrown out. And
probably because the authorities assumed that the same amount
of poison would be found present in the body of the dead woman's
husband and so be similarly rejected by a jury, they decided not to
waste the court's time in bringing further charges.

Despite his parents having been poisoned and the finger of
blame having pointed at his wife, John Creighton did not leave
Mary; instead they moved to Long Island with their young
daughter Ruth, where they became friendly with another couple,
Everett and Ada Appelgate, who after some time moved in with
them. Allegations were later to be made, not only that Everett
seduced 15-year-old Ruth Creighton and wanted to marry her, but
that Ruth and Everett were having an affair. Whether either of

these was the motive or not, sufficient to say that Mary reached for the poison bottle labelled 'Rough on Rats', and little by little supplemented Ada's eggnogs with its contents until Everett found he had become a widower.

This time, however, Mary's phenomenal luck had run out. Charged with murder, she stood trial and not only confessed to the crime, but also accused Appelgate of actually helping to administer the poison. After three hours' deliberation by the jury, both were found guilty and sentenced to death.

In the condemned cell in Sing Sing Prison Mary gave few signs of despair; on the contrary she was obviously buoyed up at the prospect of a favourable result being reached by the Court of Appeal. But when news came through that the original death sentence had been affirmed, her nerves gave way completely. Eating little but ice cream, she lay on the bed in her cell crying and moaning; she rarely slept but when she did she would wake up screaming, 'I can't stand it, I can't stand it!' What further exacerbated her already fragile mental condition was that while she was thus incarcerated, no fewer than ten men were electrocuted for their crimes within the prison, events that could not possibly be kept concealed from the other inmates. The strain on her emotions was such that two days before she was due to be escorted to the execution chamber, she became bedridden and hardly able to move.

A special commission was authorised to examine her both physically and mentally, its results stating:

We find no evidence of organic disease of the central nervous system or the body as a whole. Mrs Creighton is well developed, well nourished and muscular. If she has lost weight, it is not apparent. Her disturbances in motor power, in sensation and in speech are in part hysterical. They are grossly exaggerated by conscious malingering. Her mind appears to be clear and she fully appreciates her present position. She is suffering from a type of disability which would improve rapidly if she were encouraged, and get worse if she were discouraged. Her condition is the reaction to the situation in which she finds herself.

The executioner was Robert G. Elliott, not only an expert in his profession, but also noted for his humane and compassionate attitude towards his victims. When on 16 July 1936 he reported to the prison, he was shocked to find Mrs Creighton in a state of total collapse. Clad only in a pink nightdress and black dressing gown, wearing black slippers and holding a rosary, she was placed in a wheelchair – the first time a victim had ever been transported in that manner on such an occasion – and in the execution chamber was lifted into the electric chair. Limp and unresisting, her eyes closed and all the colour drained from her face, she was obviously unconscious and the warders had no difficulty in strapping her into the chair and attaching the electrodes. After checking that all necessary connections had been made, Mr Elliott gently raised her head and, pressing it back against the rubber headrest, secured it in position.

To block the view of the helpless woman from would-be photographers among the official witnesses in the audience, the guards placed themselves between the chair and the observation window, and as soon as they did so the executioner moved swiftly to throw the switch – and Mary Frances Creighton died without even knowing.

As an indication of the heat that is generated in a person being electrocuted, one of the warders on duty that night suffered severe burns on coming into contact with Mrs Creighton's body while releasing her from the chair; normally this would have been prevented by the thick clothing usually worn by the victim, but on this occasion her flimsy apparel proved inadequate.

American tabloids were never averse to giving criminals lurid labels, especially the female ones, as evidenced by those given to murderess Ada LeBoeuf by one southern newspaper in the 1920s, 'the Siren of the Swamps', 'Louisiana's Love Pirate' and 'Small Town Cleopatra' being just a few. Nor were the details of her appearance ignored, repeated allusions to her entertaining guests in her cell wearing a white organdie dress, and when someone suggested that she have her long black hair bobbed, she allegedly answered, 'Oh no, bobbed hair suits some women but I don't think I'd like it; I've never had my hair cut and I don't intend to now.'

D

Davy, Margaret (England)

A man named Richard Roose was indirectly instrumental in Margaret Davy being executed in a particularly gruesome manner, for in 1531 he added poison to the yeast in some porridge which had been prepared for the family and servants of the Bishop of Rochester, and for the poor of the parish, causing serious illness in many victims and two deaths. The Bishop himself was not affected, he not having partaken of porridge that day.

MARTYRS, MURDERESSES AND MADWOMEN

Henry VIII was so appalled at such a secretive and indiscriminate method of killing people that he caused an Act to be passed in that year, to deal with the crime, chapter 9 stating in part that:

> *Our Sayde Sovereign Lord The Kynge, of his blessed Disposicion, inwardly abhorrying all such abhomynable offences because that in no persone can lyve in suretye out of daunger of death by that meane yf practyse thereof shulde not be exchued, hath ordeyned and enacted by auctorytie of thys presente parlyment that the sayde poysonyng be adjudged and demed as high treason [...] and requyeth condigne punysshemente for the same, and it is ordeyned and enacted by auctoritie of this presente parlyment that the sayd Richard Roose shalbe therfore boyled to deathe.*

And because that was the penalty for poisoning, poor Margaret Davy, who was found guilty of poisoning three households in which she had been employed, was similarly 'boyled to death', being immersed in a cauldron of water in the marketplace in Smithfield, London, on 17 March 1542 and watched by crowds of ghoulish spectators. Whether the water was boiling at the time or subsequently heated was not disclosed.

> *By the nineteenth century condemned women, having mounted the scaffold and being positioned on the drop, had their arms and ankles tied, the latter thereby preventing their long skirts rising as they fell. Regrettably this precaution was not in force in 1751 when well-educated though naive Mary Blandy met her end. She had succumbed to the blandishments of Captain William Henry Cranstoun who was intent on securing her dowry; her father objected so she agreed to put a potion, sent by the*

captain, in his food, which poisoned him. She was tried at Oxford, found guilty and sentenced to death.

A makeshift scaffold had been constructed which required the victim to climb a high ladder instead of the usual flight of steps, and as Mary ascended it local men surged forward in an attempt to peer beneath her ankle-length skirts. Overwhelmed by embarrassment, she reached the platform and exclaimed to the waiting executioner as he positioned the noose around her neck: 'Please don't hang me high, for the sake of decency!'

Deshayes, Catherine (France)

If Catherine had ever written a recipe book, the contents would have given the diner rather more than a queasy stomach-ache, for the ingredients included bat's blood, blister beetles and desiccated moles! Her culinary prowess proved more than useful, for the seventeenth century was an era in which love potions and philtres were the cocktails with which to entice reluctant lovers to succumb to one's charms, or to dispose of enemies, all supplied by the local witch – at a price, of course.

There was little doubt that Catherine Deshayes, also known as La Voisin, was one of the most renowned members of that particular profession. In her early thirties she decided to solve her severe financial difficulties by practising sorcery and fortune-telling, concentrating on clients needing advice on attracting the opposite sex and retaining their affection. Having made an initially favourable impression in Parisian circles, her business flourished to the extent that she was able to buy a house on the outskirts of the city, a stately residence which became a venue for the lovelorn among the aristocracy. In *Archives de la Bastille*, written by the celebrated author François Ravaisson and published in 1873, Catherine explained how:

> *Some women asked whether they could not soon become widows, because they wanted to marry someone else; almost all asked this, and came for no other reason. When those who come to have their hand read do ask for anything else, they nevertheless always come to that point, given time, and ask to be ridded of someone, and when I gave those who come to me for that purpose my usual answer, that those they wished to be rid of would die when it pleased God, they told me that I was not very clever.*

It then became obvious to her that if she was to maintain her superiority among the other practising soothsayers and palmists, she would have to show some results of her prognostications. She had already amassed a considerable inventory of 'magical' aids, Tarot cards, crystal balls, charts of the heavens and astrological tables, but in order to offer more tangible means whereby her clients' problems could be solved, she became a purveyor of poisons at prices which could be afforded only by the most affluent of Paris. Her efforts to satisfy her clientele resulted in an unidentifiable ailment sweeping the city, fatally affecting, curiously enough, older, unattractive men and women whose spouses just happened to have fancied someone else, and pregnant women who wished to lose their unborn children. Other potions benefited lovers, both men and women, much to their delight, who found their erotic performances considerably enhanced after having unknowingly partaken of one of La Voisin's secret and extremely expensive philtres, administered by their partners.

Swept along on a highly lucrative wave of sorcery, Catherine indulged in black magic at its very darkest. She gathered around her a veritable coven of other witches, sadists and perverts; animals were slaughtered, their entrails, suitably boiled and flavoured, providing infallible medicines; newborn babies were sacrificed during Black Masses; and she became so eminent among the elite that eventually word of her mystic powers reached the ears of the Marquise de Montespan, mistress of King Louis XIV, whose beauty was as much renowned as her volcanic temper was feared. Jealous of any possible competitors for the royal favours and fearing that the King might discard her for a younger woman, she paid La Voisin tens of thousands of francs for potions with which to remove suspected rivals from the scene – permanently. Nor was that all; the Marquise even took part in the Satanic rites arranged by Catherine, ceremonies involving severed limbs which La Voisin procured from her lover, the Paris executioner.

But as reports of these clandestine orgies circulated, priests belonging to the Order of St Vincent de Paul, dedicated to tracking down and converting heretics, started to investigate such irreligious activities. On learning of this, the Marquise immediately assumed that their enquiries had been instigated by the King so that, having incriminated her, he could replace her with one of the younger and more tempting beauties of the royal court.

At that, her already ungovernable temper knew no bounds; so venomously determined was she to prevent anyone else assuming her role as Louis' mistress that, hastening to La Voisin, she presented her with a veritable fortune in gold and demanded that she poison the King.

Made richer than she had ever been, Catherine formulated a plan whereby she would impregnate a scroll of paper with toxic fluids and hand it to the King as a petition; mixing with his perspiration, the poison would attack his nervous system and kill him within a short space of time. But before she could act, one of her circle of Satanists betrayed her to the police, who promptly arrested her. Loyal to her many aristocratic clients, when interrogated she refused to name names, but her daughter, doubtless hoping that by laying the blame on others, her mother would escape serious involvement, identified the hundreds of high society members who had participated in her mother's demonic ceremonies.

Most of the aristocrats she named were rounded up and put on trial, scores being subsequently imprisoned. As for the Marquise, she desperately begged Louis for mercy, artfully reminding him of the seven children she had borne him; her plea saved her life for the King banished her, forbidding her ever to return to Paris.

But no such good fortune or royal clemency favoured La Voisin. Retribution was demanded, and in the Middle Ages that was rather more than a reprimand and a smack on the wrist. Catherine Deshayes was taken away and after being severely racked, she was strapped immovable into the torture chair, an iron structure with spiked seat, back and armrests, under which a fire could be lighted. Nor were her legs neglected, for she was later subjected to the dreaded boots, metal legging which could be tightened, crushing the limbs until the wearer's shin bones splintered and fractured. Even incoherent protests were out of the question, for her sentence also included the amputation of her tongue.

Her ghastly torture ended on 22 February 1680, when the authorities prepared her execution in accordance with regulations. After erecting the stake, a circular wall consisting of alternate layers of straw and wood was built around it, a passage being left for access to the centre. Catherine Deshayes, clad only in a sulphur-smeared tunic, was led to the stake, to which she was bound with ropes and chains. Before leaving the pyre the executioner heaped more combustible material around her, and, after closing

The Torture Chair

the passage with further supplies of wood, he and his assistants ignited all sides of the kindling at the same time.

Regardless of her crimes, one can only hope that the rising smoke brought suffocation before the leaping flames devoured her flesh; whichever horrific way she perished, she paid the price of her wickedness in full.

 During the French Revolution Mme Marie Jeanne Roland had been condemned to death by the Council and when visited by executioner Sanson who was to cut away the long black hair from her neck so that it would not impede the falling blade, she murmured, 'At least leave me enough for you to hold up my head and show it to the people, if they wish to see it!'

Dick, Alison (Scotland)

Witches also existed in Scotland in the seventeenth century, their presence being suspected when cattle died, droughts occurred or illness spread through the residents of a village. To prove a woman was indeed a witch, they needed a witch-finder. There was no shortage of these 'experts' for they moved around the country, their travel expenses being paid by those who engaged them, plus about twenty shillings for each conviction. On arrival in a village the bellman would advertise the fact by walking round the streets announcing it to all and sundry. Suspects would then be arrested, or vengeful neighbours would inform on their enemies. It also worked in reverse, a woman anticipating being reported bribing her likely informer to keep quiet, or even bribing the witch-finder to find her innocent.

In many cases the witness's evidence was sufficient to prove guilty; if not, the fact that witches were secretly marked by Satan made it necessary to find the sign on the witch's body. There were two kinds of marks, visible and invisible. The former was simple to locate, for after the suspect had been stripped naked and all her hair had been shaved off, all one had to look for was a pimple, mole or birthmark to prove her guilt. It was the invisible mark that called for all the professional expertise of the witch-finder. Based on the fact that the flesh where the invisible mark existed was not susceptible to pain and would not bleed, even under pressure from a sharp instrument (James I himself stated that the absence of blood was an infallible sign), he would proceed to probe her entire body with a long sharp needle. His search was usually successful, because as the time passed, continued prodding caused the flesh to become insensitive. Some witch-finders, determined not to be deprived of their fees, would use a spring-loaded instrument, the needle of which would retract into its holder when pressed against the skin, the suspect of course experiencing no pain.

Sometimes additional measures had to be employed, such as that used on a suspect in 1591: 'By tightening the pilliwinckes [thumbscrews] on her fingers they, upon search, found the enemy's mark to be in her fore-crag, or forepart of her throat, and then she confessed all. In another witch, the Devil's mark was found upon her privates.'

One of those who thus suffered was Alison Dick who, found guilty of practising witchcraft in Kirkcaldy in 1633, was burnt to death on 19 November of that year, together with her male colleague William Coke, the itemised bill submitted to the treasurer of the local council being as follows:

For ten loads of coal to burn them – £3.6.8
For a tar barrel – 14.0
For towes [kindling] – 6.0
To him that brought the Executioner – £2.18.0
To the Executioner for his pains – £8.14.0
For his expenses here – 16.4
For one to go to Tinmouth for the Laird [to preside over the burning] – 6.0
Total – £17.1.0.

Although her real name was Mary Young, she became known as Jenny Diver because of the dexterity with which, as an expert pickpocket, she could dive her hand in and out of her victims' pockets without being detected. Her sleight of hand was truly remarkable, although that phrase should be in the plural, because at times she had four of them! To further reduce the risk of being caught, she paid an amateur sculptor to make her two false arms, which she secured within her coat sleeves, and when seated she crossed the false gloved hands demurely in her lap. Slits in the sides of her coat allowed her to slide her own hands out and into the pockets or handbags of those sitting on each side of her in church or theatre. Similar ruses, such as graciously accepting assistance from men on crossing a muddy road, then deftly sliding the rings from their fingers as she did so, brought her a veritable fortune. In fact, the only thrift she ever experienced was when meeting hangman John Thrift on 18 March 1740; then, her false arms discarded, her real arms bound in front of her, she felt the noose tighten around her slim neck 'neath the gallows at Tyburn, and the trap fall away from beneath her feet.

Druse, Roxalana (USA)

When William Druse first met Roxalana Teftt in 1863 he was struck by her attractive figure and completely lost his head to her; twenty-one years later he was struck again, this time by the axe she wielded – as she beheaded him!

Dominant by nature, Roxalana ruled the roost. With their teenaged daughter Mary she entertained men after William had gone to bed, giving rise to much gossip among the neighbours, as did the commotion caused by the couple's repeated rows. Matters came to a head, in more ways than one, when, during a furious argument, Roxalana handed a revolver to her 14-year-old nephew, Frank Gates, and told him to shoot his uncle. Whether too scared to disobey, or in order to protect her from being attacked by her husband, he did so, both shots only inflicting flesh wounds. William collapsed on the floor, but Roxalana, seeing he was still alive, picked up the axe from where it lay by the stove and struck him on the head. Not content with that, she then aimed at his neck with such force that she severed his head completely.

Where any other woman would have been aghast at what she had done, or sought medical assistance, Roxalana calmly picked up the head and, rolling it up in her apron, she put it to one side. Then she and Mary proceeded to dismember the decapitated corpse, using the axe and a kitchen knife, throwing the body parts and limbs into the already lighted stove. Apparently loath to part with what was left of her dearly beloved, she dumped the head in a sack of wheat which was stored in the corner of the room, after which she and nephew Frank disposed of the weapons in a nearby pond.

However, the young boy could not keep silent about what had happened that awful night, and word reached the authorities. Roxalana was arrested but, under questioning, remained silent, as did Mary. The testimony submitted by Frank, the presence of ashes and charred bones in the stove, and the discovery of William's head, were so overwhelming that defence in court was futile and she was found guilty of murder and sentenced to death.

As the following months went by, appeal after appeal was heard and rejected. The media had a field day, some being against capital punishment per se, others calling for the execution of the perpetrator of such cold-blooded slaughter. Meanwhile, in the condemned cell, Roxalana had outbursts of bad temper, even ordering the priest, there to give her spiritual support, to leave her alone.

It was not until 28 February 1887 that the scaffold was made ready in the grounds of the gaol and the executioner detailed to attend. Hardly surprisingly the prisoner had slept but little, and on rising, dressed herself in what was described in the newspapers as 'a narrow satin skirt, having a tight fitting basque. The hem of the skirt was ruffled, her sleeves having white ruching at the cuffs, repeated at the neckline, where she had pinned a bunch of roses'.

As she was led out to the yard it became obvious to the official witnesses and large number of reporters that her cold, almost remote attitude had finally been overcome, for tears ran down her cheeks and she trembled almost uncontrollably. Mounting the scaffold steps she paused and, as the priest said his final words of support, two deputies advanced, one of them swiftly slipping the black hood over her head. Even as muffled shrieks commenced beneath the tightly drawn fabric, the signal was given and as the noose tightened its stranglehold 'there was a rattle, a jar and a strangled cry', and Roxalana's lifeless body swayed from side to side in the cold winter's wind.

 Obsessed with jealousy, Mary Bolton suspected that her meek, ordinary-looking husband was having secret affairs with other women, and she attacked

him on several occasions, but eventually her uncontrollable emotions got the better of her. Going into his office one day in June 1936 she pointed a revolver at him, then proceeded to fire every round into his body. Somehow he managed to drag himself out into the corridor and exclaimed to horrified colleagues: 'Keep that woman away from me!' Totally unconcerned, his wife walked past him saying scornfully as she did so, 'Take no notice of him – he's just putting on an act!'

Found guilty of murder, Mary Bolton was given a life sentence and committed suicide in prison some years later.

Du Barry, Marie (France)

What must it have felt like to have to behead a woman you loved, knowing that if you refused you would be replaced by someone much more brutal? That was the appalling dilemma that faced Charles-Henri Sanson, the Paris executioner, on 6 December 1793.

Sanson had first met Marie in 1766 when a close friend, Abbé Gomart, who happened to be dining with him, expressed his fears regarding a young lady he described as his niece, although in actual fact she was his daughter. Her name was Marie Jeanne de Vaubernier, and, he said sadly, her morals were causing him increasing concern. Convent educated, she had left to become apprenticed to a famous costumier in Paris, and whilst working there, had become acquainted with some of the elegant ladies of the court, their somewhat wayward lifestyle encouraging her to act likewise. Ravishingly beautiful, his friend explained, she had begun to lead a life of sin and dissipation.

Charles-Henri agreed to help and so met Marie, instantly conceding that the young lady was indeed overwhelmingly alluring.

Despite having no motive in mind other than to help her mend her ways, he was nevertheless deeply attracted to her; his attentions, however, were not reciprocated, for the lady was aiming far higher than a liaison with the public executioner.

They parted, and she soon ingratiated her way into fashionable society where she won the attention of Louis XV who, in order to elevate her status, arranged that she should marry the Comte Guillaume du Barry. And it was as Jeanne Gomard de Vaubernier, Comtesse du Barry, that she achieved what was undoubtedly the pinnacle of her life's ambition, that of being the King's mistress.

The years passed, and Marie's lifestyle and those of thousands of others were to change forever with the advent of the French Revolution. The main targets of the revolutionaries were of course the King and Queen, together with the members of the royal family and all those who associated with them. After the death of Louis XV, du Barry went to live in England, but following the Revolution she returned to her home country, believing that no harm would come to her; being the daughter of a priest and a dressmaker, she could not be condemned as a hated aristocrat. But the Tribunal thought otherwise; as a royal mistress she had squandered the treasures of the State, and was known to have mourned the late, guillotined, King Louis XVI.

In Charles-Henri's diary for 6 December 1793 he described the harrowing scenes in heartfelt detail:

Madame du Barry was sentenced to death last night and executed this morning. We arrived at the Hall of Justice punctually but had to wait as the convict [du Barry] was with the judges who were taking down her confession. Then she was brought in; her legs could hardly carry her. It was some twenty years since I had seen her, and I could hardly have known her. Her features had become coarse.

When she saw me she shrieked, covered her eyes with her hands and sank down on her knees, crying, 'Do not kill me!'

She rose to her feet again. 'Where are the judges?' she exclaimed. 'I have not confessed everything; I want to see them.' The judge and his clerk were sent for, and she said she had concealed several objects of value in her country house, but she broke down and sobbed at every word. The clerk kept saying, 'Is that all?' and tried to make her sign the confession, but she pushed the paper away, saying that she had something more to add. She perhaps thought that, in reason of the immense wealth she was giving up, she might be reprieved.

At last the judge said she must submit to the court's decision and make up by her courage for the ignominy of her past life as a member of the royal court. One of my assistants approached and attempted to cut her hair, but she resisted, and the other assistants had great difficulty in binding her hands. She at last submitted, but she cried as I never saw a woman cry before.

Vast crowds had assembled, and many cries were raised, but her shrieks were louder than any. She exclaimed: 'Good citizens, free me! I am innocent; I am of the people, good citizens, do not let them kill me!' No one moved, but men and women hung their heads and silence prevailed at last.

Du Barry was so faint that my son Henri had to support her. She often spoke to me, begging for mercy. I was more moved than anyone, for this unfortunate woman reminded me of my younger days, of the time when I knew her . . . When she saw the guillotine she became overwrought and struggled with my assistants and tried to bite them. She was very strong, and three minutes elapsed before they could carry her up on to the platform. She was frightful to look at, and to the very last moment she struggled.

Although most French aristocrats retained their dignity on the scaffold and went to their deaths without flinching, one can understand Marie's frenzied emotions, and feel for the man who once loved her, but also had to behead her.

Before Queen Marie Antoinette was guillotined she wrote a farewell letter to her sister-in-law Princess Elizabeth, which found its way into the hands of Robespierre, then Leader of the Revolutionary Assembly. Rather than take any humane action by giving it to the Princess, he concealed it under his mattress. When later he, in turn, was guillotined, the letter was found by a revolutionary deputy, M. Curtois, who kept it as a souvenir, the Princess already having been beheaded.

Twenty years later, hopeful to exchange it for a pardon for his revolutionary past, he handed it, together with a lock of the late Queen's hair, to the then King, Louis XVIII, only to be promptly arrested. The relics were seized, and Curtois was banished for life to Belgium. The letter was then given to Mme Royale, the late Queen's daughter, and on seeing the pitiful, tear-stained pages written by her mother under such tragic circumstances, she fainted.

Dugan, Eva (USA)

In England, the year 1874 heralded a new era in execution technique when, having just taken over the scaffold, hangman William Marwood realised that breaking the felon's spinal column would bring death faster than the current slow strangulation method brought about by using the 'one length of rope fits all' method. To achieve this, and thereby alleviate the victim's suffering, it would be necessary to vary the distance he or she dropped, having first taken into consideration their age, weight, physical development and similar factors. This method of calculation was refined and improved by subsequent hangmen, and was in fact the basic measure used until capital punishment was eventually abolished.

However, it would seem that Marwood's ideas were not embraced in America until much later, many states in the USA still adhering to the original system until well into the following century, much to the horror and distress of the spectators attending the execution of Eva Dugan.

Eva had been found guilty of the brutal murder of her employer, A. J. Mathis. At her trial she accused another alleged 'employee' named Jack, of the murder, letters signed by Jack later coming from Mexico, confessing to the crime; no explanation of how Eva arranged for these missives was forthcoming, if indeed she was responsible in any way for them. They had no effect on the jury's deliberations, the verdict being one of guilty.

The inevitable petitions were submitted to the Arizona state governor, Eva even claiming to be insane in order to be granted a reprieve, but to no avail. In gaol she was reported as being full of bravado, one journalist quoting her as saying that she was going to die as she had lived, and that people loved a good sport but hated a bad loser.

On 21 February 1930 Eva stood on the scaffold, hooded and bound. The executioner positioned the noose around her neck and operated the drop. The trapdoors opened, the body dropped, but then the rope swung back up again – empty. Witnesses saw Eva's torso sprawled in the pit, her hooded head lying some distance away. And as her heart had continued beating for some little time, copiously flowing blood was very much in evidence.

Eva had been given too long a drop, due regard not having been given to her physical condition, for subsequent examination revealed that the debacle had been caused by her having a flabby neck. Had prior checks such as those advocated by Marwood and further improved by a successor, James Berry, been in force, a shorter drop would have resulted in a 'normal' execution. However, the severance of her head would have been so rapid that Eva would have suffered for only an infinitesimal length of time. Bearing that fact in mind, it is ironic to note that mainly due to that catastrophe, the Arizona authorities decided to dispatch victims by the gas chamber instead – a method in which victims usually attempt to hold their breath for as long as possible, and so suffer visibly for a number of seconds before and while inhaling the toxic fumes.

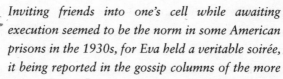

Inviting friends into one's cell while awaiting execution seemed to be the norm in some American prisons in the 1930s, for Eva held a veritable soirée, it being reported in the gossip columns of the more popular papers that 'she was gracious as a society woman entertaining at a tea, the conversation positively sparkling with the repartee'.

Durgan, Bridget (USA)

Eva Dugan, whose tragic end is described above, slew her employer and fell to her death from the scaffold; Bridget murdered her employer's wife and met her death by rising!

Bridget was a servant in the New Jersey residence of a Dr William Coriell and his wife Ellen. Among the possible reasons which later emerged as to why she should have repeatedly and savagely stabbed the doctor's wife to death and then attempted to burn the house down, was that she had been reprimanded for not doing her job satisfactorily, or that she had been secretly in love with the doctor. What credence was given at the trial to the fact that she suffered from epilepsy, and whether this might have had any bearing on the crime, is not known, but the jury did not hesitate to bring in a verdict of guilty; nor did the judge hesitate to sentence her to death by hanging, his words being greeted with applause by those in the public gallery, their cheers being drowned by the condemned woman's hysterical screams, which could be heard by passers-by outside the building.

Media attention was widespread and intensive, it being reported that hundreds of applications were received from those who wanted to be present at her execution, and on the actual day, 30 August 1867, scenes resembling those at Tyburn, London, two centuries earlier, were very evident. The area surrounding the gaol was packed with spectators, some clambering on roofs and clinging on to ledges, hoping to get a glimpse of the condemned woman as she was led out of the prison block. Inside the yard mayhem reigned, for a further thousand or more had managed to gain admittance, cheering, pushing, even fighting to get a better viewpoint; a mob totally out of control of the officers who were attempting to preserve some sort of order.

The execution mechanism was of unusual design in that, after being hooded and noosed, Bridget, instead of falling through the drop trapdoors, was jerked violently upwards, the other end of the rope being attached to a heavy weight that was suddenly released (for greater detail see Appendix 2). As that happened, onlookers variously described her as having her neck instantly broken, others claiming that she struggled madly, panting for breath, her writhing hands becoming discoloured. That the execution method left much to be desired was evidenced by a report that she took nearly thirteen minutes to die, although the movements seen could have been attributed to muscular spasms after death.

When eventually the weight was released and her body slowly lowered, it was noticed that her eyes were protruding and, to be expected, her face was suffused with blood. Having earlier expressed a wish that a post-mortem should not take place – she feared being dissected – her body was placed in a coffin and she was interred in a nearby Catholic cemetery.

Bridget's choice of clothes for her final appearance was as modest as could be imagined, consisting as it did of a plain brown long-sleeved frock with a lace collar, white gloves and matching stockings. The one incongruous note was that she had decided to wear what were known as 'lasting' slippers – hardly necessary, one would have thought!

Dyer, Amelia Elizabeth (England)

That a man should kill a child is appalling; that a woman should kill a child is unthinkable; but a woman who kills eight children and perhaps many more . . .

Amelia Dyer was known as the Reading Baby-farmer; having once been a member of the Salvation Army, she was a figure of trust to those parents or guardians who, over the years, accepted her offer to adopt unwanted children, and were more than happy to pay her the regular boarding fees for their upkeep. But their trust was badly shaken when in 1885 a boatman on the Thames noticed something unusual floating in the water. Rescuing it, he was shocked to find that, wrapped in a brown paper parcel, was a dead baby, with a tape tied tightly round its neck. The parcel bore an address: Mrs Thomas, Piggotts Road, Lower Caversham.

The police immediately went to the address, only to discover that their quarry had moved away and had, moreover, changed her name. Worse was to follow, for within the next few days two more bodies were found floating in the river, each in a separate parcel, each having been strangled by the tape around its throat.

In the widespread hunt that ensued, Mrs Dyer, alias Thomas, alias Harding, alias Stanfield, was found, and when arrested on a charge of murdering a little girl named Fry, admitted her guilt, adding, 'You'll know all mine by the tapes around their necks.' That statement was tragically borne out when no fewer than a further four small corpses were fished out of the Thames, and it was suspected that there could have been many more similarly strangled over the years during which she had been a baby-farmer, four more children having recently disappeared.

It would appear that she would place an advertisement in local papers, worded as follows:

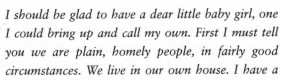

I should be glad to have a dear little baby girl, one I could bring up and call my own. First I must tell you we are plain, homely people, in fairly good circumstances. We live in our own house. I have a good and comfortable home. We are out in the country and sometimes I am alone a good deal. I do not want a child for money's sake but for company and home comfort. Myself and my husband are dearly fond of children. I have no child of my own. A child with me will have a good home and a mother's love and care. We belong to the Church of England. Although I want to bring the child up as my own, I should not mind the mother or any other person coming to see the child at any

time. It would be a satisfaction to see and know the child was
getting on all right. I only hope we can come to terms.

The latter offer of access was impossible, of course, Amelia Dyer repeatedly changing her name and address. Women who responded to the advertisement usually handed over a parcel of clothes, ten pounds in cash, a considerable sum in those days, and the baby – which she never saw again.

When her house was searched by the police, no less than three hundredweight (336 lb) of children's clothes were found, together with a large number of pawn tickets for baby clothes.

In May 1896 Amelia appeared in court charged with murdering a four-month-old baby girl named Doris Marmon and a boy, Harry Simmons. Her plea, that she was insane, was not accepted, the jury taking only five minutes to find her guilty, and she was sentenced to death. Confident of a reprieve, doubtless because of her age – she was 57 – she spent her time in the condemned cell praying and writing poems, one of which survives:

By nature, Lord, I know with grief,
I am a poor fallen leaf Shrivelled and dry, near unto death
Driven with sin, as with a breath.
But if by Grace I am made new,
Washed in the blood of Jesus, too,
Like to a lily, I shall stand
Spotless and pure at His right hand.

And not content with the hypocritical tone of the verse, she had the appalling gall to sign it 'Mother'.

In accordance with the regulations, which stipulated that executions should take place at 8 a.m. on the first day after the intervention of three Sundays from the day on which the sentence was passed – in this case 10 June 1896 – Amelia herself was taken into care, James Billington, the public executioner, a muscular ex-coalminer, having temporarily adopted her. He escorted her up the steps of the scaffold behind the high walls of Newgate Prison and there guided her on to the trapdoors, where he hooded her. The prison bell had already been tolling for the past fifteen minutes and would continue to do so for the same length of time after the execution had taken place. Crowds had gathered outside, waiting to see the regulatory black flag which would be raised on the prison's flagpole at the moment the trapdoors opened, and also, within the next few minutes, to read the Certificate of Death which had to be displayed near the principal entrance to the prison. They did not have long to wait, for Billington, never one to linger, and no doubt recalling the manner in which Amelia Dyer had strangled her helpless charges, positioned his version of a tape, the noose, around her neck and swiftly operated the drop – sending the cold-blooded killer plummeting into the depths of the pit.

Whether Amelia's spirit departed with her, though, is another matter, it being rumoured that her ghost haunted the chief warder's office for some years following her execution.

Dyer, Mary (USA)

In England members of the Society of Friends, founded by George Fox (1624–1691), were unpopular with the populace because they opposed the Presbyterian system in force at the time. As a result of his unceasing and public protests, Fox himself spent some time in prisons in Lancaster, Nottingham and Scarborough. It was hardly to be wondered, therefore, that some Quakers, as they became known, sailed to the New World as colonists in order to spread their beliefs.

Their activities were far from welcome, many of them being persecuted and harshly punished, in particular by the Puritans in Massachusetts. One of the Quakers was Mary Dyer who, together with two male colleagues, was sentenced to be hanged for returning after being earlier driven out of the colony. On 27 October 1659 they were escorted under armed guard to Boston Common. On attempting to address the large crowd which had assembled, army drummers drowned out their voices – interestingly enough, the same tactics which were used over a hundred years later in France when the Revolutionaries guillotined their king.

The method of the trio's execution was identical to that in use at the time at Tyburn, London. After her companions had been executed, Mary, having been blindfolded, was forced to climb the ladder propped against the branch of the tree, the noose already in place around her neck, the other end tied to the branch. The crowd fell silent as the hangman gripped the ladder, preparatory to turning it and causing her to hang, when suddenly it was announced that she had been reprieved. So strong was her faith that almost reluctantly she descended the ladder, to be returned to gaol and from thence to Rhode Island.

However, the challenge to spread Quaker beliefs was too strong for her. Having already brushed shoulders with death she was aware of the appalling risk she was taking; nevertheless, a few months later, she returned to Boston, only to be arrested again. Clemency was shown once more and she was urged to go into exile again. She would not, so they hanged her.

 At that time, Quakers were indeed cruelly treated. Following the ordeal suffered by one, Mary Clark, it was recounted how: 'Her tender Body the Hangman

unmercifully tore with twenty stripes of a three-fold-corded-knotted whip, as near as he could, all in one place, fetching his Stroakes with the greatest Strength and Advantage.'

E

Edmonson, Mary (England)

Mary was the daughter of a farmer who lived near Leeds, Yorkshire, but had gone to live with her widowed aunt, Mrs Walker, at Rotherham. There Mary lived a decorous way of life and, being a religiously minded young lady, went to the local church regularly. What she was alleged to have done later was totally out of character – if, as some believed, she was indeed guilty of the horrendous crime.

It seemed that a lady teacher named Toucher had been spending the evening with Mrs Walker, and Mary escorted her across the darkened street afterwards. Some time later a woman who sold oysters and had been crying her wares in the locality, saw that the house door was open and heard Mary call out: 'Help! Murder! They have killed my aunt!' Other neighbours, hearing the commotion, ran to help, as did some men who had been drinking in a nearby tavern. On entering the house they were shocked to find Mrs Walker lying on the floor, her head covered with a piece of linen. On removing that, it became horribly apparent that her throat had been cut.

Mary, apparently almost incoherent, explained that four men had entered the house through the back door and that one of them put his hands round her aunt's neck. Another man, tall and dressed in black, she said, swore that he would kill her if she spoke a single word.

Just then one of the neighbours noticed that one of Mary's arms was cut, and on being asked about the wound, Mary said that one of the men, when leaving, jammed her arm in the door. This sounded so much beyond belief that another neighbour shook his head and accused the girl of committing the murder herself. At his words, Mary fell into a fit and, being carried to a nearby house, was blooded by a surgeon. She remained there until the next day when a coroner's inquest took place; the verdict being wilful murder, Mary was forthwith committed to prison.

Investigating her statement that the four mysterious men had entered the house to steal valuables, the police searched every room, only to find a watch and other items alleged to have been stolen, hidden beneath the floorboards in the privy. Mary was held in Kingston Prison until her trial, at which, damned by such evidence, any convincing defence was out of the question.

On 2 April 1759, only two days after being convicted, she was taken by carriage to the Peacock Inn on Kennington Lane. After a glass of wine there, she was put in a cart and driven to Kennington Common, the public execution site for the county of Surrey. Near St Mark's Church stood the scaffold (where, only a few years earlier, some of the Jacobite rebels had been hanged, drawn and quartered). There, ignoring her continued assertions of innocence, the hangman, probably Thomas Turlis, deftly hooded and noosed her. To somewhat muted cheers from the crowd, he operated the drop, and after she had hanged for some time, her body was cut down and taken to St Thomas' Hospital, Southwark, and there dissected 'in accordance with the laws respecting murderers'.

 In order to control certain 'stews' (brothels) in Southwark, London, in 1162, it was ordained by parliament that:

'No *stew holder [brothel keeper] or his wife should prevent any single woman [prostitute] from coming and going freely at all times, whenever they wished.*

To take no more for the woman's chamber in the week [rental] than fourteen pence.

Not to keep his doors open [for clients] upon the holidays [holy days].

No single woman to be kept against her will that would leave her sin

[change her way of life].

No stew holder to receive any woman of religion [nuns, etc.] or any man's wife.

No single woman to take any money to lie with any man, unless she lies with him all night till the morrow.

No man to be drawn or enticed into any stew-house.

The constables, bailiff and others, every week, to search every stew-house.'

F

Flanagan, Catherine and Williams, Margaret (England)

If you have to discuss your latest crime, then whatever you do, do not discuss it within earshot of a policeman! This is the lesson to be learned from this case, which involved Catherine and Margaret, sisters who, in the 1870s, hit on the brilliant idea of taking out insurance policies on various people, without telling them, of course, then murdering them and collecting the insurance money, which they shared out between them.

As Margaret was housekeeper to a Mr Higgins, it made sense to start with him. Accordingly they took out a policy on him and decided that, while they were at it, they might as well take out one on his elderly aunt – with a different company, naturally. What made it easy was that both their intended victims lived in the same house in Liverpool, so Margaret added a modicum of arsenic, not too little, not too much, first of all to the aunt's food, and confidently ordered some black attire ready for the funeral. When the time came to wear it, Margaret, as befits a faithful servant, was overcome with grief at the graveside; after which, she contacted the insurance company and shared the proceeds with her sister.

Mr Higgins was the next to savour one of his housekeeper's special recipes, the result being one that no amount of liver salts could cure. Catherine, wishing to play her part and earn her fifty per cent, joined Margaret at the funeral service, suitably sobbing into her black-edged hanky. Another insurance company subsequently paid up.

From then on it was all systems go; it is not known how many friends and relatives were assisted in shuffling off this mortal coil with a nasty taste in their mouths, nor how many more cheques signed by the treasurers of insurance companies would have dropped through their letterboxes, had not the two, like sisters all over the world, argued with each other. Perhaps the sister who bought the arsenic thought the percentage should be 60/40 in her favour; maybe the one who actually stirred it into the spicy bowl of soup thought she was doing all the work and so deserved 75 per cent. And if they were going to argue at all, the last place in which the disagreement should have taken place was in the cellar where they usually met to decide the division of the spoils. As sometimes happens in family rows, abusive language was used, voices were raised, and a vigilant policeman, patrolling the street, paused to listen intently to the heated disagreement which was coming via the grating at his feet. He did not need to be Sherlock Holmes to realise exactly what was being debated so vehemently, nor who was involved; entering the house he promptly arrested both of them.

During the subsequent post-mortems carried out on the corpses of Mr Higgins and his aunt, arsenic was found to have been the cause of death. Both sisters were sentenced to be hanged on 31 August 1874, that date bringing what little luck they had left, for had they been found out and sentenced prior to July of that year, their hangman would have been William Calcraft, the rope they would have been suspended by would have been little more than three feet in length, and they would have died by being painfully and slowly strangled. As it was, Calcraft had just retired, his place on the scaffold having been taken by William Marwood, a more humane man who varied the rope length by gauging the victim's weight and similar factors, thereby bringing death almost, though not always, instantaneously.

In that respect at least, the sisters Margaret and Catherine were a lot luckier than their victims.

In the court at Taunton, Somerset, in 1746, Mary Hamilton, alias Charles Hamilton, alias George Hamilton, alias William Hamilton, appeared accused of marrying no fewer than fourteen members of her own sex! Mary Price, her latest 'spouse' swore that she was lawfully married to the prisoner and that they had lived and bedded together as man and wife for more than three months, 'during which time, so well did the impostor assume the character of a man that she still actually believed she had married a fellow-creature of the right and proper sex.

At length she became distrustful and on comparing certain circumstances with her neighbours, became convinced that Mary Hamilton had acted the part of Charles Hamilton towards her by the vilest and most deceitful practices.'

After hearing the evidence, the judge decreed 'that the he, she, prisoner at the bar, is an uncommon cheat, and we, the Court, do sentence her or him, whichever he or she may be, to be for imprisoned for six months and during that time to be whipped in the towns of Taunton, Glastonbury, Wells and Shepton Mallet.'

Oh, to have overheard the conversation between Mary Price and her neighbours!

G

Gaunt, Elizabeth (England)

One day in 1683 Charles II and his brother James, Duke of York, visited the races at Newmarket. Their route home led past Rye House Farm in Hertfordshire, and it was there that an ambush had been prepared, with the intention of assassinating both royals and replacing them with a Protestant monarch. At one point hedges lined the road, and it was planned that horsemen, charging from both directions, would suddenly attack the party. However, the attempt failed, both King and Duke managing to escape.

One of the would-be killers was a man named James Burton; frantic to avoid capture for the sake of his family, he sought refuge with a poor widow, Elizabeth Gaunt, who gave him food and shelter. Out of Christian charity she contacted friends who arranged a passage to Holland for him.

Two years later James, Duke of Monmouth, raised a small and ineffectual army of peasants and marched to London in a futile bid to overthrow King James. One who joined his forces was James Burton, back from Holland. The attack on London was a disastrous failure and Monmouth was beheaded on Tower Hill by order of the King. Burton managed to escape and, remembering the sanctuary given to him on the previous occasion, again sought Elizabeth Gaunt's help. For some reason she was unable to do so; however, a woman neighbour of hers persuaded her husband, Mr Fernley, a barber, to give him shelter. But the lot of Good Samaritans is a hard one, for when Burton was eventually captured, to save his own precious skin he named his benefactors and in court gave fatally incriminating evidence against them.

The result was inevitable. Elizabeth was found guilty, the judge, in pronouncing the death sentence, saying:

The said Elizabeth Gaunt, well-knowing one James Burton to be a False Traitor and Rebel, in a certain House to the jurors unknown, did knowingly and traitorously sustain and maintain with Meat, Drink and Five Pounds in money, for the maintenance and sustenance of the said James Burton, did maliciously and traitorously deliver against the Duty of her Allegiance.

In the condemned cell Elizabeth composed her last speech:

I did but relieve an unworthy, poor, distressed family, and lo, I must die for it; well, I desire in the Lamb-like nature of the Gospel to forgive all that are concerned, and to say, Lord, lay it not to their

charge; but I fear it will not; nay I believe, when He comes to make inquisition for blood, it will be found at the door of the furious Judge: my blood will also be found at the door of the unrighteous Jury, who found me guilty upon the single oath of an out-lawd man.

The barber Fernley was also sentenced to death, and was hanged at Tyburn in October 1685, where, on the 23rd of that month, Elizabeth Gaunt was burned at the stake. Quaker William Penn, himself once a prisoner in the Tower, was at Tyburn that day and afterwards told a colleague that 'she laid the straw about her for burning herself speedily, and behaved herself in such a manner that all the spectators melted in tears.'

Unfortunately the fate of James Burton is not known, but he is hardly likely to have been given a medal.

Because in earlier centuries people in general were so poor and owned few possessions, theft was considered a heinous crime and was severely punished. In Doncaster on 23 May 1789 Mary Ashford found out how true this was when, having stolen two pieces of muslin, she was sentenced to be publicly whipped through the marketplace. She was tied with cords to the back of a horse-drawn cart and taken from the gaol along St Sepulchre's Gate, Baxter Gate, Market Place, Scot Lane, High Street, and so back to the gaol, having received a thorough flogging from the under-gaoler. 'Salt and brandy were applied to her lacerated back and shoulders' the prison records stated.

Graham, Barbara (USA)

Doomed to an unhappy life from the very beginning, Barbara Graham's end was equally tragic. Born in 1923, she was brought up by neighbours when her mother was imprisoned. She ran away and when caught, was held in the same reformatory as was her mother. After release she was repeatedly arrested on minor charges such as luring passers–by into gambling dens, vagrancy and prostitution, and was introduced to drugs by her fourth husband Henry Graham. Going morally downhill fast, in March 1953 she joined three criminals in a planned robbery on the residence of an elderly widow, Mrs Mabel Monahan, in Burbank, California, and during the raid she repeatedly struck the woman with the gun she carried in an attempt to find out where her victim's jewels were hidden. She was later caught and arrested on a charge of murder, the widow having died in hospital.

In order to make her incriminate herself, an undercover agent offered to provide her with an alibi for the night of the robbery; she accepted, and in doing so, demolished whatever defence she might have brought in court. As if that weren't sufficient to bring about her ultimate downfall, one of her criminal confederates, in order to be granted immunity, threw all the blame for the killing on her.

Because of her relative youth – she was only 32 – and her wretched upbringing, much of the media and the public supported her claim that she was innocent. In San Quentin's condemned cell she wrote poetry and listened to classical music, while outside petitions were raised and appeals held. But all to no avail, for on 3 June 1955 she rose and breakfasted. Replenishing her bright red lipstick, at 10 a.m. she prepared to be taken to the gas chamber – when news came that because her lawyer was still making efforts on her behalf before the State Supreme Court, the execution was postponed.

Filled with hope, though doubtless tinged with apprehension, Barbara was returned to her cell – only to be informed 45 minutes later that her lawyer's request had been rejected. Again the warders started the regulation procedure preparatory to leading her to the gas chamber, and just as they were securing the pad of the stethoscope over her heart that would signify when the gas had done its work, she was told that a further delay had been granted so that a new petition could be considered. What state her mind must have been in at this stage can only be imagined.

'Why do they torture me?' she exclaimed piteously. 'I was ready at ten o'clock.' And it was not until 11.30 a.m., all pleas having failed, that Barbara entered the sinister green-painted room where the chair, with the ominous-looking receptacle positioned beneath it, waited.

Rather than have to meet the eyes of the many official witnesses seated on the other side of the large glass window, Barbara had requested that she be blindfolded; gently guided to the chair, straps were then secured around her body, arms and legs. The rubber tube extending from outside the chamber was connected to the stethoscope positioned over her heart, and the warders left the chamber. The valves of the mixing bowls were opened to allow sulphuric acid and distilled water to flow into the receptacle by the chair; the cyanide eggs were released, their immersion in the acid allowing the toxic gases to rise; and Barbara died.

With head bowed, her body, slumped against the restraining straps, was left there for a further two hours after the doctor had confirmed that he could hear no further heartbeats.

Although many American newspapers sided with Barbara Graham, others denigrated her, variously describing her as a 'rat' and a 'rattlesnake' who 'took her last walk as if going on a shopping trip, clad in a skin-tight dress and wearing jangling, dangling earrings'.

Grese, *Irma* (*Germany*)

Although born in the same year as Barbara Graham, 1923, Irma Grese was of a totally different calibre. Brutal, ruthless and sadistic, she became a supervisor in the Ravenbruck, Auschwitz and Belsen concentration camps during the Second World War, a post which gave her the opportunity to punish without reason or restraint, any of the thousands of men and women who were incarcerated therein. Well-built and muscular, she gloried in donning the essentially masculine Nazi SS uniform and high boots, a pistol at her waist and whip in hand. Barbara Graham might have been called a rattlesnake – Irma Grese was given the unenviable title of the 'Beast of Belsen', one in which she undoubtedly gloried. Any excuse – or often none at all – was sufficient to allow her to terrorise the inmates with her two half-starved Alsatian dogs, never hesitating to let them off the lead.

When the prisoners were eventually liberated in 1945, appalling stories of her innate cruelty were related; accounts of her sadistic taunting of those about to be marched to the gas chambers, the chimneys of which belched smoke continually; of shooting prisoners for even looking at her; of obtaining the skins of dead prisoners to use as lampshades 'because human skin was tough and durable, but let the light through perfectly' one army journalist reported her as saying.

After capture she maintained her cold, inhuman attitude. As far as she was concerned, the prisoners were little more than animals, far inferior to the pure-blooded members of the Third Reich, the chosen race. She admitted without a hint of remorse that she maltreated them, and listened unmoved as the death sentence was passed on her.

On 13 December 1945 she was brought out of her prison cell in Hamelin, a small, medieval town nestling on the banks of the River

Weser. Even with death so near, she retained her almost robotic disinterest as Albert Pierrepoint, the English hangman who had been given the task of executing many of the Nazi war criminals, approached her. Any qualms he might have had about hanging a young (she was only 21) and outwardly attractive woman must have been quickly dispelled by the knowledge that she had used her authority to slaughter at least thirty inmates a day. He dropped the noose over her head. 'Schnell!' ('Do it quickly') she exclaimed. He did.

At the height of the French Revolution the scores of headless corpses were carted away to cemeteries where they were stripped and flung into deep pits. During this operation, wood fires were kept burning and thyme, sage and juniper were thrown on to the flames to mask the appalling stench of decomposing flesh that permeated the air. Worse was reported by the historian Montgaillard, who described how 'at Meudon there was a Tannery of Human Skins for such of the Guillotined as seemed worth flaying, of which perfectly good wash-leather was made for breeches and other uses. The skins of men were superior in toughness and quality to shamoy [chamois]; that of women was good for almost nothing, being so soft in texture.'

Gurdemaine, Margery (England)

It all started when a certain highly ambitious lady named Elianor Cobham, daughter of Reginald Cobham, Lord of Stirbridge, listened intently to Roger Bolingbroke, the renowned mathematician and astronomer of the day who, after studying the stars, forecast that Humphrey, Duke of Gloucester, the youngest son of Henry IV, Great

Chamberlain of England, would eventually become King. This, she decided, was an opportunity like none other; she had to get closely acquainted, very closely acquainted with Humphrey, despite his being married to Jacqueline of Hainault, and so prepare herself to become Queen of England. Accordingly she contacted a London witch, Margery Gurdemaine, who, after concocting a mixture of various secret ingredients known only to the trade, supplied her with a variety of aphrodisiacs. Elianor managed to have these administered to Humphrey, and so potent were their properties that he succumbed to her charms and made her his mistress.

How well they got on together – or how sustained the supply of the love philtres became – is evidenced by the fact that in 1428 'Good Duke Humphrey', as he became known, had his marriage to Jacqueline annulled, and forthwith married Elianor. She had achieved her first ambition, that of becoming Duchess of Gloucester; now for the Throne itself!

She went back to discuss with Margery the best means whereby she could actually sit on that imposing piece of regal furniture, in view of the fact that Margaret, Consort of Henry VI, was currently occupying it. The sorceress came up with a sure-fire solution: she would make a waxen image of Henry and insert pins into various parts of the anatomy, thereby bringing certain death.

The weeks became months, then years, Elianor having to put up with being merely a Duchess. And then in 1441 disaster struck: Roger Bolinbrooke, together with Thomas Southwell, a canon of St Stephen's Chapel at Westminster, and others were arrested on treasonable charges. During interrogation the astronomer accused Elianor of dabbling in witchcraft and, despite her husband's efforts to intercede on her behalf, she too was punished for being 'hurtful to the King's person'.

Because of her quasi-royal position in society, instead of being executed she was ordered to pay penance, it being described by the historian John Stow:

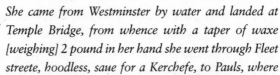 *She came from Westminster by water and landed at Temple Bridge, from whence with a taper of waxe [weighing] 2 pound in her hand she went through Fleet streete, hoodless, saue for a Kerchefe, to Pauls, where she offered her taper at the High Altar. On the Wednesday next she landed at the Swan in Thamis streete, and then went through Bridge streete, Gracechurch streete, to Leaden Hall, and so to Christ church by Aldegate. On Friday she landed at Queene Hiue, and so went through Cheape [Cheapside] to Saynt Michaels in Corne hill, in forme said [clad as before]; to all which time the Maior, Sherifes and Crafts of London receiued her.*

This being done she was committed to the ward [guardianship] of Sir Thomas Stanley, wherein she remained during her life in the castle of Chester, hauing yerely 100 markes for her finding [upkeep]. In 22 of Henry sixt [1444] she was remoued to Kenilworth to be safely kept, a woman whose pride, false couetise [coveteousness] and lechery, were cause of her confusion.

She remained incarcerated there until her death in about 1446.

It was all right for her, relatively speaking, but what of the others? Of those imprisoned in the Tower of London in 1441, Thomas Southwell died in his cell, but Roger Bolinbrooke was carried from the Tower to Tyburn to be hanged, drawn and quartered. Roger's head was displayed on London Bridge, his quarters being sent to be exhibited on the city gates of Hereford, Oxford, York and Cambridge. Ironically, Henry VI, whose continued existence thwarted Elianor's ambitious plans, was murdered in the Tower of London – but not until 1461!

As for Margery; alas, on scouring ancient records, it was found that:

There was taken also Margery Gurdemaine, a Witch of Eye besides Westminster, whose sorcerie and witchcrafte the said Elianor hadde long time vsed, and by her medicines and drinkes, enforced the Duke of Gloster to loue her, and after to wedde her, wherefore, and for cause of relapse, the same Witch was brent [burned at the stake] in Smithfield, on the twentie-seaven day of October 1444.

Voicing one's opinions in public could bring the magistrate's wrath down on one's head, but Ann Walker forgot this when, on meeting Andrew Shaw, who had recently brought a prosecution against her father, she called him a cuckoo. And so, on 4 October 1614, she found herself in court in Wakefield, Yorkshire, to hear judgement passed 'that the Constable of Wakefield shall cause ye said Ann Walker, for her impudent and bold behaviour, to be runge through ye town of Wakefield with basins before her [these being struck to attract everyone's attention] as is accustomed for common scoldes.'

H

Hahn, Anna (USA)

Many people believe that the number thirteen is unlucky; it certainly was for the thirteen people murdered by Anna Hahn. Being of German descent, she concentrated on befriending German men, usually elderly ones, writing their cheques out for them – and also 'helpfully' signing them. Eventually she would add a little toxic flavouring to the meals she cooked for them, thereby acquiring their money and valuables.

So George Gsellmann, Albert Palmer, George Oberndoefer, Jacob Wagner and others all involuntarily helped to pay her gambling debts and embellish her lifestyle. Nor were men the only ones to sample the food she prepared. Ollie Koehler and Julia Kresckay also died of acute poisoning. So much evidence mounted against her that in late 1937 she was arrested and imprisoned in Hamilton County Gaol. Confident of convincing the courts of her innocence, she invited journalists into her cell one morning, one reporter describing her immaculate appearance, her hair carefully brushed, her fingernails polished, her attitude almost carefree as she exclaimed that this surely was the weirdest breakfast chat she had ever had.

Searches in the homes of the various victims revealed bottles of poison and stolen belongings, this being testified at her trial which opened on 11 October 1938. Much attention was paid to her appearance by the press; fashion editors dwelling on her brown crêpe dress, the shade of her lipstick, her stylishly long skirt. Eventually the jury retired and needed less than three hours to reach a decision – guilty, with no recommendation for mercy.

So assured was she that she would be found innocent, that before the trial she had packed her belongings ready to take home; now, her complacency shattered, she broke down in her cell and sobbed uncontrollably, her hair awry, her voice breaking with the shock of the judgement.

Prior to execution day, one of her pyjama legs had been slit to permit the attachment of one of the electrodes. On the morning of the day itself, another warder cut away some of the hair on the back of her neck to accommodate the other electrode. As the time approached she was so near to collapse that she had to be supported as she was led to the execution chamber. There,

Anna collapsed completely. Her escort managed to prevent her from falling to the floor, and as quickly as possible placed her in the electric chair, stopping her from slumping forwards while the guards strapped her into it. Momentarily recovering, she cried, 'Don't do that to me!' but the prison warden, sympathetic despite the appalling crimes she had committed, replied, 'I'm sorry, but we can't help it.'

As the black mask was placed over her face she felt her hand held by the priest; although doubtless longing to have his comforting grasp until the very last moment, nevertheless she realised the risk: 'Be careful, Father, you'll be killed!' she exclaimed.

As he moved away, the warden gave the signal, and she jerked against the restraining straps as the powerful current surged through her body. In accordance with regulations, two doctors monitored her condition using stethoscopes, and within seconds confirmed her death.

Let it never be said that women are more squeamish than men! If proof were needed, one need look no further than the case described above. Eleven of the jury were women, yet not one of them apparently batted an eyelid when the exhibits were passed round for them to examine, despite them consisting of a jar containing Albert Palmer's brain, and bottles filled with some of Jacob Wagner's internal organs!

Hamilton, Mary (Scotland)

Also known as Mary Lennox, she was so short of money that she stole £20 from her sister-in-law's bank by forging her signature.

Then, on 7 June 1849, either having been found out or fearing discovery, she poisoned her relative with arsenic.

On 31 January 1850 she was led from her cell to the gallows, which had been positioned in front of Glasgow's High Court. There, hangman John Murdoch waited, and on seeing him she pleaded with him to be gentle and not to hurt her. Then nervousness overcame her and she fainted. With one warder each side of her, holding her upright until the last minute, Murdoch, despite being 82 years old and needing a walking stick to climb the scaffold steps, was not too decrepit to operate the drop, and his unconscious victim descended into the pit.

Prison reformer John Howard visited Berkshire's County Gaol at Reading in the 1770s, where he found that women prisoners were not only chained together by their wrists but also had heavy irons on their ankles when they were taken to the court house. For clothing they were issued with 'linsey woolsey gowns and petticoats, flannel petticoats for winter, two dowlas shifts and two pairs of yarn hose.' Their own clothes were labelled and put away until the quarter assizes, to be worn again when they appeared on trial. When prisoners were discharged, the regulation clothing was washed, mended and purified in an oven for the use of future occupants.

Harris, Phoebe (England)

It must have been a macabre sight to the throng, reportedly twenty thousand people, massing outside Newgate Gaol on 22 June 1786 when, as so vividly described by the *Chelmsford Chronicle*:

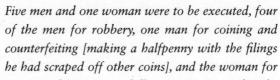*Five men and one woman were to be executed, four of the men for robbery, one man for coining and counterfeiting [making a halfpenny with the filings he had scraped off other coins], and the woman for assisting in counterfeiting some shilling pieces. Soon after the men had died, twelve people clambered on to the scaffold and had the hands of the deceased repeatedly rubbed by the hangman on their faces and necks as a supposed cure for the protuberances called wens, or warts.*

About a quarter of an hour afterwards, the woman, Phoebe Harris, was led out of Newgate by two warders. She was a well-made little woman, something more than thirty years of age, of pale complexion, and not disagreeable in features, and she appeared both languid and terrified, and trembled greatly as she advanced towards the stake, where the apparatus for the punishment she was about to experience seemed to strike her mind with horror and consternation to the exclusion of all power of recollectness in preparation for the awful approaching moment.

The stake had been fixed in the ground about midway between the scaffold and the pump. The stake was about eleven feet high and at the top of it was inserted a curved piece of iron to which the other end of the rope around her neck was tied. The prisoner stood on a low stool which, after the prison Ordinary, the chaplain, had prayed with her for a short while, was taken away, leaving her suspended by the neck, her feet being scarcely more than twelve or thirteen inches from the pavement. Soon after the signs of life had ceased, two cart loads of timber were placed around her and set alight. The flames presently burned through the halter and the victim fell a few inches and was then sustained by an iron chain which had been secured around her waist and affixed to the stake.

*Some scattered remains of her body were perceptible in the fire
at ten o'clock; the fire had not quite burnt out even at twelve.'*

Phoebe Harris was the last female to be burned at the stake, that
barbaric method of execution being abolished by statute in 1793.

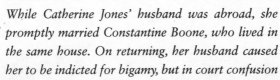 *While Catherine Jones' husband was abroad, she
promptly married Constantine Boone, who lived in
the same house. On returning, her husband caused
her to be indicted for bigamy, but in court confusion
arose, for how could the 'marriage' between two women be
classed as bigamy? But Catherine claimed that Constantine
was in reality a hermaphrodite and had been exhibited as such
at Southwark and Bartholomew Fairs, doubtless in company
with two-headed lambs, so-called mermaids, assorted giants
and dwarfs. As recounted in the* Newgate Calendar, *a witness
stated that 'he knew Boone when a child, and that his, or
her mother dressed it in girl's apparel until the age of twelve,
when it turned man and went to sea.' However, because other
witnesses testified that Boone was more female than male, the
offence could not have been bigamy and the jury acquitted the
prisoner. The* Calendar's *account concludes by saying: 'We can
only express our astonishment that a hermaphrodite should
think of such a glaring absurdity as the taking of a wife!'*

Hayes, Catherine (England)

One must feel sorry for poor Mr Hayes, hen-pecked as he was
by Catherine, for she was a sharp-tongued harridan who never
ceased nagging him. Briefly, she and their two lodgers, Billings and

Wood, plotted to kill him for his money, so, getting him drunk on potent 'red biddy', the two men then took turns in using an axe to cleave his skull. To avoid identification of the remains Catherine suggested cutting the head off, and held the bucket to catch the blood while Wood did so. The men then threw the head into the Thames, and the parts of the dismembered torso were dropped into a pond near Marylebone.

Catherine Hayes Decapitating Her Husband

When the head was eventually found, the authorities had it impaled on a high pole in Westminster so that it could be identified; friends recognised it, and when it was taken down and put in a glass jar, Catherine saw it and, bursting into tears, said, 'Yes, it is my husband.' Whereupon the surgeon extracted it from the jar and gave it to her to hold.

All were arrested, Wood and Billings confessed, the former dying in gaol, the latter being hanged and gibbeted, his corpse suspended from a tree in an iron cage. On 9 May 1726 Catherine was tied to the stake and burned alive, the executioner, beaten back by the roaring fire, being unable to strangle her.

At most executions, together with ale and cake purveyors, accounts of the crimes, written in execrable doggerel and set to popular tunes of the day, were published by local printers. These were sold for the crowds to sing while waiting for the show to start. One such poetic masterpiece hawked round Newgate that day has survived the ravages of time, moths and mildew, and describes in melodramatic style the 'Orrible Murder.

The Head of Catherine Haye's Husband

A BALLAD ON THE MURDER OF MR HAYES BY HIS WIFE

In Ty-burn road a man there lived
A just and honest life,
And there he might have lived still,
If so had pleased his wife.

Full twice a day to church he went,
And so devout would be,
Sure never was a saint on earth,
If that no saint was he!

This vext his wife unto the heart,
She was of wrath so full,
That finding no hole in his coat,
She picked one in his scull.

But then heart began to relent,
And griev'd she was so sore,
That quarter to him for to give,
She cut him into four.

FEMALE EXECUTIONS

All in the dark and dead of night,
These quarters she conveyed,
And in a ditch in Marybone,
His marrow-bones she laid.

His head at Westminster she threw,
All in the Thames so wide,
Says she, 'My dear, the wind sets fair,
And you may have the tide.'

But Heav'n, whose pow'r no limit knows,
On earth or on the main,
Soon caus'd this head for to be thrown
Upon the land again.

The head being found, the justices,
Their heads together laid;
And all agreed there must have been
Some body to this head.

But since no body could be found,
High mounted on a shelf,
They e'en set up the head to be,
A witness for itself.

Next, that it no self-murder was,
The case itself explains,
For no man could cut off his head,
And throw it in the Thames.

Ere many days had gone and passed,
The deed at length was known.
And Cath'rine, she confess'd at last,
The fact to be her own.

God prosper long our noble King,
Our lives and safeties all,
And grant that we may warning take,
By Cath'rine Hayes's fall.

Catherine Hayes at the Stake

This advertisement in an issue of the *London Morning Post* read:

 Mrs De St Raymond, Dentist, takes the liberty to recommend to the Nobility and Gentry, her well-known skill in the performance of chirurgical operations for the various disorders of the mouth, especially the lightness of her hand in removing all tartarous concretations, so destructive to the teeth, and her dexterity in extracting stumps, splints and fangs of teeth. She also draws, fills up, fastens and preserves teeth, corrects their deformities, transplants them from one mouth to another, grafts on, and sets in human teeth; likewise makes and fixes in artificial teeth, from one to an entire set, and executes her own newly invented masks for the teeth and obturators for the loss of the palate.

The lady also made an even more attractive offer, if possible, to those with vacant areas of gum space, by stating that she had the necessary expertise 'to transplant teeth from the jaws of poor lads into the head of any lady or gentleman.'

And before you say that this quirky quote hardly falls into the category of torture, I should point out that it was advertised in 1777 – but that the first practical application of anaesthesia in dentistry, that of using nitrous oxide, was not until 1844, ether was not used until 1846, and sufferers preferring cocaine had to wait until 1879 – ouch!

Hereford, Nan (England)

In the 1600s highwaymen lurked on every lonely street – and one of the fiercest and most demanding was Nan Hereford. Big-boned and unattractive, it didn't really matter; she sat well on a horse and hid her features behind a forbidding black mask. Like her male compatriots she wore a cloak, shirt and breeches, with a wide-brimmed hat pulled low over her face. Unlike them, however, she never resorted to using a pistol; her very appearance in front of a coach was sufficient to make the driver rein in the horses, his companion to throw down his blunderbuss, and the unfortunate passengers to hand over their valuables, any tardiness being overcome by a few well-aimed blows from her fists. Following a hold-up or two, she would retreat to a tavern by arrangement, the inn-keeper being only too willing to give her refuge until any pursuit died down. There, to make doubly sure, she would change into women's attire and return to the city, biding her time until taking to the highways again.

But the horse patrols eventually caught up with her. In Newgate she proved almost impossible to control, fighting with the warders and even setting part of the gaol on fire. She was going to be hanged for robbery anyway, so it mattered little that arson was also a hanging offence.

On 22 December 1690 the hangman had quite a busy day. In addition to hanging sixteen felons at Tyburn for various crimes, highwayman William Davis, known as the 'Golden Farmer', had to be dispatched in Fleet Street, his cadaver afterwards to be suspended in chains on Bagshot Heath. After that the executioner had to go to Newgate, where Nan Hereford was waiting for him on the scaffold. 'Stand and deliver!' might have been her usual demand – but this time it was the hangman who stood there and delivered her into the next world!

One would have thought that even a murderer such as Wanda Jean Allen, who brutally killed her room-mate in 1988, would have behaved with a certain degree of decorum and shown some penitence in her

final moments before being executed, but not Wanda; she just smiled broadly at her lawyer and the prison chaplain – and stuck her tongue out derisively!

Housden, Jane (England)

The moral of this story is if you're a man and you have to shoot someone, don't shoot them in a crowded courtroom; if you're a woman, don't encourage him in the dire deed no matter how much you care for him – with so many witnesses, even the finest defence counsel in the world could not get you acquitted!

Jane was a hardened criminal from the word go, as was her paramour, William Johnson. A jack of all trades, an ex-sailor, William turned his hand, and his horse's head, towards the highway and held up coaches to rob the passengers. He was caught, tried, but for some reason, was pardoned. He had a lot in common with Jane, for she too had previously been arrested and tried on a charge of coining (counterfeiting), and had also received a pardon. This merciful gesture did not deter her; there was money to be made, literally, from coining and so she repeated the offence. No leniency was shown this time, and she was brought to the bar in the Old Bailey.

It so happened that on hearing that his lady friend was on trial, Johnson came to court in order to give her some loyal support, but as he approached the open door to the courtroom, the head turnkey (chief warder) attempted to bar him from entering, explaining brusquely that he could not speak to the prisoner at the bar until the end of the trial. Furious, Johnson made no reply but, urged on by Jane's defiant and encouraging shouts, drew a pistol and without a moment's hesitation, shot the turnkey dead, in full view of the judge, jury, officials and public gallery.

At that, the judge ordered the removal of the officer's body and the arrest of the attacker; he then decided that there was little point in proceeding with Jane's coining charge and, there being no need to call any witnesses to the crime just committed, he sentenced both of them to death, Johnson for pulling the trigger, Jane for being an accessory during the fact.

At least the two lovers were together when, on 19 September 1712, they mounted the scaffold steps. Neither showed the slightest remorse or regret – nor did Richard Pearse, the hangman, as he dispatched them. After an hour, all twitching and writhing having ceased, their bodies were cut down. The method of disposal of Jane Housden's corpse is not known, but that of Johnson's was hanged in chains, gibbeted, near Holloway as a dreadful warning to all.

Gibbet Irons

The obtaining of evidence of conspiracy to murder is of course vital, but the lengths to which the prosecution went, in the cases of Catherine Miller and her lover George Smith, both accused of murdering her elderly husband was, to say the least, unorthodox. During the trial testimony was given that the two suspects had been allowed to share a cell for a night, and that a prison warder had, at the instigation of the district attorney, hidden himself under the bed, hoping to hear something that would incriminate them!

Hungerford, Lady (England)

Lady Hungerford started off as plain Agnes, or Alice, Cottell, and she managed to get a job in the household of Sir Edward Hungerford at his residence, Farleigh Castle, which was situated in a village appropriately named Farleigh-Hungerford near Bath. Sir Edward, Sheriff of Wiltshire, Somerset and Dorset, Commissioner of Peace, was highly regarded in court circles. In addition to his castle he also owned a magnificent house in London, the family name later being commemorated in the capital by Hungerford Stairs and Hungerford Street – the latter being the thoroughfare in which Charles Dickens, as a child of ten, began his working life by sticking labels on bottles of blacking. During the reign of Charles II, a successor built Hungerford Market on the site of the mansion and its extensive gardens where now stands Charing Cross Station, from which southbound trains traverse Hungerford Bridge.

However, back to Agnes; what impression she made on her employer is not known; suffice it to say that the capacity in which she ultimately served was higher up the menial scale than that of a kitchen maid or even a housekeeper, and it soon occurred to her that a landowner as wealthy and aristocratic as Sir Edward would seem to be a worthwhile catch; he was a widower, his late wife, Jane, daughter of John, Lord Zouche of Haryngworth, having recently died. But Agnes' problem was that she already had a husband. However, to someone as ruthless and ambitious as Agnes Cottell, that was a mere bagatelle, and on 26 July, under her guidance and supervision, William Inges and William Mathewe, two of the Hungerford servants, murdered the unfortunate John Cottell and disposed of all traces of his cadaver. And then, by making herself indispensable, probably in more ways than one, she married Sir Edward.

The perpetrators of the crime went undetected, and Lady Agnes became a member of a social life of which she had previously only dreamed. Three memorable years passed and then, on 14 December 1521, Sir Edward made his will. By it, after leaving a few minor legacies to various churches and friends, 'the residue of all my goods, cattalls [chattels], juells, plate, harnesse, and all other moveables whatsoever they be, I freely geve and bequeath to Agnes Hungerford my wife'. He also made her the sole executrix. Oddly enough, six weeks later, on 24 January 1522, he died.

Whether Lady Agnes was betrayed by an unsuccessful blackmailer, as was likely, or suspicion borne by the authorities over John Cottell's disappearance somehow bore fruit, is not known, but on 25 August 1522, as recorded in the *Coram Rege Roll* for Michaelmas term, 14 Henry VIII (1523), the two servants, Inges and Mathewe, were indicted with:

> *Having with force and arms made an assault on John Cottell at Farley, by the procurement and abetting of Agnes Hungerford, late of Heytesbury in the county*

of Wilts., widow, at that time the wife of the aforesaid John Cottell. And that a certain linen scarf called a kerchief which the aforesaid William and William then and there held in their hands, put round the neck of the aforesaid John Cottell and with the aforesaid linen scarf did then and there feloniously throttle, suffocate and strangle the aforesaid John Cottell, so that he immediately died, and afterwards the aforesaid William and William did then and there put into a certain fire in the furnace in the kitchen of the Castle of Farley the body of the aforesaid John Cottell, which did then burn and consume it.

Agnes herself was charged with 'well knowing that the aforesaid William Mathewe and William Inges had done the felony and murder aforesaid, did receive, comfort and aid them on 28 December 1518.' It was later recorded that a charge of actually murdering her husband was also brought against her.

While awaiting trial all three were confined in the Tower of London, records showing that the cost of guarding and providing for Agnes for the duration of her imprisonment was ten shillings a week. There they remained until, as ancient documents stated, 'and now, to wit, on Thursday next after the quinzaine of St Martin [27 November 1522] in the same term, before the Lord the King at Westminster, in their proper persons [themselves], came the aforesaid William Mathewe, William Inges and Agnes Hungerford, brought to the bar by Sir Thomas Lovell, Constable of the Tower of London, by virtue of the writ of the Lord the King, to him thereupon directed.'

At the trial Lady Hungerford and her two accomplices were found guilty and sentenced to death. In addition, everything bequeathed to her in Sir Edward's will was forfeited to the King.

At last the day of execution arrived, and as reported in the *Grey Friars Chronicle*:

This yere 1523 in Feverelle [February] the 20th day was the lady Agnes Hungerford lede from the Tower unto Holborne and there put into a carte at the churchyerde with hare servantes and so carried unto Tyborne, and there all were hongyd, and she burryd at the Grayfreeres in the nether end of the myddes of the churche on the northe syde.

In London there are surely no tourist attractions more macabre than the one which was displayed to visitors in Westminster Abbey's Lady Chapel for nearly three hundred and fifty years, for they were the remains of Queen Katherine of Valois, King Henry V's wife! After her death in 1437 the coffin was wrapped in lead taken from the roof, and because the lid was not replaced, her body, naked from the waist up, lay fully exposed. Described by the historian Dart as 'continuing to be seen, the bones firmly united and thinly covered with flesh, like scrapings of fine leather', regrettably it was not until 1776 that decency prevailed, and her corpse was interred in the Abbey's vaults.

Hutchinson, Amy (England)

Poor Amy! In 1746 when she was sixteen years of age, slim and attractive, she fell in love with a young man, much against her father's wishes. Her father was right, for her lover 'seduced her under promise of marriage'. He then went to London but said he would marry her when he returned. Shocked by his infidelity, she allowed herself to be courted by another, much older man, John Hutchinson, and although he treated her unkindly at times, caught on the rebound, she agreed to marry him. But just as the newlyweds were leaving the church, who should turn up but Lover No.1!

All Amy's old feelings returned and, unable to love John, she clandestinely resumed her intimacy with – well, we'd better call him George, since the Newgate records do not name him. John, suspecting his wife's cold attitude towards him was due to her first love, became jealous and, taking to drink, resorted to force, frequently beating her. Inflamed with passion for 'George', Amy continued her close relationship with him, so close that eventually she wanted to be with him all the time, and so she decided to get rid of John.

To do this, she purchased some arsenic, widely available in the eighteenth century for domestic and indeed, some cosmetic purposes, and when John happened to complain of suffering from the ague, she gave him a tankard of ale, having first added some of the poison. Then, under the pretext of going shopping, she went to tell her lover what she had done to ensure their happy future. Far from being horrified, George told her to give John another dose in case the first one was not strong enough! But that turned out to be unnecessary, John dying by dinnertime of the same day, and buried shortly afterwards.

The day after the funeral, George promptly visited Amy, his continued presence in her house giving rise to so much scandalised gossip among the neighbours that the authorities were alerted. Amy was arrested, John's corpse exhumed, and the discovery of arsenic traces in his body spelled the end of Amy's romance, and ultimately her life.

After being tried and convicted of murder, she confessed and acknowledged the enormity of her crime. Willing to make atonement, she left a paper with the clergyman who attended her in her last moments, on which she had written the following advice to other susceptible young ladies:

First, to warn all young women to acquaint their friends when any addresses [advances] are made to them; and, above all, if any base or immodest man dare to insult you with any thing shocking to chaste ears.

Secondly, that they should never leave the person they are engaged to, in a pet [moment of anger], nor wed another to whom they are indifferent, in spite; for, if they come together without affection, the smallest matter will separate them.

Thirdly, that, being married, all persons should mutually love, forgive and forbear; and afford no room for busy meddlers to raise and foment jealousy between two who should be as one.

On 7 November 1750, for her sins, Amy was burnt and strangled at Ely.

It would certainly seem that in the seventeenth century, Barnsley, in Gloucestershire, was probably the village that most strictly observed the Lord's Day, for not only were little children forbidden to walk or play out, but in 1652 it was reported that:

Two women, who had been at Church both before and after the hour of noon, did but walk in the fields for their recreation, and were then charged with having indulged in profane walking. They were given the choice either to be fined sixpence, or to be secured for one hour in the stocks. The peevish, wilful women, even though they were able enough to pay, in order to save their money, chose the latter and sat one hour locked in the stocks, a warning to all.

J

Jaffrey, Elizabeth (Scotland)

Why Mrs Jaffrey should want to poison her lodger Ann Carole in October 1837 with arsenic allegedly bought to kill rats is not known, although it was suspected that she owed some money to her other lodger, Hugh Munro, but wanted to see how effective the dosage was by first testing it out on the girl. It certainly worked with Ann, who succumbed to a fatal cocktail of meal, arsenic and whisky, but Hugh was evidently made of sterner stuff, for he ate his arsenic-laced porridge with apparently no ill effects. However, Elizabeth increased the amount she stirred into his rhubarb, and to her satisfaction was no longer in his debt.

Although she refused to admit her guilt, the jury thought otherwise, and she was hanged from the Glasgow gallows on 21 May 1838. For her final public appearance she wore a shawl in the Rob Roy plaid, a decision which resulted in that particular pattern going out of fashion for many years afterwards.

It could have been a music-hall joke when Tilly Klimek, on being measured for a mourning dress and asked when her husband had died, replied, 'In ten days time.' However, the results were deadly serious, for when the police were informed they discovered that husband Anton was indeed in peril of his life, arsenic having been administered to him. Further investigation revealed that her four previous husbands had died in a similar fashion. Sometimes it just doesn't pay to make facetious remarks.

Jegado, Helene (France)

To be able to control precisely one's lachrymal glands, to cry on demand, is a great advantage after having poisoned someone. This ability was used to the full by French peasant Helene Jegado when, as repeatedly happened, members of the families of her various employers for whom she worked as a cook, unexpectedly died. Seemingly overcome with grief, she would leave, taking with her the bottles of wine and sundry valuable articles she had stolen, and gain similar employment elsewhere, with the same deadly results.

In 1830 she took a job in the household of Professor Bidard at Rennes. Unaccountably another maid fell ill, and Helene devoted all her spare time to nursing her friend, but all to no avail, for her patient died. Again the crocodile tears flowed, but it wasn't long before she made a new friend, Rosalie Sarrazin, who had filled the now vacant post. A rift soon appeared in their relationship, for Rosalie was better educated than Helene and so she was put in charge of the household accounts, but fate remedied the situation – the remedy being arsenic powder – and within months poor Rosalie complained of stomach pains. The complaints did not last long, however, and neither did the new maid.

Helene might have been good at crying, but not at being able to control her guilty conscience, for when the police came to the house to investigate the sudden death, Helene opened the door and, on seeing them, exclaimed, 'I am innocent!' To which the officer replied, 'What of? Nobody has accused you of anything!'

Helene Jegado was tried at Rennes in December 1831 on three charges of murder and a similar number of attempted murders. No poison was found in her possession, and because no doubt she had sold all the valuables she had stolen, no apparent motive was found. But when her employment record was checked and found to coincide with nearly two dozen mysterious deaths, the court came to but one conclusion, and in 1832 Madamoiselle Jegado kept an appointment with Madame Guillotine but did not keep her head.

In England most of the clothes belonging to his victims were the perquisite of the executioner, but not in France during the Revolution. Most garments were cut into pieces and used for the cleaning of the scaffold, which rapidly became soaked with blood and fragments of flesh. But what of the hair, shorn from the necks of those about to be guillotined? It was reported at the time that:

> *A new sect has lately been formed in Paris; in their zeal to associate themselves with the counter-revolutionaries by every possible means, the initiates, who are animated by a pious respect and tender devotion to the guillotine, have the same desires, the same sentiments, and in these days, the same hair; toothless women are eager to buy the locks of any golden-haired young spark who has been guillotined, and to wear such tresses on their heads. It is a new branch of commerce, and a perfectly new kind of devotion too, so let us respect these blonde locks; our late aristocrats will at least have been of some use – their hair will hide the bald heads of a few women!*

Jones, Mary (England)

The annals of Tyburn contain no more poignantly tragic account than that of Mary Jones. Young and attractive, with thick tresses of auburn hair, she was happily married until the day her husband was caught by the press-gang (seized without warning by government recruiting men and forced on board short-staffed naval vessels to serve abroad). In order to raise money for sustenance she sold the furniture and finally her home, the records reporting how she had 'neither bed to lie on, nor food to give her two young children, who were almost naked.' In sheer desperation she stole some lengths of muslin from a draper's shop on Ludgate Hill, and was arrested.

The record continued:

At her trial she said, 'I have been a very honest woman in my lifetime. I have two children; I work very hard to maintain my two children since my husband was pressed.' Her beauty and poverty proved Mary's averment that she had been a very honest woman, but when the jury gave in a verdict of guilty, Mary cursed the judge and jury, for [being] a lot of 'old fogrums'. It was really for this that she died on the gallows. The theft had not been completed; she was arrested in the shop and gave up the goods. It was her first offence. Her neighbours in Red Lion Street, Whitechapel, presented a petition on her behalf, but there was against her the record of her 'indecent behaviour' in court. One of the two children was at her breast when, on 16 October 1771, she set out in the cart on the journey from Newgate to Tyburn. Her petulance had gone, and she met her death with amazing fortitude.

One of the victims of English hangman James Berry (1884–1892) was, coincidentally, a woman having the same surname – a woman he had also met socially some years earlier. As can be imagined, it was with great difficulty that he managed to keep the situation on the essentially impersonal level, and so perhaps he can be excused for his actions when, having executed her with as little delay as possible, he then cut a lock of her long auburn hair to keep as a memento. But as time passed he felt that it was having a baleful influence on him, one that affected him so adversely that he eventually disposed of the macabre souvenir.

K

Kidden, Frances (England)

On 2 April 1868 William Calcraft, who, by the time he retired in 1874, would have served 45 years on the scaffold (more than any other in his profession), achieved the distinction of being the last executioner to hang a woman in public. His victim was Frances Kidden, an attractive young woman whose happily married existence was marred only by the fact that she and her husband had not been able to have a baby. Her outraged reaction upon discovering that her husband had had a child by another woman can therefore be well imagined, a reaction that drove her to kill the man she loved, the man who had so cruelly deceived her. And so, on that day in April, she stood silently on the drop in the marketplace in Maidstone, Kent, resigned to her fate, as Calcraft, much as he hated having to execute a woman, hooded and noosed her; then, having deprived her unfaithful husband of his life, she forfeited her own.

 Lest it be thought that only men could be so hard-hearted as to execute their fellow human beings, at least one woman wielded the whip and tightened

the noose. Known as 'Lady Betty', she was described in the Dublin University Magazine *of January 1850 as a middle-aged, stout-made, swarthy-complexioned but by no means forbidding-looking woman, well-educated though possessing a violent temper. She was the mother of a boy and had treated him so harshly in his youth that he ran away from home and joined the army. After overseas service he had come home but, recalling his mother's fiery temperament, disguised himself, and when she opened the door he asked for lodgings for the night. She showed him to a room and later, while he was asleep, she murdered him for his savings.*

She was sentenced to death with other criminals, but there was no hangman available and, as the Magazine *sarcastically reported, 'time was pressing, and as the sheriff and his deputy, being men of refinement, education, humanity and sensibility, who could not be expected to fulfil the office which they had undertaken, and for which at least one of them was paid, this wretched woman, being the only one who could be found to perform the office of executioner, consented!'*

It would seem that, unlike other hangmen who disguised themselves with false beards and wooden humps on their backs to avoid recognition and retribution, Lady Betty deigned not to do so. She thoroughly enjoyed her new role, flogging and hanging with gusto whenever the occasion demanded. After she had hanged a felon she would cut down the body, load it into a cart and accompany it to the town square of Roscommon; there, helped by the gaolers, she would hoist the corpse, its arms outspread gibbet-fashion, to the two high poles erected there. Local parents would warn their disobedient children to behave themselves by saying 'Huggath á Pooká! – here comes Lady Betty!'

King, Jessie (Scotland)

In the nineteenth century life was hard, social conditions appalling, the lower classes poverty-stricken, and as there was no such thing as birth control, families became bigger and, in many cases, unaffordable. Women, single or married, having illegitimate children, were stigmatised and virtually outcast by society; all this gave rise to the flourishing and lucrative cottage industry of baby farming, women such as Amelia Dyer, previously described, adopting babies at a price, then getting rid of them by strangulation or drowning.

In Scotland 28-year-old Jessie King was one of that murderous breed of women. On 18 February 1889, before the High Court of Edinburgh, she was found guilty of murdering two children committed to her charge, although she was suspected of many similar crimes. Suspicion had led to investigation and bodies were found wrapped in sacking in her landlord's house. This evidence, together with the testimony given against her by her elderly lover Thomas Pearson, was sufficient, and Jessie King was arrested. It was not even necessary to prove that the 'football' kicked around by small boys a year earlier, which turned out to be a baby's body wrapped in an old coat, was her handiwork, although the finger of suspicion certainly pointed in her direction.

The jury took less than an hour to reach their verdict, and when it was read out in court Jessie screamed and moaned hysterically, eventually collapsing in a fainting fit. She was carried from the dock by two policemen to the cells, from where she was taken to the condemned cell in Calton Gaol.

While awaiting execution, which had been appointed to take place on 11 March, she attempted to commit suicide on two occasions, first by using a long pin, which she had probably concealed in her hair and with which she might have opened a vein and bled to death had it not been discovered by a wardress; another time she was found in possession of a length of rope, intending to hang herself before the executioner could.

Throughout her long sojourn in the prison she hoped she would escape the scaffold, a belief borne out by the number of petitions raised on her behalf and delivered to the Home Secretary, signatures perhaps obtained because she would be the first woman in Scotland to receive the death penalty in nearly 40 years, rather than for belief in her innocence. When the death penalty was confirmed, she was overcome, but surprisingly she met her end with fortitude, walking without faltering to where the Bradford hangman James Berry waited. After being cut down, her corpse was interred within the grounds of Calton Gaol. Fame of a kind resulted from her infamy, in that she was the last woman to be hanged in Scotland.

 Women awaiting execution in Britain wore prison dress and were confined to the condemned cell, constantly guarded by two prison officers who stayed in the cell day and night. After the executions their bodies were placed in coffins and lime was then poured over them before burial took place within the confines of the prison. Although the locations of the burials were not marked in any way, they were easily identifiable, for the soil gradually sank lower than the surrounding earth and had to be periodically 'topped up' by prisoners on outdoor working parties.

Kurschnerin, Marie (Germany)

Master Franz Schmidt, executioner of Nuremburg 1571–1617, related in his *Diary* how, on 10 January 1583, 'Maria Kurschnerin of Nuremburg, also known as "Silly Mary", a prostitute, who was a musketeer's daughter, and a handsome young creature who thieved considerably, was here pilloried and afterwards flogged out of town.' It subsequently transpired that she had her ears cropped, but had obviously not learned her lesson, for the executioner's entry for 11 February 1584 reported that 'the thief and whore Marie Kurschnerin, together with thievish youths and fellows, had climbed and broken into citizens' houses and stole a mighty quantity of things. It was an unheard of thing for a woman to be hanged in this city and it had never happened before. Such a dreadful crowd ran out to see this, that several people were crushed to death.'

Nor did Margaret Brompton learn her lesson. She was whipped in Leeds on 7 August 1641, at a cost to the council of fourpence, and before the weals had properly healed up, she was back fifteen days later for a second dose, when she was again whipped by the beadle – and another fourpence came out of the rates!

L

Lee, Jean (Australia)

Jean Lee, deservedly described as a gorgeous redhead, was a much sought after prostitute in Australia in the 1940s who, not content with the payment handed over by clients, thought up a scheme whereby she could obtain everything else of value the punters might have in their possession. Accordingly she teamed up with a minor criminal named David Clayton and embarked on what, in the jargon of the Victorian criminal underworld, was known as the 'buttock and file' game; she would lure a man into a highly compromising situation and Clayton, purporting to be her husband, would 'surprise' them. Under the threat of humiliating exposure to the press and the authorities, the victim would hand over his wallet and valuables. Any necessary reinforcement was provided by Norman Andrews, the heavy member of the villainous trio, who was endowed with particularly persuasive fists.

However, one man who was determined not to be robbed, come what may, was William Kent. On 7 November 1949, after enjoying Jean's voluptuous charms and a drink or two in a hotel bedroom, he fell asleep, only to wake up to find her going through his pockets. He resisted strenuously, but was knocked out by a blow to the head with a bottle deftly wielded by Jean. Summoning her two confederates, she then searched their victim, but on finding nothing worth stealing, the trio tied him up and proceeded to torture him with a broken bottle before leaving.

Kent's dead and badly lacerated body was discovered the next day by hotel staff, who described the two men and the redhead so accurately to the police that it was only a matter of hours before all three were arrested and charged with murder. Despite a desperate appeal, Jean Lee and her criminal companions were hanged on 19 February 1951 in Sydney.

Women convicts in the Australian penal colonies were harshly punished for misbehaving, some sentenced to spend hours on the treadwheel, pacing ever upwards to keep the huge paddle-steamer-like wheel turning, their legs throbbing, panting for breath, with only minimal breaks to recover.

Lefley, Mary (England)

Was she guilty or wasn't she? Certainly circumstantial evidence, if nothing else, was against her; she had earlier been a close friend of Priscilla Biggadike, a woman who had been hanged at Lincoln for poisoning her husband, and here was Mary Lefley using the same method to rid herself of her husband. There was some doubt, of course. It was declared in court that she had left the farm to go to the market, having first prepared some rice pudding for her husband, ready for his return from work; all he had to do was to put it in the oven and cook it. A neighbour then took the witness stand and testified that Mr Lefley had come to his house for help, obviously in great pain; a doctor had been summoned, but alas too late, for the distressed man died before medical help arrived. Recognising the symptoms described by the neighbour, the doctor took possession of the food left on the table and sent it for forensic analysis, the laboratory technicians subsequently reporting the presence of arsenic in the uneaten portion.

Mary was arrested and charged with her husband's murder. Despite the fact that she pleaded innocence; that there was no apparent motive; that no poison was found by the police anywhere in the house; and that no evidence emerged that she had ever purchased any arsenic, local gossip was against her, it being intimated that in the past she had been popular with the local youths, and anyway, she'd known Priscilla Biggadike, and look what she did! No wonder, after the jury, having deliberated all night to bring in a guilty verdict, did Mary Lefley exclaim, 'They are hanging me for my past!'

In Lincoln Prison's condemned cell Mary prayed constantly, convinced that truth would prevail but on 26 May 1884, when hangman James Berry entered the cell, she shouted, 'Murder!

Murder! Don't hang me, or you will commit another murder!' The female warders guarding her had to pull her out of the bed and forcibly dress her in her prison garb, and her frantic shrieks echoed round the prison's stone walls as she was led to the scaffold between the warders. Her cries of innocence were abruptly stilled as Berry operated the drop – but that was not the end of this tragic story.

Nine years later, in 1893, it emerged that a local farmer had confessed, on his deathbed, that he was the real murderer. Bearing a grudge against Mr Lefrey over a business deal, he had bided his time until, on seeing Mary leave for market, he had gone into their house and mixed some of the arsenic he had bought to exterminate rats into the rice pudding.

The practice of English hangmen selling short lengths of the rope as souvenirs after dispatching notorious criminals was not entirely confined to that country. Following the wide publicity in America given to the crime and execution of Emiline Meaker in 1883, not only did the spectators queue up for hours to enter the prison and see the actual gallows from which she had been suspended, but requests were also made to the warden for pieces of the rope, the applicants insisting on receiving certificates authenticating the use to which they had been put.

Line, Anne (England)

Harbouring clerics of the 'wrong' religion carried just one penalty – death, as Anne Line found out in 1601. The ancient records reveal that:

FEMALE EXECUTIONS

 On the 27th of February a Gentlewoman called Mistress Anne Line, a widow, for relieuing [giving relief to] a priest contrary to statute; that, Mass having been said in her house, she assisted the priest in his escape.

Her weakness was suche that she was caryed to the said sessions betwixt two, in a chaire. Havyng been condemnede, she was carryed the next daye to her execution, many tymes on the waye being stayed and urged by the minister, who urged what meanes he could, to perswade her to convert from her professed faithe and opinion; he most constantlie persevered therin, and she was brought to the place of execution [Tyburn] and there shewed the cause of her coming thither [the gallows], and being further urged among other thinges by the minister that she had bene a common receavor of many priests, she aunswered 'Where I have receaved one, I would to God I had bene able to have receaved a thousand.' She behaved herself most meekely, patiently and vertuously to her last breath. She kissed the gallowes and before and after her private prayers blessinge herself, the carte in which she stood was drawne awaye, and she then made the signe of the crosse uppon her, and after that, never moved.

Religious feelings also ran strongly on the other side of the Atlantic, sympathy being extended, albeit too late, to Mary Tompkins, Anna Coleman, Alice Andrews and Alice Ambrose, four seventeenth-century 'rogue and vagabond Quakers'. The constables of twelve Massachusetts and New Hampshire towns received their instructions, viz. 'You are enjoined to make them fast to the cart-tail and draw them through your several towns, and whip them on their naked backs, not exceeding ten stripes in each town, and so convey them from Constable to Constable on your Peril.'

Lisle, Dame Alice (England)

Another woman whose qualities of charity and humanity towards others were ultimately responsible for her execution was Alice Lisle. The daughter of Sir White Beckenshaw, in 1630, aged sixteen, she married John Lisle, a Member of Parliament and barrister. John Lisle was so esteemed by Oliver Cromwell that he was appointed to organise the trial of King Charles I in 1649. But when Charles II regained the throne, he fled to Switzerland to evade arrest and trial as a regicide, although Fate dogged his footsteps even there, for he was later murdered in Lausanne.

After her husband had left the country Dame Alice lived a quiet life in Dorset, but in 1685 James, Duke of Monmouth led an ill-assorted army of peasants equipped with pitchforks and cudgels through that county, heading for London, hoping to overthrow James II and claim the throne for himself. The attempt was abortive; James, Duke of Monmouth, was beheaded, five strokes of the axe being necessary. His followers scattered across the country, the King ordering Judge George Jeffreys to deal with them, an invitation relished by the Hanging Judge, no fewer than 330 being executed. As described by Sir Edward Parry:

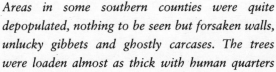

Areas in some southern counties were quite depopulated, nothing to be seen but forsaken walls, unlucky gibbets and ghostly carcases. The trees were loaden almost as thick with human quarters as with leaves; the houses and steeples covered as close with heads as at other times with crows or ravens. Nothing could be liker hell; caldrons hissing, carcases boyling, pitch and tar sparkling and glowing, blood and limbs boyling and tearing and mangling, and Jeffreys the great director of all.

In Lyme Regis, where Monmouth had started his ill-fated attempt, the mayor had been ordered to build gallows and provide nooses to hang the prisoners 'with a number of faggots to burn the bowels of the traitors and a furnace or caldron to boil their heads and quarters and salt to boil them with to preserve them on display; and tar to tar them with, and a sufficient number of spears and poles to fix and place their heads and quarters.'

Throughout all this turmoil, Alice Lisle lived an undisturbed life at her house, but throughout the county hundreds of Monmouth's supporters frantically sought refuge from the soldiers hunting them. One night two of them turned up at Alice's door, one a preacher named Hicks, the other a man called Nelthorp. Filled with compassion she took them in, fed them and gave them shelter, but the next day the local Justice of the Peace arrived with an escort of soldiers; Hicks, Nelthorp and Alice were arrested.

Dame Alice appeared in court on 27 August 1685, the charge being 'that on 28 July, knowing that one John Hicks, clerk, to be a false traitor, and to have conspired to the death and destruction of the King, and to have levied war against him, did, in her dwelling house at Ellingham, Dorset, traitorously entertain, conceal and comfort the said John Hicks and cause meat and drink to be delivered to him, against the allegiance, the King's Peace, etc.'

Alice was extremely deaf and the charge had to be repeated loudly to her; upon which she pleaded not guilty. Colonel Penruddock, the JP, testified that on searching the house with the soldiers, he had found Hicks and later discovered Nelthorp hiding in a hole by the chimney. In her defence Dame Alice said she knew warrants were out for Hicks but did not know he was a Monmouth supporter; further, that she was loyal to the King and that her son was actually serving with the government forces. The legal point was also raised that she could not be accused of harbouring a traitor until Hicks had been convicted as one. But all this was brushed aside by the irascible and irrational Judge, who sent the jury out to consider their verdict. However, they returned shortly afterwards, the foreman saying that they doubted whether the accused knew Hicks was in Monmouth's army. Jeffreys, never one to heed a questioning jury, promptly sent them out to think again. Once more they returned to announce that she was not guilty, but the Judge, outraged by their apparent defiance, threatened them with dire consequences if they failed to take notice of his 'judicial recommendation'. Not daring to risk being accused of being traitors themselves for disagreeing with His Worship, they speedily brought in a verdict of guilty. Satisfied, Jeffreys urged Dame Alice to confess, adding that she was to be burned at the stake that very afternoon. However, sentence was postponed until 2 September, and although she did not confess, a petition sent to the King resulted in his gracious consent that, rather than being consumed by the flames, she could be beheaded by the axe instead.

The ghastly execution was carried out in the marketplace in Winchester, the frail 71-year-old lady kneeling over the block and submitting to decapitation without resistance, onlookers averring that 'she died with serene courage'. Only one blow of the axe was necessary.

Although a happy ending to this tragic episode is not possible, it is of some consolation to know that the baddies got their come-uppance. Following the Revolution of 1688, James II went into exile on the Continent, William and Mary accepted the Throne of England, and Parliament annulled the judgement passed on Dame Alice Lisle (not that it did much good). The hunt was on for Judge Jeffreys and he was captured in a tavern near the Thames, imprisoned in the Tower of London, and sentenced to death. He was known to suffer from cirrhosis of the liver due to his lifelong addition to brandy, and regrettably escaped the axe, for on the morning of 19 April 1689 he was found dead in his cell in the Bloody Tower.

Once Quakers had been banished from a town, they were forbidden to return. The Colonial Records of Massachusetts for the year 1657 defined the penalties to be paid by those who defied the law: 'A Quaker, if male, for the first offense shall have one of his ears cutt off; for the second offense have his other ear cutt off; a woman shall be severely whipt; for the third offense they, he or she, shall have their tongues bored through with a hot iron.'

M

MacLauchlan, Mary (Australia)

Mary was one of the many hundreds of women convicted of minor crimes in England to be transported to the penal colonies of Australia, the punishment being additionally severe in her case, since she was separated from her husband and children. In Tasmania the women worked in factories and, not unnaturally, became acquainted with male transportees and established residents. It so happened that Mary, as a consequence of one such relationship, had a baby and, terrified of the punitive consequences, and doubtless in a confused state of mind having just given birth, she attempted to dispose of her newborn son by flushing him down the toilets in the building. The deed being discovered, she was tried, found guilty of infanticide, and sentenced to death.

On the dreaded day she was taken to the scaffold clad in a long white gown with a black ribbon about her waist. It was strongly suspected that the man in question was a 'gentleman' rather than a fellow convict, and the prison chaplain, the Reverend William Bedford, an ex-Ordinary of Newgate Prison, managed to persuade her not to name the transgressor as the executioner positioned the noose about her neck. Some of the immense crowd gathered round the scaffold reported that 'her mental agony was truly awful' and that as she fell through the opening trapdoors she screamed, 'Oh my God!'

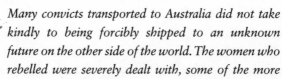 *Many convicts transported to Australia did not take kindly to being forcibly shipped to an unknown future on the other side of the world. The women who rebelled were severely dealt with, some of the more violent being put in irons for days, and even tied to the grating and whipped. One such was Elizabeth Dudgeon, of whom it was reported in Massey's* Journal Book, *1796, 'the corporal did not play with her, but laid it [the whip] home, which I [the lieutenant in charge] was very glad to see; she has long been fishing for it, which she has at last got, to her heart's content.'*

𝓜𝓪𝓬𝓛𝓮𝓸𝓭, Margaret (Scotland)

This lady was short of ready money but was cunning enough to obtain some without becoming personally involved; instead she used her wiles on a man friend named Household, to the extent that he agreed to forge a bill of sale apparently signed by the Duchess of Gordon. Margaret then obtained £58 from a Mr Henderson, an Edinburgh merchant, in exchange for the bill of sale.

The document was found to be false, probably by the Duchess's auditors, and Mr Henderson, although totally innocent, was arrested and charged with fraud. Released on bail, and realising the predicament into which he had been manoeuvred, he fled the city to avoid trial.

The trail led back to Margaret, and she too was arrested. The details of the case were scrutinised by the Lord Advocate's office (the chief prosecutor) and it was then that sheer coincidence intervened, one that even Margaret, with all her guile, could not possibly have foreseen. It so happened that the Lord Advocate was having a house built in the city, and on visiting the site he discussed progress with the builder. During the conversation the builder happened to mention that one of the carpenters he employed, a man called Household, had appeared agitated on learning of the lawyer's visit and had left abruptly. When asked whether the workman had given any reason, the builder said that Household had mentioned something about a forgery!

Putting two and two together, the Lord Advocate ordered a police search. It resulted in the arrest of the fugitive carpenter, and he, to save his own skin, admitted the part he had played, but accused Margaret MacLeod of being the instigator of the plot. In court, despite the part he had played in the fraudulent transaction, the jury absolved him from all blame. Margaret, however, was not as fortunate; charged and found guilty, she was sentenced to be hanged.

Her appearance on the scaffold, that day in 1726, brought a murmur of admiration from the many onlookers: self-assured, showing not the slightest sign of weakness or apprehension, she carried a white fan, which, together with her necklace and brooches, she then handed to the prison chaplain before taking the noose from the hangman and positioning it around her neck. With a smile, she said calmly, 'I am ready to die!' There was little doubt that she had dressed meticulously for the occasion, for she wore a black crinoline supported by a huge hoop – and one can only assume that the drop trapdoors must have been made extra wide to accommodate her descent betwixt them.

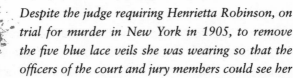

Despite the judge requiring Henrietta Robinson, on trial for murder in New York in 1905, to remove the five blue lace veils she was wearing so that the officers of the court and jury members could see her face, she obstinately refused to do so, though did lift them momentarily, only to conceal her face with her handkerchief. Wild rumours spread through the press that her hair grew abnormally low over her forehead, that her skull was misshapen, that her jaw line was deformed, and the mystery deepened further when, sentenced to life imprisonment, she continued to hide her features from visitors to the gaol. The identity of the person who sent her regular supplies of blue veils was never discovered.

Malcolm, Sarah (England)

Most female murderers use poison to dispose of their victims; whether this is because they have greater opportunity to add it to the food they are preparing, or that they recoil from employing actual weapons, is not known, but 22-year-old Sarah Malcolm from Ireland certainly did not waste time going to the chemist for arsenic under the pretext of needing it to kill rats; she much preferred her bare hands and a sharp knife – if indeed the findings of the court were correct.

On first coming to London she worked in the Black Horse Inn, near Temple Bar, where she met two brothers, Thomas and James

Alexander, men of somewhat dubious character. Subsequently she obtained a job as a laundress in a set of lawyers' chambers in the Inns of Court, one of her employers being a young Irishman named Mr Kerril, and another, Mrs Lydia Duncomb, a reputedly wealthy 80-year-old lady who had two maids, Elizabeth Harrison, aged 60, and 17-year-old Ann Price. On 3 February 1733 Sarah called at Mrs Duncomb's chambers in Tanfield Court in the Inner Temple, ostensibly to visit Elizabeth Harrison, who had been ill, although it was later surmised that her actual motive could have been to make sure there had been no changes to the layout of the rooms.

The following day a friend of Mrs Duncomb's called at the block of chambers but, on getting no reply, contacted a woman working in the next room, who, by dint of climbing out of her employer's room and breaking a window in Mrs Duncomb's chambers, succeeded in gaining an entrance. When the two women went in, they were horrified at the gruesome sight that greeted them, for there, to quote the *Newgate Calendar* 'was the body of Ann Price, lying on her bed, wallowing in blood, with her throat cut from ear to ear'. In the next room lay Elizabeth Harrison, who had obviously been strangled, as had Mrs Duncomb in an adjoining room. A chest, in which the old lady had kept her valuables, had been broken into and the contents removed.

The news spread swiftly round the locality and Mr Kerril, on going to his quarters, found Sarah Malcolm there, lighting the fires. He noticed a bundle lying on the floor and on querying its contents, she replied that it was her gown, together with other garments and she said she hoped decency would deter him from opening it. So, of course, he refrained from doing so. However, two watchmen, the police officers of the day, started to search the building, and on finding some of Mr Kerril's belongings hidden in her rooms, Sarah was arrested. A further search by her employer revealed more linen, and a silver tankard with a bloodstained handle concealed in the lavatory. On being interrogated, Sarah alleged that they belonged to her mother and that the blood was from her hand, having cut her finger that morning.

Such excuses being regarded as frivolous, Sarah was taken to Newgate Prison, and in accordance with regulations she was searched. On doing so, Mr Johnson, the turnkey, was astonished to find a small bag containing coins amounting to over a hundred pounds in value hidden beneath the thick coiled tresses of her hair. At the discovery, Sarah admitted that the money belonged to Mrs Duncomb, adding brazenly, 'I'll make you a present of it if you will but keep it to yourself and let nobody know of anything of the matter; for the other things against me are nothing but circumstances, and I shall come off well enough.

So I only desire you to let me have threepence or sixpence a day till the court sessions are over, and then I'll be at liberty to shift for myself.' Johnson, however, was a man of integrity; yielding not to temptation, he promptly sealed up the bag and locked it away to await her trial.

In court Sarah claimed that the murders had been committed by the Alexander brothers; that having all the keys to the chambers, as required by her job, she had admitted them to Mrs Duncomb's rooms, but had taken no part in the crimes but had watched from the stairs. Whether this account was true or not, so overwhelming was the evidence of the bloody-handled tankard, and the clothing and money in her possession, that the verdict was not long forthcoming. She was found guilty and sentenced to death.

On 7 March 1733 she was taken in the horse-drawn cart from Newgate, accompanied by the hangman 'Laughing Jack' Hooper, to the set of gallows erected near Fetter Lane in Fleet Street, it being the custom in those days to execute a murderer as near as possible to the place of the crime. An onlooker said that Sarah had rouged her cheeks heavily to conceal her prison pallor, and was wearing a black gown, white apron, a hood made of sarsenet (a fine soft silk fabric) and black gloves; she appeared very serious and devout, crying and wringing her hands in an extraordinary manner. She was helped in her devotions by the Reverend Peddington of the Church of St Bartholomew the Great, and Mr Guthrie, the Ordinary of Newgate Prison went with her in the cart en route to the scaffold. Another observer declared that 'at one time that she was in the cart, what with praying, Agony and Passion, she fell down, but was immediately rais'd, and laid her head against hangman John Hooper, and Mr Peddington read to her.'

On arrival she called out to the bellman who had been ringing his bell to warn everyone of the vehicle's approach, and gave him a shilling with which to buy himself a bottle of wine; she then declared to the crowd 'that her employer Mr Kerril knew nothing of her intentions of the robbery and the terrible deeds that followed' and also said that 'she had given Mr Peddington a letter in which she related what she had to say about the fact'.

On the scaffold she was seen to sway momentarily but swiftly recovered as Hooper dropped the noose over her head and tightened it. Climbing down out of the cart, he gave the horse a sharp slap on its flanks, causing the steed, and the cart, to move away and leave Sarah swinging and kicking for some little time in the empty air. At length she was cut down and taken by coach back to Newgate and buried.

The inevitably vast crowd watched Sarah's execution and so great was the surging and jostling after she had been cut down that the scaffold itself almost collapsed; the gangs of thieves who usually attended such profitable events seized the opportunity to enhance their bank balances, and many of the more affluent of the spectators found their pockets empty, their purses and watches gone.

Manning, Maria (England)

Despite being married, Maria, an alluring 28-year-old Swiss woman, fell in love with Patrick O'Connor, a middle-aged money lender, a relationship that was accepted seemingly wholeheartedly by her husband Frederick. O'Connor, using his business acumen, recommended that the Mannings should rent a public house in Shoreditch, but when the concern failed to make any profit, Maria accused O'Connor of cheating them and demanded compensation. On 8 August 1849 she invited him to visit them at their home at No. 3 Minerva Place, Bermondsey, in order to discuss the situation; instead she cold-bloodedly shot him through the head. It would seem that the couple had formulated their plan in advance, for when O'Connor appeared to be still alive, Frederick picked up the crowbar he had bought with the intention of using it to bury their victim, and proceeded to batter O'Connor to death. He then used the makeshift weapon to lever up some of the paving stones in the kitchen, and with Maria's help, concealed the body beneath them.

Whether Maria then deliberately decided to double-cross her husband, or whether she panicked at the murder they had committed and made up her mind to go abroad, is not known, but, saying nothing to Frederick, she went to O'Connor's house and after stealing cash and valuables, including some railway stock, she caught the train to Edinburgh. Meanwhile their victim's absence had been reported to the police and on tracing O'Connor's last movements they visited the Mannings' residence. During a detailed search of the premises one of the officers noticed the fresh cement around some of the flagstones in the kitchen and, on lifting them, they discovered a man's body, his wrists bound behind him, his legs doubled up and tied to his haunches. Quicklime had been poured over the corpse in an attempt to prevent any identification, but dental checks on the set of false teeth found in the remains confirmed that the victim was indeed O'Connor. That the death was not accidental was evidenced by the single bullet discovered within the mutilated skull.

On reaching Scotland, Maria later attempted to sell the railway stock she had stolen, and, the alarm having been raised among the brokers, she was arrested. Frederick, realising that his wife had deserted him, also took to his heels, only to be similarly taken into custody in Jersey.

At their trial each blamed the other for the crime, although the facts that the shares were found in Maria's possession, and that she could not possibly have buried O'Connor's body singlehanded, left the jury in little doubt that both were equally culpable. After just 45 minutes a verdict of guilty was announced.

Defending herself to the last, Maria furiously declared that she was innocent, and the only man she would have killed would have been that man – pointing to her husband – who had made her life a hell on earth. On both being sentenced to death, Maria gave vent to a furious tirade against Judge Cresswell and British juries, claiming that such an injustice would never have happened in Switzerland! Her outburst was ignored by His Worship; 'Take them down,' he ordered, and the couple were escorted below, and from thence to Horsemonger Lane Gaol, the county gaol for Surrey, situated near the Elephant and Castle in Southwark, there to await execution.

Even in the condemned cell Maria refused to give up her fight for freedom. She had once been a servant in the household of Lady Blantyre, whose mother, the Duchess of Sutherland, had been a close friend of Queen Victoria, so she sent a letter to Her Majesty, appealing for mercy. Not receiving a reply, desperately she attempted to take her own life. Taking advantage of a moment in the middle of the night when her three wardresses were dozing, she tried to pierce her windpipe with her sharp pointed fingernails. One of the wardresses, waking up, realised what was happening, and it took the efforts of all three to tear her hands away from her throat and subdue her.

On Tuesday morning, 13 November 1849, the doomed couple met in the prison chapel and it was reported that as they stood before the altar, Frederick expressed his wish that they should not part in animosity; she replied that she had none, and then kissed him. The Ordinary administered the last sacrament, after which Frederick said, 'I think we shall meet in heaven.'

The veteran executioner William Calcraft then appeared and pinioned the arms of his prisoners. It was a bitterly cold morning and the hangman tried to show some solicitude for his female victim, urging her to allow the wardress to wrap her cloak around her, but Maria refused; instead she asked that her black silk handkerchief be tied about her eyes beneath the black veil she already wore, so that she would not have to see the waiting gallows, or the vast crowds, whose hubbub she could hear in the distance. Thus blindfolded she was led by Mr Harris, the surgeon, in the sombre procession, the sonorous bell tolling the while along the seemingly endless passageways and up the steep steps to where the scaffold had been erected.

Horsemonger Lane Gaol had a flat roof and so provided a perfect stage for the drama due to take place. Below was a veritable sea of upturned faces, more than 30,000 spectators filling every available space on the cobbles, in balconies and clinging to chimney stacks on rooftops, with no fewer than 500 police constables attempting to maintain some semblance of order.

Journalistic hyperbole, not necessarily factual, was extensively used in the newspapers of the day when describing an execution, but this time a more authoritative description was penned by none other than Charles Dickens and printed in the next edition of *The Times*. He wrote:

> *I was a witness to the execution at Horsemonger Lane this morning. I went there with the intention of observing the crowd gathered to behold it and I had excellent opportunities of doing so at intervals throughout the night, and continuously from daybreak, until after the spectacle was over. I believe that a sight so inconceivably awful as the wickedness and levity of the immense crowd could be imagined by no man, and could be presented in no heathen land under the sun. When I came upon the scene at midnight, the shrillness of the cries and howls that were raised from time to time, denoting that they came from a concourse of boys and girls already assembled in the best places, made my blood run cold.*
>
> *When the day dawned, thieves, low prostitutes, ruffians and vagabonds of every kind flocked on to the ground, with every variety of offensive and foul behaviour. Fightings, faintings, whistling, imitations of Punch, brutal jokes, tumultuous demonstrations of indecent delight when swooning women were dragged out of the crowd by the police, with their dresses disordered, gave a new zest to the general entertainment. When the sun rose brightly – as it did – it gilded thousands upon thousands of upturned faces, so inexpressibly odious in their brutal mirth or callousness, that a man had cause to feel ashamed of the shape he wore, and to shrink from himself, as fashioned in the image of the Devil.*

His account was endorsed by a *Times* reporter, who described 'the disorderly rabble smoking clay pipes and muzzy with beer, pickpockets plying their light-fingered art, little ragged boys climbing up posts, a ceaseless din of sounds and war of tongues'. He went on to paint a picture of the couple's last moments:

> *And when Frederick Manning ascended the steps leading to the drop his limbs tottered under him and he appeared scarcely able to move. Upon his wife approaching the scaffold, he turned round, his face towards the people, while Calcraft proceeded to draw over his head the white nightcap and adjust the fatal rope. The executioner then drew another nightcap over the female prisoner's head and, all the necessary preparations being now completed, the scaffold was cleared of all its occupants except the two wretched beings doomed to die.*

The mob fell hushed and silent as Calcraft swiftly drew the bolt, all eyes fixed on the two hooded and noosed figures silhouetted against the morning sky; the trap opened and the bodies dropped, swaying and twisting slowly with the momentum of their fall, and dying almost immediately. Dickens, with his literary flair for words, wrote how 'the woman's fine shape, elaborately corseted and artfully dressed, was quite unchanged in its trim appearance as it slowly swung from side to side'.

After an hour the Mannings' corpses were cut down and buried, ironically enough, beneath the same type of paving stones within the prison as those under which they had buried Patrick O'Connor. And the multitudes of scaffold aficionados slowly drifted away, savouring the morbid memories of what they had just witnessed, and looking forward with sadistic anticipation to the next occasion on which human beings would be so primitively dispatched into the next world.

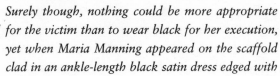

Surely though, nothing could be more appropriate for the victim than to wear black for her execution, yet when Maria Manning appeared on the scaffold clad in an ankle-length black satin dress edged with black lace, with black silk stockings completing her ensemble, and hangman William Calcraft allowed her to have her eyes covered with her black handkerchief beneath the black veil she wore, it is hardly surprising that material of that colour rapidly went out of fashion for many years to come.

One satirical magazine quoted a model in Madame Tussaud's Chamber of Horrors saying to another, 'I've got a nice black dress I've only worn once!' And Punch *printed an acerbic item entitled 'Fashions for Old Bailey Ladies' reporting, tongue-in-cheek, how: 'At the elegant reunion on the occasion of the late Matinée Criminelle at the Old Bailey, the lovely and accomplished Lady X [...] carried off les honneurs with her lovely Manteau á la Mannings, trimmed with ruche en gibbets and têtes de port bouffonées. The neck is surmounted with a running cord, la Calcraft, which finishes in a noeud couland in satin, under the left ear. With the chapeau is worn a bonnet de pendue; this sweet cap can be arranged to cover the whole face and is likely to be thus worn during the approaching season.'*

Marek, Martha (Austria)

Marrying Martha Lowenstein cost young Emil Marek an arm and a leg – well, a leg anyway, and later his life and that of his baby daughter. It all started when Emil, a young engineering student, met 20-year-old Martha. She was quite wealthy, having some years earlier met Moritz Fritsch, a rich dress shop owner, who enjoyed her company so much that he made her his ward and in order to give her a good upper-class education, sent her to finishing schools for young ladies in England and France. When she returned she lived with Moritz, but then, in 1924, she met and fell in love with Emil. Fortune smiled on them, and a fortune came their way, for her elderly benefactor died and left her his estate and all his money. The young lovers promptly married and wasted little time in squandering the assets on the good things in life.

Eventually funds ran low, so low in fact that they concocted a plan which, although it entailed a sacrifice on Emil's part, would bring them a large amount of cash. The first step was for Martha to take out a £10,000 policy insuring Emil against accidents. This would be followed, some weeks afterwards, by the young man losing a leg while using an axe to cut down a tree; except that it would happen not when Emil was wielding the axe accidentally – but when Martha was wielding it on purpose!

One can only conjecture the mentality of a woman who could deliberately aim a blow with an axe at someone's leg, not just once, doubtless because it only caused a flesh wound, but then strike twice more until the limb was so badly mutilated that a surgeon had to amputate it below the knee. In his subsequent clinical write-up, the medical man reported his findings: that the injury was caused not by one, but three separate blows, and the angles of the wounds were inconsistent with being struck by the alleged holder of the axe. At that, Martha, seeing the prospects of the £10,000 rapidly slipping away, tried to bribe one of the surgeon's assistants into testifying that he had seen the surgeon deliberately create the additional wounds at the instigation of the insurance company. This attempt failed, and the couple were sentenced to four months in gaol for bribery, Emil probably being excused hard labour while his drastically shortened leg was healing. As a result of the fraud, the insurance company charitably paid out only £3,000, which was rapidly dissipated by the legal costs the Mareks had incurred.

They were once more in the poverty trap, made worse by the fact that by now they had two young children, but Martha pinned all her hopes on the life insurances she had taken out on her husband and offspring, one hope being realised when Emil suddenly died, the doctors diagnosing tuberculosis. The relatively small amount of insurance money she received was further increased when, only weeks later, their seven-year-old daughter Ingeborg also passed away.

Her faith in the insurance system now fully restored, Martha became a companion to an aunt, Susanne Lowenstein, ingratiating herself in the old lady's affections so much that when her relative died, as she soon did, Martha inherited all her aunt's property, which consisted mainly of a well-furnished mansion. As much a spendthrift as ever, Martha spent what money had been left to her, then had no option but to rent out some of the rooms in the house, one of the lodgers being a Frau Kittenberger. It is hardly necessary to mention that Martha, as forward-looking as ever, took out a policy on her tenant's life, nor that the lady died shortly afterwards.

Perhaps Martha could have gone on insuring everyone she met and reaping the rewards without ever being detected, but she changed her tactics and instead insured the many valuable pictures in the house. She then sold many of them to art dealers and subsequently claimed to the insurers that they had been stolen. The insurance firm, by now suspicious, called in the police, whose success after circulating details of the paintings throughout the art world spelt the end for Martha Marek. Even worse was to follow, for further suspicions were now raised concerning the other insurance claims she had made; highly alarmed, the government authorised the exhumation not only of the lodger Frau Kittenberg, but also of Martha's aunt Susanne Lowenstein, her daughter Ingeborg, and even her husband Emil. Post-mortems revealed that all had died of thallium poisoning, a soft, white, highly toxic metallic element which brought death, first by slow paralysis of the limbs and eventually of the internal organs. Any defence Martha may have made by accusing others of administering the thallium was nullified when the chemist who had sold her the poison was traced.

On 6 December 1938 mass-murderer Martha Marek mounted the scaffold in Vienna and knelt over the block. She had insured her victims before they died, and the executioner ensured that his victim also died, achieving it much more accurately than she had done – with but one blow of the axe.

Another pact between partners that went wrong involved Ginette Vidal and Gerard Osselin. Although both were married, with families of their own, in 1972 they fell in love and, settling down together in a little French town, they agreed that, to prove their devotion and loyalty towards each other, should either of them double-cross their partner, the betrayed one was entitled to kill the deceiver. Whether Gerard did not really believe in their pact, or thought he could get away with it, is not known, but when Ginette found a note written in Gerard's wife's handwriting, she did not hesitate; she shot him through the head.

Ginette made no attempt to report what had happened; on the contrary she stayed in the house with her lover's corpse, cooking for them both as if nothing had happened. Eventually Gerard's family raised the alarm and the body was discovered by the gendarmes. When questioned, Ginette was surprised at their accusations; she explained she had acted in accordance with their agreement, and as evidence she produced the document each had signed. Unfortunately the visiting magistrate did not see it that way, and she went to prison for ten years.

Masset, Louise (England)

The victim in this case was not a husband or a rival, but a son; the weapon was not poison or a blunt instrument, but a heavy piece of stone; and the motive was illicit love.

Louise, a Frenchwoman, had an illegitimate child while in France. Louise, a highly intelligent, 36-year-old woman, then became a governess in London and, to avoid the inevitable gossip, arranged for her son Manfred to be cared for by a Miss Gentle. All went well; Louise was a loving mother and frequently visited her son, but she became acquainted with Eudore Lucas, a young French clerk who lived nearby, a friendship which rapidly matured into an intense love affair.

Varied accounts were given as to what happened next. According to the confession she made while in the condemned cell to Miss Ellen Hayes, Inspector of Prisons, she was so deeply concerned about the derogatory names which would be aimed at Manfred as he grew older – she averred that he had already been a target of abuse – that she killed him out of mercy and compassion. Yet this was decidedly at odds with the other account – that she wanted to marry Eudore and so cold-heartedly decided to free herself of any baggage, human or otherwise.

What was indisputable was the fact that on 27 October 1899 a woman walked into the ladies' toilets at Broad Green Station and found a boy's body lying there, wrapped only in a black shawl, and nearby was a large piece of stone. A post-mortem revealed that he had been stunned by a single blow, then strangled to death.

The corpse was identified by Miss Gentle as that of Manfred Masset, and Louise was arrested and charged with murder. In court, evidence was given that she had informed Miss Gentle that she would be collecting her son on that particular day to take him to his father in France. She also told her lover that she would meet him in Brighton on the following day. Among the witnesses called was Miss Gentle who stated that when collected, the little boy had been dressed in a blue serge tunic – and that his mother had wrapped him in a black shawl to keep him warm during the Channel crossing. Other witnesses stated they had later seen the couple in the refreshment room on London Bridge Station.

In her defence Louise agreed that she had indeed gone to that railway station to buy Manfred something to eat, but the main object of her being there was to give the boy into the care of two sisters named Browning who had previously promised to bring him up in an infant school they ran, for a fee of £12 a year. But when she was asked by the prosecution how she could explain the discovery of Manfred's clothes in the waiting room at Brighton Station, she remained silent. And when the police stated that they had found no trace of the Brownings or the alleged infant school, and Louise was unable to produce a receipt for the alleged payment she had made, the members of the jury were in no doubt as to her guilt.

In the condemned cell Louise Masset said calmly, 'I can only win peace by meeting my death bravely.' On 9 January 1900 she was hanged on the Newgate scaffold. Later, Miss Hayes, the Prisons Inspector, declared: 'Louise had done her best to face, with becoming courage, that fate from which the very bravest might shrink.'

 Violette Nozière, found guilty of murdering her father, listened calmly as the French judge sentenced her to be taken to the place of execution, barefoot and wearing only a chemise, there to be publicly beheaded

by the sword. As she was being escorted by warders from the court room, Violette, eternally feminine no matter what the circumstances, suddenly stopped and exclaimed, 'Wait – I must have left my handbag in the dock. It's got my powder and rouge in it – let me get it!' At a later appeal against her sentence, the court, impressed by her unconcerned attitude towards her fate and with the traditional French chivalry towards the fair sex, showed clemency, and reduced her sentence to one of life imprisonment.

Masson, Margaret (Scotland)

To wax cynical, it was surely merciful of the court, on finding Margaret pregnant, to wait until she had given birth five months later – and then hang her! But the law in 1806 was harsh and unrelenting, and when Margaret, in company with her lover, John Skinner, the father of her unborn baby, was charged with poisoning her husband John with arsenic on 9 May, a panel of midwives in Edinburgh's High Court certified that she was indeed with child. Sentence was postponed for five months, and in November, as she stood at the bar with her child in her arms, she was sentenced to be hanged, her execution being carried out shortly afterwards. And her fellow murderer and lover John Skinner? He absconded from the city and was never caught.

 A bill of indictment was found against Elizabeth Carr of Brampton, Cumberland (now Cumbria), for stealing 2½ pence from the pocket of Margaret Hepworth. Although Elizabeth pleaded not guilty the jury thought otherwise 'and she, being with child, was only ordered to strip to the waist by the Common Beadle, to

have four lashes, and then to be turned out of the town by the Mill Bridge'.

Meteyard, Sarah (England)

Like the brutal maltreatment of young servants inflicted by Elizabeth Brownrigg, described elsewhere, Sarah Meteyard was arrested for exactly the same appalling offences. Sarah employed girls aged between eight and thirteen years old in her millinery shop in Bruton Street, London; girls provided by the local Poor Law authorities, who were only too pleased to reduce their maintenance costs. These children were kept in atrocious conditions, ill-fed and ill-treated both by Sarah and her daughter Sally, but in 1758 things started to go badly wrong for the evil pair. One of the 'apprentices', Ann Naylor, managed to escape into the street where, on meeting a milkman, she beseeched him to help her to get away, saying that if she had to go back she would be severely punished. But Sally Meteyard, suddenly aware of the girl's absence, rushed out and, grabbing the girl by the neck, dragged her back into the shop. Taking her to an upstairs room, she then held Ann down while Sarah beat her with a broom handle before tying her hands behind her and fastening her to the door with another rope around her waist so that she could neither sit nor lie down.

The other apprentices were not allowed near the room until, several days later, one happened to go in to find Ann Naylor slumped against the door, her whole weight taken by the ropes; her frantic shouts were answered by Sally Meteyard, who exclaimed, 'If she won't move, I will make her move!' and then proceeded to take off one of her shoes and beat the motionless girl over the head with it. On seeing no signs of life she summoned her mother and, cutting Ann down, they attempted to revive her – alas, too late, for the girl was already dead.

Worse was to follow, for the two women carried the body into the attic, then told their staff that she had had a fit and was confined up there to stop her from running away again; to substantiate their story, Sally even took a plate of food upstairs to the room. Later, the pretence was furthered by mother and daughter putting the corpse in a box; then, leaving the attic door open, they announced that Ann had run away again.

The body remained in the locked chest for two months when, the smell of the decomposing flesh becoming overwhelming, on Christmas Day the two women cut the corpse into pieces, tying the head and torso up in one large cloth and the limbs in another – excepting one hand, a finger of which had been amputated before death, which they burned later. They had originally intended to dispose of all the body parts in the same way, but, worried that the smoke and smell would attract unfavourable attention, they carried the makeshift parcels out of the house and dumped them by the common sewer in nearby Chick Lane. Some hours later the bundles were found by the watchman who, assuming they had been discarded by a hospital surgeon, had them buried locally.

Four years passed, and had mother and daughter maintained a loving family relationship, the tragic death of Ann Naylor would have passed unavenged. However, quarrels developed, and after being subjected to beatings from Sarah, Sally walked out and went to live in the house of a neighbour, Mr Rooker. Sarah, however, refused to let the matter rest, and frequently visited the Rooker residence, abusing and cursing both of them. These occurrences became so frequent that eventually Mr Rooker and Sally, who by now had become his mistress, moved to another house in Ealing, only to be followed by Sally's mother, bent on causing further trouble. Matters came to a head on 9 June 1762 when, on one visit, she thrashed her daughter so severely that Sally blurted, 'Remember, mother, you are the Chick Lane Ghost!' After Sarah had left, Mr Rooker urged Sally to explain her cryptic retort, whereupon Sally burst into tears and confessed everything to her lover. But the horrified Mr Rooker informed the authorities, and not only was Sarah Meteyard arrested, but further enquiries also led to Sally being taken into custody in the Gatehouse Prison.

In court both sought to incriminate the other, both thereby incriminating themselves even further. Sally pleaded that she was pregnant, but the panel of matrons who examined her soon discounted that as being merely an excuse to avoid the gallows. They were both sentenced to death and their bodies to be handed over to Surgeons' Hall for subsequent dissection (rather more skilfully than the manner in which they had carved up poor Ann Naylor).

They were hanged side by side at Tyburn on 19 July 1768, the *Newgate Calendar* describing how, from the time of leaving Newgate for the scaffold, the daughter wept uncontrollably. As for her mother, it related how 'Sarah Meteyard, being in a fit when she was put into the cart, lay at her length until she came to the place of execution, when she was raised up, and means were used for her recovery, but without effect, so that she departed this life in a state of insensibility'.

When the nineteenth-century executioner William Marwood gave a lecture about his profession he waxed lyrical, saying how 'the Wheel of Time is constantly casting people into Eternity', but was somewhat disconcerted when a member of the more rowdy element of the audience shouted back, 'Yes, and so's the rope!'

M'Lachlan, Margaret (Scotland)

Why go to all the trouble of constructing a scaffold and gallows when rivers and the sea were available? In 1685, when Margaret M'Lachlan, aged 63, was charged with declaring that James VII of Scotland was not entitled to rule the Church in the manner in which he wanted to, the authorities simply took her to the River Bladnoch in Wigtown and there tied her to a stake. As the tidal waters slowly rose, had she agreed to support the King's religious intentions, her life would have been spared, but true to her beliefs and principles, she refused and drowned.

The Ducking Stool

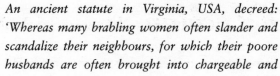

An ancient statute in Virginia, USA, decreed: 'Whereas many brabling women often slander and scandalize their neighbours, for which their poore husbands are often brought into chargeable and vexacious law suits and cast in great damages, be it enacted that all women found guilty be sentenced to ducking.'

Moders, Mary (England)

A warrant dated 17 October 1670 to Sir William Morton, Justice of the King's Bench, and the Recorder and Sheriffs of London, contained instructions 'to reprieve Mary Moders alias Carleton alias Kirton alias Blacke, who has been a second time condemned to death for felony, and to cause her to be inserted in the next general transportation pardon for convicts of Newgate'.

Mary Moders was nothing if not a colourful and fascinating character. Born in Canterbury on 22 January 1642, her father was a chorister in the cathedral in that city, but she was to claim her birthplace to be that of Cologne and her father of being Henry Van Wolway, 'a Licentiate and Doctor of Civil Law, and Lord of Holmstein, a man esteemed for his services done to the City of Cologne in mediating their peace, security and neutrality, in the Swedish and German War'. Whether such a gentleman actually existed is not known; nevertheless, having 'created' him, she thereby claimed to be a German princess.

When she was sixteen years of age Mary married Thomas Stedman, a cobbler, by whom she had two children, both dying in infancy. She lived with him for about three years but, getting bored with him, she left with what valuables he had, and eloped with a mate of a ship bound for the Barbados, but Thomas swore out a warrant against her, and she was arrested and imprisoned in Dover Castle. When eventually released, she went abroad for two years, on return marrying a surgeon, Mr Day. But having committed bigamy, she was tried, though for some reason acquitted. Off she went again, this time to the Continent, where she picked up a smattering of French and German, having employed her considerable charms in a brothel. Insisting on having her own personal boudoir, she consorted only with very rich clients, extracting fees appropriate to the regal services she had bestowed on them.

She came back to England in 1662 and met a man named John Carleton, as much a charlatan as her, for she was pretending to be a German princess and he a gentleman of quality. They married on 21 April 1663, but he found out that she was already married and she found herself arrested for bigamy – again! Awaiting trial, she was committed to Newgate and, as quoted in *Howel's State Papers*, 'After she was arraigned and going to gaol, her husband told her he must now bid her adieu for ever, to which she replied, couplet-wise, "Nay, my Lord, 'tis not amiss, Before we part, to have a kiss." And so saluted him, saying, "You cheated me and I cheated you; you told me you were a Lord, and I told you I was a Princess. And so I think I fitted you." And so saluting each other, they parted.'

Her case caused a great deal of interest, and for a time she was the talk of the metropolis. Samuel Pepys went to the prison on 29 May 1663, writing in his *Diary*: 'Then with Creed, to see the German Princess at the Gate-House at Westminster.' At the time, prisons were akin to present-day zoos, in that the public could satisfy their curiosity by viewing the inmates. After being acquitted for the second time, she appeared on the stage of London's Duke's Theatre, and once performed in a play bearing her own name, *The German Princess*, Pepys being in the audience, not applauding but deploring her acting ability.

More adventures followed. Mary pretended to be an innocent damsel newly arrived from the countryside, claiming to have a £1,000 dowry from an uncle. A Mr Woodson of Islington walked straight into her net, a useful catch, he having an income of £200 per annum and £500 in ready money; she assumed extreme coyness, but by guile and promises reduced his cash flow by £300 before changing her address to one in Houndsditch. There the records show that:

She told the landlady that a Country Gentleman of her Acquaintance, happening to fall sick in an Alehouse in the City, died, and some friends of his, and her together, had thought it convenient to remove the Corpse to a House of more Credit, in order to arrange a handsome Burial. The landlady readily granted the use of her best Chamber, whither the 'Corpse' was brought, and an undertaker in Leadenhall Street laid hold of the Jobb, having received an unlimited Commission to perform the Funeral, that nothing should be lacking to make as complete as possible. Accordingly he provided a good Quantity of Old Plate for an Ornament to the Room, where the Body lay, these being two large Silver Candlesticks, a Silver Flagon, two Silver Bowls and several other pieces of Plate. But the night before the intended burial, Madam and her maid (a baggage as unscrupulous as she) handed out to the Comrades all the Man's Plate, together with the velvet pall, and then got away by a Ladder that was placed to the Balcony. Upon opening the Coffin, which had been brought from the Alehouse ready nailed up, it was filled with nothing but Brickbats [pieces of brick].

Mary's audaciously fraudulent career knew no bounds. She would order new gowns and robes, invite the dressmaker to bring them to a big party she was having, then by getting the woman hopelessly drunk, would abscond with every garment that had been delivered. She often changed her lodgings

and would visit Taverns and Alehouses, stealing silver Tankards, Bowls, and other drinking Vessels in abundance, but for some of these Offences she was detected and found Guilty, and exiled to Jamaica, from whence she returned, unlawfully, in a little more than a year, heavy with child, and was delivered soon after, of a fine boy, in her cell in Newgate, it being intimated that the child saved her life, because that way she evaded the Execution of her Sentence of her Death, by pleading her Belly.

Among later fraudulent activities, she took lodgings at Charing Cross, where a rich watchmaker also lodged, and invited him, the landlady and her daughter to see a play, then took them all to the Green Dragon Tavern on Fleet Street. Under the pretext of joining a party of friends in another room in the hostelry, she sped back to the house and stole £200 and thirty expensive watches to the value of £400 or more. Her maid, meanwhile, was stealing everything she could from the party in the tavern, and then met her mistress at a pre-arranged rendezvous.

Despite disguising herself, such was her reputation that the finger of suspicion pointed at her. Seventeenth-century documents described her decline by saying:

This was her last Project, her appointed time was drawing nigh, her Glass had but few more Sands to run. She fled across town and lodged in St George's

Fields, where one named Fisher, a bailiff, searching after a felon called Lancaster, came across Her Highness, who was walking in her Chamber in a rich Night Gown, with a Letter upon her table addressed to an accomplice, one Mr Hyde, a notorious Robber.

Mary was arrested and brought to Newgate Prison. On 17 January 1678 she was tried at the Old Bailey on one charge of stealing a piece of valuable plate from a tavern in Chancery Lane and, being found guilty, was sentenced to death.

Mary Moders was executed at Tyburn on her thirtieth birthday, 22 January 1678. Before being noosed she drank a glass of gin and appeared unconcerned at her fate. It was said that she died penitent, and that on the scaffold she carried a small picture of her husband John Carleton pinned to her wrist, 'which she put in her Bosom when she was going to be turned off, requesting that it might be buried with her, which was complied with accordingly, at St-Martin-in-the-Fields churchyard'.

 Had Mary's claim to royalty been authentic she would have been interred in Westminster Abbey; as it was, a humble grave in St Martin's Churchyard, received the coffin, an engraver possessing a sense of humour carving her epitaph:

'The German Princess, here against her will, Lies underneath and yet, oh strange, lies still.'

N

Newell, Susan (England)

A woman who committed an inexplicable murder in 1923, and the hangman who executed her attempting to commit suicide ten months later, proved to be the news headlines of the decade. Susan was charged with murdering John Johnstone, a 12-year-old schoolboy who delivered newspapers for pocket money, a crime that seemed totally motiveless.

It all started in June 1923 when Mrs Helen Elliott was about to leave her house to go shopping. A lorry had pulled up a little further along the road and she noticed the driver climb out and help a woman lift a small handcart out of his vehicle. He then drove away, but as the woman manoeuvred the cart on to the pavement, Mrs Elliot noticed something else, something that made her gasp in disbelief, for from the wrapped-up bundle in the cart protruded a head and a foot. Hardly believing her eyes, she called to her sister who was nearby and, at a discreet distance, they followed the woman as she went down a narrow alleyway, to see her dump the bundle in a corner. Fortunately a policeman was passing by and, summoned by the two sisters, he proceeded to arrest the woman, a Mrs Susan Newell. On unwrapping the contents of the bundle he found that it contained the doubled-up and mutilated body of the aforementioned newsboy. Subsequent forensic examination showed that the boy's body had been burned while he was still alive, and then violently throttled.

Susan, her husband John and their eight-year-old daughter Janet, lived in a Glasgow lodging house, and on the morning of 21

June 1923 the landlady not only noticed that the front door was open, but also that the handcart she owned was missing. At about the same time, a lorry driver along the street had noticed a woman pushing what was obviously a heavy cart and offered to give her a lift; further into town she asked him to stop, saying that she did not have much further to go. Had she waited a mile or so before speaking, Helen Elliott would not have had such a horrific story with which to regale her neighbours for months to come, and the police would have been faced with an unsolvable crime. As it was, Susan was questioned, her only explanation being that she was disposing of the body to protect her husband, who had actually committed the murder. That this was a falsehood became clear when John was able to prove that he had been away in another town during the two days previous to his wife's arrest.

The prosecution at this stage faltered for the lack of evidence; Susan Newell could have been charged with being an accessory to a murder, but nothing more serious than that. But then Susan's young daughter provided the evidence, if not the motive, for she recounted how she had seen the boy arrive to deliver the papers but had not seen him leave. She had then been taken by her mother to a nearby public house, and on returning with her later, saw him lying in a chair. Little realising, at her age, that what she was saying virtually condemned her mother to death, the girl described how she had helped to wrap up the body, and had watched her mother lift it into the cart.

Despite a plea of insanity, Susan Newell was found guilty by the jury on a majority verdict, albeit with a recommendation for mercy. The judge agreed with the first decision but rejected the adjunct, and sentenced her to death.

Susan made no confession and gave no reason why the boy had to die, and on 10 October 1923 in Duke Street Prison, not far from where she had attempted to leave the corpse of her victim, she came face to face with John Ellis, the executioner, as he drew the hood down over her head and positioned the noose. Unresisting, her hands and ankles pinioned, she stood motionless as he moved to the lever, her body falling through the aperture, death coming within minutes.

As for the hangman himself, although he always denied that that particular execution had affected him in any way, in the following December he resigned, having been executioner for 23 years. Shortly afterwards, apparently suffering from depression, he attempted to commit suicide by shooting himself. In the years that followed he appeared on the stage in the role of a hangman and also gave talks about his experiences on the scaffold, but in September 1932, by then a sick man, he killed himself by cutting his throat.

The profession of executioner was generally regarded with revulsion and disgust, hangmen being frequently abused, even violently assaulted. This irrational attitude of the public was challenged by the late French executioner Henri Anatole Deibler, who wrote sarcastically: 'To kill in the name of one's country is a glorious feat, one rewarded by medals. But to kill in the name of the law, that is a gruesome, horrible function, rewarded with scorn, contempt and loathing by the public.'

P

Pearcey, Mary Eleanor (England)

Mary Eleanor was another woman who pushed a small cart, a pram in this case, into which she had crammed her victims, one being that of a woman, the other of the woman's baby, in an attempt to dispose of them. The dead woman's body, covered in blood, the head almost severed, was discovered on a building site in a street in Hampstead, London, by a policeman. A search for clues was immediately instituted but it was not until the following day that, some distance away, a small child's corpse was found together with a heavily bloodstained pram.

Descriptions of the victim's clothing were circulated, a young woman by the name of Clara Hogg coming forward to claim that they resembled those sometimes worn by her aunt, Mrs Phoebe Hogg. When asked to come and identify the body she persuaded a friend of her aunt's, 24-year-old Mrs Mary Pearcey, to accompany her. The friend was very reluctant to do so; so reluctant that, on seeing the corpse, she exclaimed that it was not that of Phoebe. However, Clara, on seeing the face of the dead woman, confirmed that the body was indeed that of her aunt.

The police visited the murdered woman's house and interviewed her husband Frank, who told them that his wife had taken Jeffrey, their 18-month-old son, out in the pram for a walk. As Frank did not appear to be as upset over his wife's gruesome death as would have been expected, they searched the premises for any clues and discovered a key which they ascertained to be the door key to Mary Pearcey's house nearby. Following this up, the police then visited Mrs Pearcey herself, to be greeted by a ghastly sight, for the kitchen resembled a slaughter-house, the walls and floor splashed with blood, furniture overturned and shards of crockery scattered around the room. When asked to account for the scene of devastation Mary blandly replied that she had been chasing mice, accompanying her words by playing on the piano! The weapons used, a bloodstained chopper and a poker, were found among the debris, hairs on the latter matching those found on the cushions in the pram.

The truth then emerged that although Mary entertained other gentlemen of the neighbourhood, and Phoebe's husband had the reputation of being a womaniser, nevertheless she and Frank had been having a long-term intense and clandestine love affair. The relationship was known to and accepted by Phoebe, and the two women remained firm friends, at least until Mary invited her friend to visit her in October 1890. Accordingly, Phoebe washed and dressed the baby and wheeled it in the pram to Mary's house. What happened there between the two was never discovered. Mary could have been suddenly overwhelmed with uncontrollable jealousy; Phoebe may have finally resented some possessive comment inadvertently made by her friend.

The attack, seemingly one-sided, was brutal and savage, Mary wielding the chopper and poker, then cutting her victim's throat, almost severing her head. After ascertaining that Phoebe was dead, Mary then put the body on top of the baby in the pram, its mother's weight eventually suffocating it. Draping a raincoat over the bodies, she pushed the pram out of the house, passing neighbours as she did so, even speaking to some of them as she headed through the streets, first to deposit Phoebe's body where it was eventually found, then continuing to the wasteland, where she abandoned the baby and the pram.

Arrested and charged, there was no mercy shown towards her, any vestiges of compassion vanishing when it was learned that, when taken into custody, she wore two wedding rings on her finger – but only the impression of one remained on the finger of the murdered Phoebe. In court she pleaded not guilty on the grounds of circumstantial evidence, the defence also claiming insanity, but the jury did not hesitate and nor did the judge. Finding her guilty, he sentenced her to death.

Mary showed no reaction on being taken away, her icy composure only finally breaking down when, from the condemned cell, she wrote to her lover asking him to come and visit her; her letters were returned unanswered. However, she soon resumed her self-assured attitude, outwardly at least; needing to assess her weight in order to decide on the length of 'drop' to give her, hangman James Berry walked past the cell and quickly glanced in, whereupon she said casually, 'Oh, was that the executioner? He's in good time, isn't he – is it usual for him to arrive on the Saturday for the Monday?' And when Berry came to collect his prisoner on that day, 23 December 1890, she shook hands with him. He then asked whether she had any last statement to make, to which she cryptically replied, 'The sentence was just, but some of the evidence was false.' Requiring to prepare her for execution, Berry then said politely, 'If you are ready, madam, I will get these straps round you.' Without any hesitation she said, 'I am quite ready, Mr Berry.' When the female warders moved to walk each side of her in the macabre procession, she remarked, 'I need no one to assist me; I can walk by myself and there is no need for you to come.' One of the officers said that they didn't mind in the least accompanying her, to which she answered, 'Oh well, if you don't mind coming, I shall be glad to have you.' On arriving at the scaffold she kissed the women goodbye, surely a highly emotional moment for the officers.

On the trapdoors, supported by two male warders standing on the planks that bridged the gap, and holding the ropes suspended from the overhead beam with their free hands, she maintained her almost uncanny air of complete composure as Berry hooded and noosed her. The end came rapidly as he operated the drop, the rope straightening taut and spinning slightly as she dropped into the pit.

One mystery still remains unsolved. On her instructions Mary's solicitor caused a message to be published in a Spanish newspaper, reading: 'M.E.C.P. Last wish of M.E.W. Have not betrayed.' The latter three initials were those of her real name, Mary Eleanor Wheeler,

Pearcey being the surname of a man, John Charles Pearcey, with whom she had lived for some years. But who was M.E.C.P? Why Spain? Who was it she had not betrayed? And of doing what?

Did she in fact commit the murder? There were no reported signs of any injuries she might, indeed *should* have sustained during the violent struggle in the kitchen, so was M.E.C.P. one of her men friends who was so enamoured with her that at her request he killed her rival for Frank's affections and then fled to Spain? And knowing that, in his absence, she could neither prove his existence, nor have him extradited from abroad, was that why she affected insanity by playing the piano and claiming that she had been killing mice, in the last final hope of a reprieve? We will never know.

The saying that 'Mother knows best' was never more true than in the case of the woman who said to her son, who was shortly to be executed, 'Well, be a good boy; the hangman will claim your clothes, so don't wear your best ones, but let me have them. I had better have your red waistcoat now.'

Perry, Joan (England)

There have been many miscarriages of justice in the past, but surely none so weird or far-fetched as the one called the 'Camden Wonder' of 1660, involving as it did a titled lady, an outright liar, Turkish pirates, a doctor's slave, and three people hanged although completely innocent!

It all started when Viscountess Camden, Lady of that manor, sent her 70-year-old steward William Harrison around the estate to collect the rents from the tenants. When he failed to return, his wife, fearing that he might have met with an accident, asked another servant, John Perry, to go and look for him, but he too failed to come back that day. The mystery deepened when, on the following day, one of the women who lived in the village found a bloodstained hat and scarf which belonged to Harrison. Some time later John Perry returned, and when taxed to explain his absence he said that a mist had come down and, losing his way, he sheltered beneath a hedge overnight.

The police were called in to investigate, and it became obvious to them that Perry knew the old steward would have collected a large sum of money, and so they arrested him. When questioned, whether through sheer panic or seeking to shift the blame in order to save his own skin, he blurted out that William Harrison had indeed been murdered – by John's own mother Joan and his brother Richard! He even alleged that he had seen them killing the old man, had tried to protect him but had been pushed aside by Richard, the latter then strangling the steward with some cord and throwing the body into a local pool known as the Great Sink.

The pond was searched, with negative results, but Mrs Joan Perry and Richard were arrested. Both were charged with murder, John with being an accessory to murder; the jury did not hesitate to find them guilty, and despite their pitiful protestations of innocence, all three were sentenced to death. In the hopes that Richard would make a full confession, the executioner hanged Joan Perry first, but the youth continued to insist that he and his mother had nothing to do with the crime, so he too was hanged. And when it came to John's turn, he struggled frantically, swearing that he had lied, that he didn't know what he was saying when he accused the others. It didn't make any difference, because he also swung from the gallows.

Eventually the village gossip subsided and the inhabitants got on with their work, toiling in the fields, grinding the corn, and duly paying their tithes to the Lord of the Manor. Then two years later, from out of the blue, suddenly appeared the old steward, William Harrison, with an almost unbelievable tale to tell. He claimed that while walking down the lane leading to the village that day, three horsemen had suddenly appeared and had attacked him, then carried him away, minus his hat and scarf, to Deal, in Kent, where he was sold to the captain of a ship. He alleged that the vessel had then sailed for foreign parts, eventually docking in Smyrna, where he was sold as a slave to a doctor. To a rapt and incredulous audience, he then described how he had later managed to escape by stowing away on a ship sailing to Portugal where, in Lisbon, a kind-hearted Englishman had given him sufficient money to return to England.

Understandably, this outlandish story, worthy of Baron Munchausen himself, stretched the listeners' imaginations beyond belief. Did he abscond with the few pounds he might have collected – hardly enough to sustain him for the length of time he had been away – and if he had, why did he return? And what on earth induced John Perry to accuse the other members of his family of murder, a totally false indictment which led to three totally needless and completely unjust executions? It is true he admitted that he lied – but alas, too late for his mother, his brother – and himself.

In earlier centuries in the Isle of Man, the fate of a man who had committed rape was left in the hands of his victim; she would be invited to choose between a rope, a sword or a ring. It was entirely up to her whether he should hang, be decapitated – or become her husband!

Place, Martha Garretson (USA)

Many people aspire to achieve records, but Martha Place achieved a place in the record books for which she would rather not have qualified, for she became the first woman to be executed in the electric chair.

As Martha Garretson she was employed by widower William Place as his housekeeper, but their relationship became closer and they got married. William already had a daughter, Ida, by his first wife, and Martha resented the affection shown by her new husband towards the 17-year-old girl to such an extent that it apparently affected her mental balance, for on 7 February 1898, after an argument in which Ida had sided with her father before he left for work, she viciously attacked Ida, throwing acid into her eyes. As the girl covered her face in agony, Martha picked up an axe and felled her with several violent blows; Ida collapsed on the floor, Martha then piling pillows on her face and suffocating her. Newspapers were later to describe the force of the axe blows, how a deep gash over the top of her head reached down to her neck, her face being horribly burned by the acid.

A little while later, William came home to be the immediate target of Martha's axe; although with a severely fractured skull he managed to struggle out of the house, neighbours then sending for the police. On entering the house, the officers found Mrs Place unconscious, having turned on the gas in an attempt to commit suicide. Medical help was forthcoming, and she was revived – and arrested.

Such was the horrific nature of her crimes that at her trial her defence sought to enter a plea of insanity, but this proved unsustainable and she was declared sane. Confident that she would at least be reprieved at a retrial, her spirits sank when this was refused. In the condemned cell in Sing Sing Prison she had several hysterical outbursts, although following frequent prayer sessions with her priest, and perhaps due to his guidance, she regained her self-assurance when, on 20 March 1899, she was led to the execution chamber where the executioner Edwin Davis awaited. There, seated in the chair, she sat still and unresisting, holding a Bible in her hands while her hair was clipped short, preparatory to the head electrode being positioned. A female warder tightened the straps around her, attached the leg electrode and covered her face with the mask. Davis then sent 1,760 volts surging through her body and after about four seconds had elapsed, a further 200 volts were given, followed by a third wave of current, this series of power bringing death to the murderess Martha Garretson Place.

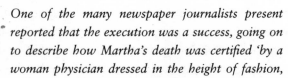

One of the many newspaper journalists present reported that the execution was a success, going on to describe how Martha's death was certified 'by a woman physician dressed in the height of fashion, immaculate in a grey dress and a huge hat with pronounced crimson trimmings'. Must have been tricky using a stethoscope.

Pledge, Sarah and Whale, Anne (England)

This scandalous story was one of an illicit relationship between two women, a tragedy that involved a poisoning and ended in a hanging, strangulation and being burned to ashes.

Anne was born in Horsham, Sussex; her father died when she was young and so she was brought up by her mother. A wayward child, on attaining her teens she got into unsavoury company but later returned home and was fortunate enough to meet a respectable young man named James Whale. It so happened that a relative had bequeathed the large sum of eighty pounds, which would become hers on reaching the age of 21. This being a promising basis for a sound marriage, their wedding took place, and the young couple went to live in a house owned by Sarah Pledge, who was distantly related to Mrs Whale. An attractive widow, she wasted no time in acting in a highly provocative manner towards James Whale. Upright and respectable, Mr Whale promptly forbade her ever to enter his private rooms again.

Rebuffed and insulted, Sarah was determined to get her revenge, and having already become close friends with Anne, encouraged her into an even more intimate relationship, to the extent that one day in June 1742 she suggested to Anne that they should dispose of her husband by giving him poison, implying that they would be much happier together without him. Anne agreed, but being amateurs, took it for granted that anything that was particularly horrible would be equally poisonous, and so they caught as many spiders as they could, and after roasting them, mixed them in his tankard of beer. The brew may have tasted nauseating, but much to the women's annoyance, James continued to live.

Sarah then came to the conclusion that sterner measures would have to be taken, and as the only real poison she had probably ever heard of was arsenic, she bought some from a chemist in Horsham. Anne agreed to administer it and so, while her husband was taking care of their child, she mixed it into the pudding she was preparing for his supper. Avoiding having any of the sweetmeat herself, she watched James eat his fill, then go to bed – and to die in excruciating agony.

But the relationship between the two women had not passed unnoticed by the neighbours, and at the news of poor Mr Whale's sudden death, the subsequent gossip reached the ears of the local police. A post-mortem was carried out and after the surgeon had reported finding the presence of a large amount of arsenic in the internal organs, the coroner's jury brought in a verdict of wilful murder. It wasn't long before another jury, this time sitting in the courtroom at Horsham at the trial of the two women, found both of them guilty of murder.

The judge then sentenced them to death, it then being reported in the *Newgate Calendar* that 'Mrs Pledge behaved in a most hardened manner, making use of profane expressions, and declaring that she would fight the hangman at the place of execution. On the contrary, Mrs Whale acknowledged the justice of the sentence which had condemned her, and gave evident signs of her being a real penitent.' However, under the spiritual guidance of the clergyman who attended them, Sarah Pledge's attitude mellowed considerably and she accepted her fate.

On 14 August 1742 an immense crowd attended the execution site in Horsham to watch with ghoulish satisfaction the sight of Sarah Pledge being hanged, and then the execution of Anne Whale who, having committed the crime of petty treason (the murder of a husband) was tied to a stake, then strangled by the hangman before the burning tinder ignited the flames which, after some hours, reduced her to ashes.

When women get together for a casual chat it is sometimes to grumble about their husbands or to exchange recipes, and that was certainly the case when Joyce, Audrey and Clestrell shared a pot of coffee in 1956 – except that the husband who was most grumbled about was Joyce Turner's, and the recipe discussed was how best to kill him. Such was the pressure brought to bear on her by her friends, that Joyce left her neighbour's

house and went home where she found her husband asleep. She promptly shot him dead. When the crime was investigated all three women blamed an intruder, but when the police discovered that the murder weapon belonged to Joyce, the game was up. She was given a life sentence in gaol – as were her two friends, being equal members of the conspiracy.

Potts, Elizabeth (USA)

Some executions are by hanging, others by decapitation; rarely did one victim suffer both methods almost simultaneously, but that was the appalling result when Elizabeth met her death in 1890.

The events leading up to this shocking disaster started back in January 1888 at a house in Nevada, when a man named Miles Faucett, who was allegedly owed money by Elizabeth and her husband Josiah, called on them to discuss the debt, but never left the premises. Some months later the Potts moved to another part of the country, and the Brewer family moved in to the Potts' old house. Mrs Brewer, her senses apparently attuned to spiritualistic activities, then reported the presence of apparitions, and of hearing spectral sounds in the house, especially in the area of the cellar. Her husband George, sceptical or not, investigated, any doubts he may have had being instantly dispersed when he discovered human remains down there, these mainly consisting of a charred and mutilated head, and pieces of what were arms and legs. A fragment of clothing being identified as belonging to Miles Faucett, the Potts pair were brought back to the town for questioning. So strong was the evidence that they were subsequently charged with murder, and on 12 March 1889 appeared in court.

Their defence, which they maintained throughout their trial, was that Faucett had committed suicide because Elizabeth had caught him in the act of assaulting their four-year-old daughter and, fearing the shame of exposure, had shot himself. Elizabeth did not explain why, if that had been the case, she and her husband had dismembered and burnt the body, rather than simply sending for the police. In the absence of any extenuating circumstances, both Mr and Mrs Potts were found guilty of murder and sentenced to death.

For the executions a scaffold was transported in sections from California, a local paper describing it as 'made of seasoned timber; the crossbeam was capable of sustaining a tremendous strain and worked like a charm when tested with sandbags'. On hearing the noise of it being assembled in the prison grounds, it was reported that both the Potts had cried, although later Elizabeth was heard swearing damnation on all concerned. Josiah apparently passed the time by playing patience, an admirable quality which, seemingly, he had a sufficiency. It was also rumoured that Elizabeth had attempted to commit suicide by cutting her wrists with a small penknife she had hidden in her hair, but had been thwarted by one of the warders.

On 20 June 1890 both faced the sheriff as he read out the death warrants, a regulation procedure which took twenty minutes. Both Josiah and Elizabeth had been given a 'reinforcing tonic', probably whisky, though a reporter described how the woman gasped in horror at the official's words. They then mounted the scaffold steps to the platform, where they had their shoes removed and were pinioned, their arms to their sides, their wrists bound in front of them. Awkwardly they shook hands with each other and kissed, Elizabeth still protesting her innocence as the hangman put the black hoods over their heads and proceeded to noose them. He then cut the cord, withdrawing the bolts which held the trapdoors in place, and the two victims dropped into the pit.

It was then that, for the officials and witnesses, the 'normal' hanging was transformed into an unforgettably ghastly nightmare, for on looking down into the pit, they saw that while Josiah's body rotated slowly on the rope, life having departed, Elizabeth's speed of descent had been too great, and as the rope about her neck abruptly tightened, the noose had acted like a cheese-cutter, slicing through the carotid artery, causing the blood to flow copiously over her body, and almost severing her head. Rather than expose the distorted features of the victims to the bystanders, the black hoods were left in place, both cadavers then being brought out of the pit and later interred, appropriately, in a potter's field. Miles Faucett's remains were also buried nearby.

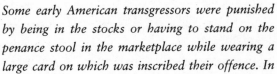 *Some early American transgressors were punished by being in the stocks or having to stand on the penance stool in the marketplace while wearing a large card on which was inscribed their offence. In May 1652, Ann Boulder, a Boston woman, was arrested for defacing a public notice and was ordered 'to stand in yrons half an hour with a Paper on her Breast marked PVBLICK DESTROYER OF PEACE.' And when Joan Andrews, a resident of York, Maine, was caught increasing the weight of a firkin of butter with two heavy stones, 'she had to stand disgraced bearing the description of her cheatery written in Capitall Letters and pinned upon her forehead.' As did Widow Bradley of New London, Connecticut, in 1673 'for her sorry behaviour, by wearing a paper pinned to her cap to proclaim her shame.'*

R

Reid, Mary (Scotland)

Some people just don't get on with their neighbours, and this was never more true than where Mary Reid (or Timney) was concerned.

She lived with her husband and family near Kirkudbright, Scotland, her neighbour being 40-year-old Ann Hannah, with whom she occasionally had violent arguments over money, but none was so violent as that which took place on 13 January 1862, for it culminated in our heroine – or villain – picking up an iron beetle, a heavy hand tool used in pounding cloth, and clubbing Ann to death.

At her trial on 8 April, before Judge Deas (colloquially referred to as 'Judge Death' because of his penchant for handing down that particular type of sentence) she pleaded self-defence, claiming that Ann Hannah had attacked her first. The jury was not convinced, the Judge lived up to his nickname, and Mary was sentenced to die.

On execution day, 29 April 1862, at Dumfries, there was a turn-out of nearly 3,000 people to watch the murderess be dispatched, but the crowd grew quiet as Mary, in a state of near collapse, had to be supported between two burly warders as she mounted the scaffold steps. On the trapdoors they remained standing on each side of her, holding her upright as hangman William Calcraft drew the white hood down over her head. So still was the crowd that most of them could hear her muffled shrieks and cries through the thin material as she begged for mercy, if only for the sake of her four young children. Calcraft, worried that the crowd's sympathies for the woman might suddenly erupt into a riotous attempt to rescue her, hastily dropped the noose over her head and reached for the lever which would operate the drop, but even as he did so, a sudden commotion stilled his hand as shouts of 'Stop!' and 'A reprieve!' came from those on the outskirts of the crowd. Aware that petitions for a commutation of her sentence had been raised and might just have been granted, the hangman stayed his hand as a man came running up the steps waving a piece of paper. He handed it to the prison governor who, together with other officials, was present on the scaffold; the officer slowly read it, while the wretched woman, unable to see what was happening and in mental anguish knowing that any second the boards would fall away from under her feet, could only wait, as did the crowd. And then, after a few breathless moments, anticlimax followed, as the governor announced that the letter was from the editor of a London newspaper requesting him to dispatch an account of the hanging as soon as possible! Realising that this could be the touch-paper should the now incensed crowd rush the scaffold, Calcraft didn't even wait for the governor's order to continue with the execution – reaching out, he released the drop and Mary's pathetic voice ceased abruptly as she dropped out of sight of the onlookers, the rope tightening remorselessly around her neck.

There has to be a legal definition of everything in the judicial system, and this of course applied to those sentenced to wear the Scold's Bridle, so in the seventeenth and eighteenth centuries a scold was defined as: 'A troublesome and angry woman who, by brawling and wrangling among her neighbours, breaks the public peace, increases discord, and becomes a public nuisance to the neighbourhood.'

Ross, Eliza (England)

With the advances in medicine in the early 1800s and the continual need for invasive operations, schools of surgery had been established in the big cities to train students, but the major setback to this was the shortage of specimens on which they could get the practice they needed in order to qualify as surgeons. There were no computer models or plastic skeletons in those days, and in order to teach their students, and also stay in business, the surgeons needed fresh, human bodies. Eliza was one of those who satisfied that demand, albeit on a small scale, by murdering, and then selling the bodies to the surgical schools in London.

Eliza was a well-known character around the area of Fleet Street where she lived with Edward Cook, himself an ex-bodysnatcher (one who dug up bodies in cemeteries and sold them to surgeons). A bad-tempered crone, she also made a living selling old clothes and animal skins, usually those donated involuntarily by local pets, and she occasionally took in lodgers. Eliza and Edward then moved to Goodman's Yard, near the Tower of London, with their lodger Catherine Walsh. One day Mrs Walsh's daughter Anne went to visit her mother, only to find her absent. Eliza said that she herself had been out shopping, and on returning she had found that Mrs Walsh had apparently left the house and gone; where, she did not know.

Worried in case her mother might have come to some harm, as time went by Anne searched the streets, enquiring in local taverns and contacting the hospitals, but with no result. Eventually, suspecting that Eliza Ross knew more about her mother's mysterious absence than she was prepared to admit, Anne then reported it to the police. Their investigations revealed that some clothes which had been sold by Eliza to her market customers belonged to Mrs Walsh, and Eliza and her 11-year-old son Ned were taken to the nearest police office.

When questioned, Eliza flatly denied any knowledge of what had happened to her lodger, but young Ned, either burdened by his conscience or fearful of the Law, described what had happened to the old lady. She had moved in, he said, and that evening he saw her lying on the bed – he also saw his mother suffocating her by holding her hand over the woman's nose and mouth until she was dead. He then saw the body carried downstairs, and later, on going into the cellar, he saw a large sack, from the open end of which protruded the head of their late lodger, the face swollen and contorted. And that night the sack had gone.

Enquiries were made in the local hospital and surgical schools regarding the possible destination of Catherine Walsh's body, but without success, and it was eventually decided that it must have been sold to the middlemen who regularly dispatched by sea large numbers of cadavers, packed in barrels labelled as pork, fish, apples, or anything similarly innocuous, to surgical schools in other major cities.

So although Eliza Ross vehemently denied the charge of murder, and despite there being no body, Ned's testimony was accepted as valid, reliable and admissible by the Old Bailey judge. The jury brought in a verdict of guilty, and Eliza Ross was sentenced to death. On 9 January 1832 hangman William Calcraft once again had the distasteful task of hanging a woman although, aware of the shocking details of her crime, no doubt he felt little sympathy for her. On the scaffold she loudly declared her innocence and cursed those witnesses who had testified against her, including her own son. Calcraft didn't hesitate to position the hood, then drop the noose over her head, the contact of the rough fibrous rope on her throat stilling her outburst; tightening, it also stilled her writhing body.

Paradoxically, surgical students also received the benefit of her corpse as well as that of Catherine Walsh, on which to practise their skills, for a statute passed in 1752 during the reign of George II was still in force, stating that:

The body of every person convicted of murder shall, if such conviction and execution shall be in the County of Middlesex or within the City of London, or of the liberties thereof, be immediately conveyed by the sheriff or sheriffs, or their deputy or deputies, and his or other officer or officers, to the Hall of the Surgeons' Company, or such other place as the said company shall appoint for this purpose, and be delivered to such person as the said company shall depute or appoint, who shall give to the sheriff or sheriffs, his or their deputy or deputies, a receipt for the same; and the body so delivered to the said company of surgeons shall be dissected or anatomised by the said surgeons or such persons as they shall appoint for that purpose; and that in no case the body shall be suffered to be buried unless after such body shall have been dissected or anatomised.

Accordingly, after being cut down by Calcraft, Eliza's body was placed in a sack and loaded into a cart. It then became the main attraction in a long procession which consisted of the sheriffs, the City Marshal and a large number of constables, which proceeded at a leisurely pace to Surgeons' Hall, the crowds lining the route yelling and jeering as they passed. On arrival it was with great difficulty that the body was carried into the Hall, the crowd more than anxious to gain possession of it themselves. Once inside, it was stripped and laid out on a slab, ready to be dissected, although before the lessons started the public were allowed in to view the corpse, long queues of eager spectators forming up outside the building.

When Irish-born Margaret Harvey was condemned to death for robbery in 1750, her friends smuggled so much strong drink to her before she mounted the scaffold that as the London executioner John Thrift dropped the noose over her head, through a bleary haze she exclaimed drunkenly, 'I wish to God I'd never stepped on to this evil country!' Well, at least being hanged saved her from having a hang-over!

S

Sampson, Agnes (Scotland)

This particular case had it all: witchcraft, the Devil's Mark, thumbscrews, a skull crusher, bridle, strangling and burning at the stake. Agnes Sampson was a much-respected citizen of Edinburgh, but was accused by a woman named Jilly Duncan of being a member of a conspiracy plot to place the Earl of Bothwell, the King's cousin, on the throne, in the event of James' death. Jilly had accused Agnes after being tortured with, among other devices, the pilniwinks, one of the Scottish names given to a type of thumbscrews, the crushing application of which on the victim's fingernails invariably encouraged him or her to confess anything required of them, whether true or false. And whether Agnes was indeed a witch is open to doubt; she was described in *The Historie of King James the Sext* as 'a grace wyff also callit the wise wyff of Keith', and by Bishop Spotswood, in his *History of the Church and State of Scotland*, as 'a woman not of the base and ignorant sort of Witches, but matron-like, grave and settled in her answers, which were all to some purpose.' She clearly had some practice as a midwife and some said she was a professed witch who was consulted by members of the gentry.

Agnes was arrested and charged with many offences, some trivial, like having foreknowledge of 'diseasit persounes', whether they would live or not; she prophesied that a certain person was 'bot a deid man' (and he died), and many she healed with 'her devilish arts.' But, of course, by reason of her profession as a midwife, she would recognise the advanced state of some diseases, and would be able to cure folk of others.

Agnes was taken to the royal palace and questioned by King James himself; she was then handed over to a witch-finder, one of the many self-professed 'experts' at identifying those who had close links with the Devil. As it was common knowledge that such women bore his Mark somewhere on their bodies, a spot insensitive to pain, the man would search for it using a long sharp needle resembling a syringe, and prod every birthmark, mole and blemish until finding one to which the victim failed to react. As his prestige – and income – depended on his success, some witch-finders would use a needle which, although apparently piercing the flesh, in reality retracted into the holder, thereby giving the same condemnatory result.

To obtain the necessary confession from Agnes, she was stripped naked, her whole body being shaved preparatory to the witch-finder starting his search. He eventually claimed success, allegedly locating the Devil's Mark on her pudenda, and having thus established that she was indeed a witch, it was then necessary to extract a full confession of the plot encompassing the King's death. She was first tortured by having to wear the Bridle, an iron cage which enclosed her head. The particular type of headgear she endured – there were others (see Appendix 1) – incorporated sharp spikes which pressed on the insides of her cheeks and on her tongue, the latter to stop her from chanting the magic spells by which she could change into a small animal and thereby escape.

As further persuasion was considered necessary to overcome her obstinacy, Agnes was then tortured by having a length of rope tied round her temples and slowly tightened a fraction at a time. Unable to endure such appalling agony, Agnes admitted that she had consorted with the Devil, and as a sign that she had become his servant, he had made his Mark on her. It is said King James was convinced of her powers as a witch when she said that she was able to repeat the exact words which passed between him and his Queen, Anne of Denmark, on their wedding night. But the words which condemned her to death for witchcraft and high treason were her admission that she, together with others, had sailed in a sieve on All-Hallows Eve 1589 in the sea between Leith and North Berwick, and while afloat the coven had cast a spell invoking a great storm that would sink the ship in which the King was bringing his new bride back to Scotland. As it happened, there was in fact a storm during their journey.

James, his superstitious beliefs overriding everything else, believed that there was but one way in which to deal with such a would-be traitorous assassin. Agnes Sampson was taken to Edinburgh's Castle Hill, where she was tied to a stake, tinder and branches being heaped high about her. Some mercy – of a sort – was shown to her, for before the flames caught hold, the hangman strangled her.

Ralph Gardner, a seventeenth-century author from Newcastle upon Tyne, wrote that 'he saw Anne Bridlestone led through the streets by an officer of the corporation, holding a rope in his hand, the other end fastened to an engine [device] called the Branks, which is like a crown, it being of iron, which was musled over the head and face, with a great gag or tongue of iron forced into her mouth, which forced the blood out; and that is the punishment which the magistrates do inflict upon chiding and scolding women; and he hath often seen the like done to others.'

Schmidtin, Gertrude (Germany)

In his diary for 20 July 1587, Nuremberg executioner Franz Schmidt wrote, 'Gertrude Schmidtin of Fach, a peasant girl and a heretic. She lived in debauchery for four years with her own father and brother, who were burnt alive at Langenzenn a week later. I beheaded her with the sword as a favour.' No doubt she appreciated his kindness.

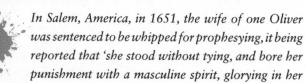

In Salem, America, in 1651, the wife of one Oliver was sentenced to be whipped for prophesying, it being reported that 'she stood without tying, and bore her punishment with a masculine spirit, glorying in her suffering. But afterwards she was much dejected by it. She had a cleft stick put on her tongue half an hour for reproaching the elders who sentenced her.'

Schonleben, Anna (Germany)

One wonders what women of earlier centuries would have done to solve their matrimonial problems or remove their enemies had arsenic not been discovered! Anna certainly had cause to be thankful, at least until the moment when the executioner's sword removed her head. In the 1790s she was employed as housekeeper to a Bavarian member of the judiciary, Judge Gläser, and forthwith decided to become one of the affluent society in which he mingled and set her sights on marrying him. Unfortunately he was already married, and any plans Anna might have had to permanently remove his wife from the scene were dashed by the fact that he was already estranged from his spouse. Undaunted, Anna was determined to manoeuvre the absent lady into a position where she could be disposed of, and by dint of many gentle hints and solicitous expressions of concern, she eventually managed to restore harmony between the two, the wife returning to the family fold – and to the housekeeper, who had wasted no time in making a welcoming cup of tea, flavoured with a little extra something. And when the judge's wife died soon afterwards, Anna attempted to make herself indispensable to the judge in more ways than one, but alas, her employer simply wasn't interested, and Anna moved on.

She went to work in the household of another judge in the town of Sanspareil; appropriately enough the quality of her arsenic was also *sans pareil*, without equal, the judge dying in agony when, instead of his new member of staff, he chose to get engaged to someone else. Luckily Anna still had ample supplies of the poison, for a local justice of the peace, whose wife was not in the best of health, was so impressed by Anna's nursing abilities that he employed the housekeeper to care for her. The JP's wife passed away far from peacefully – as did some of the servants in the household.

At that her employer, although unable to prove any involvement on her part, dispensed with her services, but Anna was determined that those she left behind would not remain long in the land of the living, and before she departed for a new job she stirred some of her favourite additive into the coffee she had made for the staff, and deposited a few spoonfuls more in the household supply of salt.

Shortly afterwards, at the sight of stricken manservants and collapsing maids, the magistrate's suspicions hardened and he sent for the police who, on examining the kitchen stocks of food, found traces of arsenic. Anna Schönleben now firmly in the frame, the bodies of her previous employers and associates were exhumed, the cause of death by arsenic poisoning being established. And any remaining doubt was dispelled when, on being arrested, Anna was found to have a further supply of the poison in her possession.

At her trial at Nuremberg in July 1811 she confessed to being a serial killer and, after being found guilty, she was taken to the marketplace, the site of the city's pillory, stocks, gallows and the wheel. Had she been a man, she would have been condemned to die by being broken on the wheel (see Appendix 2); as it was, she was first hanged, her lifeless body then exhibited to the public by being spread-eagled on the wheel until dusk.

There is little doubt that colonising a country can bring great benefits to its native population; improved methods of cultivation, education and health, to name but a few. However, the execution of Mary Ann Bilansky in Minnesota in the nineteenth century for the poisoning of her husband provided some of the native inhabitants with a different insight into the ways of the newcomers, the local newspaper describing how a few Sioux women among the spectators seemed especially interested in the manner in which the whites dealt with their criminals. The editor went on to cynically express his doubts as to whether they had been particularly impressed by what they had witnessed of the new civilisation which was being imposed on them.

Schroeder, Irene (USA)

Shoot-out in the OK Corral it wasn't, but its 1930s counterpart was similarly filled with flying lead when Irene and her lover Glenn were cornered by the police in Arizona. It was her love of violence and also for her renegade partner which, after standing up to the authorities for so long, found Irene finally sitting in the electric chair.

Born of poor parents in 1909, she married when she was fifteen and had a child, Donnie, before deserting her husband and finding work as a waitress. It was then that she met and fell deeply in love with 34-year-old Walter Glenn Dague who left his wife and children to be with her. The two, with Donnie in the back seat, then drove across the country, robbing shops and banks in isolated communities on the way, but on 29 December 1929 the alarm was raised, and on being pursued by the police, Irene, with cold deliberation, shot and killed one of the highway patrolmen in the police car. Driving away, they left Donnie with relatives, then fled across the state line.

By some means the authorities discovered the boy's whereabouts, and when Donnie was questioned, his innocent replies virtually sealed the fates of his mother and her lover for, as reported in the local press, he said, 'My mamma's killed a cop like you.' The nationwide hunt was now on, and the murderous pair were eventually surrounded by a large posse of police in Arizona. A fierce gun battle ensued, a reporter describing how 'Cracking down with a six-gun was a bobbed-hair blonde woman who faced the booming police shotguns, and hurled lead in the fracas as calmly as her gun-fighting male companion.' So furious was the combat that the couple ran out of ammunition and, fleeing in the car, abandoned it some miles away. Taking to their heels, they climbed the slopes of Estrella Mountain where, hemmed in and challenged by the police, they both surrendered and were taken to Rockview Penitentiary, Pennsylvania, it being reported that they caressed each other during the journey.

On 10 March 1930 Irene Schroeder appeared in court. 'She wore a blue dress, her hair was freshly bobbed and her face was plentifully besprinkled with powder,' a journalist wrote. That her hopes of receiving a light sentence were revealed by her reply when asked to smile for the cameras: 'How can you smile and look pretty when you are going to prison for life and are heartbroken?'

Both were found guilty of first-degree murder and sentenced to death. In his excellent autobiography *Agent of Death*, executioner Robert G. Elliott described how calmly Irene had behaved, how much she evidently loved Glenn, even to the extent of being prepared to shoulder full responsibility for the crimes if his life could be spared. When asked by the matron whether she could do anything for her, Irene answered, 'Yes, there is something – please tell them in the kitchen to fry Glenn's eggs on both sides. He likes them that way.' And, later, to the prison chaplain, she said, 'Don't worry about me, I'll be all right. You'd better go back to Glenn, I think he needs you more than I do.'

At 7 a.m. on 23 February 1931, wearing a loose, ill-fitting grey dress, beige stockings and black slippers, her hair having earlier been clipped away from the back of her head, she was escorted into the execution chamber. Elliott said that he watched her walk to the electric chair, a calm smile on her face, adding that she gave the impression that without Glenn, there was no point in going on living. As the warders tightened the straps around her and adjusted the head and leg electrodes, she closed her eyes.

In his book, Elliott, a humane and sensitive man, revealed what passed through his mind when the moment of execution approached. He wrote:

Before sending the lethal current on its journey of death, I glance at the chair to make sure no one is standing too near to it. Then I throw the switch. As I do, I often pray, 'May God have mercy on your soul.' The figure in the chair pitches forward, straining against the straps; there is the whining cry of the current and a crackling, sizzling sound. The body turns a vivid red. Sparks often shoot from the electrodes. A wisp of white or dull grey smoke may rise from the top of the head or the leg to which the electrode is attached; this is produced by the sponge lining, singed hair and, sometimes, burning flesh.

In that fashion Irene Schroeder paid the price demanded by society: two and a half minutes after the executioner had thrown the switch, the prison doctor certified her dead.

The innocence of children can best be exemplified – sadly – by Irene Schroeder's son Donnie, aged five, who, when told by his mother that he should be brave because she was going to die, was later reported to have said brightly, 'I'll bet mom will make an awful nice angel.'

Scott, Jane (England)

Twenty-one-year-old Jane Scott murdered her mother by administering rat poison to her. She was sentenced to be hanged at Lancaster Castle, Lancashire, the last woman to be executed there, and so weak and emaciated was her condition, not having eaten since the day of her trial, that a child's highchair, fitted with castor wheels, was provided by the authorities so that she could be moved around in her cell.

On 22 March 1828, the day she was to die, she was half-carried to the gallows by two female warders who held her upright on the drop while the hangman hooded and noosed her. Then upon a signal being given by him, the two guards released their hold on Jane's arms and quickly moved off the trapdoors; even as they did so, the hangman operated the lever – and the limp body descended into the pit, Jane dying within minutes.

In that era every execution was invariably used as a lesson supporting Victorian morality, and the next edition of the *Preston Chronicle* was no exception, the editor commenting that, 'It may be useful to attribute her course of criminal excess to an early departure from the path of virtue, having borne an illegitimate child when she was sixteen years of age. She also confessed to having carried out a systematic pattern of robberies on her parents, the proceeds of which she shared among the most abandoned company she could meet with.' And space for words such as 'fiendish-like depravity', brutal insensibility', 'sensual appetite' and, of course, 'terrible example' was also found in later paragraphs.

Had she been executed in London, her cadaver might well have been taken to Surgeons' Hall as a specimen to be used in dissection classes, but in this case it was purchased by Dr John Monks of Preston, doubtless for the same medical purpose. Some sixty years later he died, and Jane's skeleton, its bones wired together in their correct order, left its usual place in the corner of the good doctor's consulting room for the shop of a herbalist, Mr Livesey, who probably used it as an advertisement for his patented brand of calcium tablets, or as a warning of what would happen to children if they didn't eat their greens. Jane's appearance had been enhanced by a coat of whitewash, and she looked quite eye-catching except for a pink spot on her skull, due to rain which had dripped through a leaky roof. Later withdrawn into the living quarters behind the shop, 'Old Jane' became a member of the family, the Livesey grandchildren welcoming her as an uncomplaining and highly flexible playmate. But during a break-in the burglar stole the skull, and while some of the remaining bones were given a decent burial in the garden, others were presented to a local museum. Poor Jane!

Other times, other souvenirs: as Queen Marie Antoinette mounted the steps of the scaffold one of her shoes, of black silk but now shabby and in sad need of repair, slipped from her foot. Not stopping to pick it up, she continued on to the platform where the guillotine awaited. A soldier later retrieved the royal shoe and sold it to a souvenir collector for one gold louis.

Shuttleworth, Margaret (Scotland)

Margaret had married a sailor named Henry Shuttleworth, and they settled down in Montrose, Scotland. She was a heavy drinker, and it was no doubt due to her forceful personality and perpetual thirst that they went into business selling whisky and similar intoxicants. She might have enjoyed her tipple, but Henry bore the brunt of it, for it was common knowledge among the neighbours that when drunk, his wife turned extremely violent, hitting him with whatever came to hand. Matters came to a head – Henry's head – on 28 April 1821: Henry was found dead with a severe head wound, his clothes covered with blood. Although Margaret insisted that he must have sustained the injury by falling downstairs, the post-mortem found that the wound could only have been caused by a blow – and a bloodstained poker was found in her bedroom.

Margaret was arrested, charged with murder, and taken to Perth Prison. En route, stops were made for meals; at one inn her air of confidence was commented on, for she tucked into toast and two eggs, with numerous cups of tea. But her self-assured attitude did not support her for long; on 19 September she appeared in the Perth Circuit Court before Lord Justice Clerk Boyle and Lord Pitmilly, the jury being made up of members of the local landed gentry. Any defence that might have been made on her behalf proved ineffective, for the bloodstained poker was produced, and further evidence given that all the windows and doors of the house were found to be fastened from the inside.

The jury returned a unanimous verdict of guilty and Margaret was sentenced to be hanged between the hours of two and four o'clock in the afternoon of 7 November. However, an appeal was submitted on the grounds that there was no apparent motive, that the condemned woman was drunk when put to bed by the maid who had then gone out, and that Margaret had been the one who had raised the alarm. A one-month reprieve was granted, but to no avail.

On 7 December of that year nearly 5,000 inhabitants of Montrose and the surrounding districts gathered round the scaffold in the pouring rain as Margaret was led out of the gaol to be executed. Wearing a black dress frilled at the neck, with black stockings and gloves, a handkerchief about her head, she stood on the platform while the hangman struggled to pull the white hood over her head, it having shrunk with the rain. There was no problem in positioning the noose, however, and even as he adjusted it, she was heard to say, 'I loved my husband as I loved my life.' But just as she had lost the one, so she lost the other, as the rope holding the trapdoors was severed, bringing her world to an end.

Margaret's corpse was taken to Edinburgh, the route necessitating a crossing of the Firth of Forth, and it was reported that the Customs and Excise officers on duty there, by their very nature suspicious of possible smugglers, insisted on the coffin being opened for inspection of the contents before they allowed it to continue on its way. In the capital city it was delivered to the University where it was dissected as part of the training of students learning to become surgeons.

That there remained some doubt regarding her guilt was manifested by the entry in the parish register, for it read: 'Margaret Tyndal [her maiden name] was executed in front of the jail for the supposed murder of her husband, Henry Shuttleworth, having been condemned on presumptive evidence.' That doubt could well have been correct, for some years later an Irishman convicted of murder confessed that he, not Margaret, had killed Henry Shuttleworth. He explained that after the maid had put her mistress to bed and left the house, Henry had let him in and they had had a drinking session, during which a quarrel had developed. He had struck Henry with the poker, and in order to divert suspicion, had put it beside the woman asleep in the next room. Not only that, but he had left the house via the traditionally wide chimney, a means of entry and exit commonly used by burglars. So was Margaret innocent after all?

 Like Margaret Shuttleworth, American Emilene Meaker, awaiting execution in 1883, also enjoyed some toast and two boiled eggs – plus a potato, a doughnut and a cup of coffee. That was for lunch; earlier she had eaten a king-sized breakfast consisting of a large beefsteak, a piece of meat pie, three potatoes, and a slice of bread and butter, and of course the inevitable cup of coffee. She had obviously decided that it was far too late to go on worrying about her weight!

Snyder, Ruth (USA)

Just as Irene Schroeder had dominated Glenn Dague, so Ruth Snyder had a stronger character than Henry Judd Gray, hence her nickname in the press of 'The Granite Woman' and his of 'Putty Man'. Ruth, tall, blonde and attractive despite her ice-cold eyes, had married Albert Snyder, thirteen years older than her, but the marriage was not a success. It was hardly surprising that on meeting corset salesman Henry, weak-chinned with a nature to match, whose marriage was also on the rocks, they found much in common and started a passionate relationship. But Ruth wanted more, she wanted money, and so insured Albert for $96,000. Then she tried gassing him, adding poison to his food, and arranging near fatal household 'accidents'; when she told Henry what she was doing, he naively asked her why. 'To kill the poor guy!' she replied, and she persisted in keeping up the pressure on her lover until he agreed to help her.

On 19 March 1927 Ruth and Henry went shopping, buying a 5 lb sash weight, some chloroform and lengths of picture wire.

The next evening, while the Snyders were out at a party, Henry entered their house and hid. Husband and wife returned later, Ruth having plied Albert with sufficient drink to dull his senses; he staggered up to bed, whereupon Ruth and Henry followed shortly afterwards and Henry struck him a crushing blow with the sash weight. It didn't kill him, whereupon the would-be killer shouted desperately to Ruth, 'Momsie, Momsie, for God's sake, help!' She responded by joining in with a chloroform-soaked cloth, and when Albert had lost consciousness, they strangled him with the picture wire. Gray then tied Ruth's wrists and ankles, and after gagging her – not too tightly – left the house.

The next morning she managed to raise the alarm, telling the police that she and her husband had been attacked by a burglar who had also stolen several valuable items. Things went pear-shaped for her when, in searching the house for clues, they not only found the 'stolen' objects but also a tie-clip with Henry's initials engraved on it and his name in her address book. Taking a chance, they told her that Henry had already been arrested and had confessed everything; panicking, she then accused Henry of plotting the murder and claimed that she had only stood and watched him killing her husband.

Amid nationwide publicity they went on trial at Queens County Courthouse, Long Island City, in April 1927, thousands of people applying for tickets to see the Granite Woman and the Putty Man, and to savour the gruesome details of the crime. Outside the courthouse enterprising traders sold miniature sash weights mounted on tie-pins as souvenirs.

Both Ruth and Henry blamed each other, both were found guilty and sentenced to death. While in Sing Sing Prison each wrote their life story, Ruth's notoriety bringing offers of marriage from nearly 200 men. Executioner Robert G. Elliott also received letters, one of which read: 'If you don't want to do it, will you let me have first offer? I won't mind one bit to execute Mrs Snyder. It is just what she should get, the chair. I could execute her with a good heart. I also think that if they did have a woman executioner to execute a woman, it would take a whole lot off your mind. If you would like to have me help you the night she is put in the chair, I would be more than glad to do so. I hope to hear from you soon.' Needless to say, he didn't.

In an attempt to shift all the blame on to the adverse publicity she had received from the press and thereby obtain a reprieve by arousing public sympathy, Ruth wrote a self-pitying verse:

You've blackened and besmeared a mother
Once a man's plaything – a Toy –
What have you gained by all you've said,
And has it brought you Joy?

The ploy didn't work, and on 12 January 1928, wearing a brown smock over a black, knee-length calico skirt, she was led to the execution chamber. Her blonde hair had been freshly combed; once thick, the tresses were now so thin that it was not necessary to clip it short where the electrode was to be positioned. On seeing the electric chair she swayed and almost collapsed, a wardress having to assist her to sit in it. There, she broke down and wept: 'Jesus, have mercy on me, for I have sinned,' she sobbed. The black stocking on her right leg had been rolled down so that the electrode could be attached, and the executioner, Robert G. Elliott, parted the hair at the back of her head so that the other electrode would make good contact, then fixed it in position. As he put the mask over her face, she cried, 'Jesus, have mercy.' He threw the switch, the series of high voltage currents surged through her body, and after two minutes it was turned off to allow the prison doctor to use his stethoscope and announce that Ruth Snyder was dead.

Macabre souvenirs of executions were also all the rage during the French Revolution. The new plebeian Parisian society took the guillotine to their hearts (while aristocrats were taking it somewhat higher up). The popularity of the device was not overlooked by manufacturers, who wasted little time in bringing out miniature versions of the death-dealing device as toys for children, no doubt resulting in the early demise of many a household pet. Larger versions for adults included dolls resembling unpopular politicians which could be decapitated at the dinner party table and would exude 'blood', this being a liqueur or perfume, the latter for the benefit of the ladies present, many of whom wore silver or gold earrings in the shape of the guillotine, or brooches bearing the same image.

Spinelli, Juanita (USA)

With her spectacles, protruding ears and long nose 'the Duchess', as she became known, might have looked like 'a mouse wearing glasses', as San Quentin Warden Duffy described her, but she was tough and vicious. In the 1920–30s, when gang leaders were male, cold-blooded and ruthless, Juanita was the terrifying exception. Although then in her late thirties she dominated the gang of thugs which she and her partner Michael Simeone had recruited; physically strong, she effortlessly subdued any man who thought he could out-wrestle her. Nor was that all, for one of her favourite weapons was the throwing knife, which she used with uncanny accuracy. Ruled by fear and respect, her minions obeyed her every order implicitly, robbing shops, hijacking lorries, and mugging affluent looking residents.

But it was inevitable that sooner or later someone was going to get killed, something that, up to now, the Duchess and her gang had strenuously avoided. In one raid on a café, the proprietor was shot dead and the gang had to flee. Among those who finally holed up in an obscure hotel in Sacramento was Robert Sherrard, a young man who had recently joined the gang and who was strongly suspected by Juanita to be not as fully committed as the others – that if arrested, might break under pressure and escape the death penalty by telling everything he knew. Never one to take chances, Juanita decided to dispense with his services, so after rendering him unconscious by means of knock-out drops in his whisky, the gang took him to the Sacramento River and dropped him over the bridge.

With no evidence of violence, should the body have been washed ashore, the Duchess and members of her court could have got away with it, had not another member been arrested for a minor transgression and talked – and talked! It spelt the end of Juanita's reign of domination and terror. Taken into custody she was charged with murder and sentenced to death. Though defiant to the end – when all appeals were rejected, she snarled, 'My blood will burn holes in their bodies!' – a soft side of her nature was revealed when she requested that when executed she might have photographs of her three children and one grandchild pinned over her heart.

But few could beat her when it came to sheer coolness under pressure. While imprisoned in San Quentin Gaol the warden, Clinton Duffy, treated the inmates with kindness and humanity, none more so than when, on 21 November 1941, Juanita became the first woman in the USA to be executed by the gas chamber. The warden and guards escorted her there only to find an inexcusable hold-up – the large number of officials and others necessary to witness the execution had not arrived. Juanita stood by the open door of the chamber and studied the two chairs therein, with the cyanide containers and the jars of sulphuric acid placed in readiness for her. Refusing the offer to return to her cell until the witnesses arrived, with incredible insouciance she started to discuss the weather, for all the world as if at home having a cup of tea. When eventually the audience arrived and was seated facing the glass windows of the chamber, Warden Clinton said, 'It's time – keep your chin up.' The Duchess nodded. 'OK,' she replied and, entering the chamber, coolly took her seat in one of the chairs to await the end.

She was confirmed dead ten and a half minutes after the cyanide eggs, dropping into the acid, caused the deadly fumes to rise.

Those subsequently destined for the gas chamber in America usually wore minimal clothing to reduce the amount of cyanide gas which could be absorbed into the material and thereby pose a toxic risk to those entering the chamber afterwards to remove the corpses. Problems arose when it was decided that Bonnie Brown Heady and Carl Austin Hall, her accomplice in a kidnapping and murder case, would be executed together, it taking too long to gas one, then decontaminate the chamber before gassing the other. This was solved by allowing both to wear the standard prison uniforms. Further complications also arose regarding Bonnie's hair; being long and thick, the gas could accumulate in it, but reportedly the risk was taken, with no dire results to anyone present – other than to Bonnie herself.

Spooner, Bathsheba (USA)

A tale of a husband loyal to his new country, a wife loyal to the old country; of deserters, a lover, two generals, and an American vice-president who was imprisoned in the Tower of London; surely a scenario worthy of Hollywood itself.

The loyal husband was elderly Joshua Spooner, a fervent supporter of the revolutionary ambitions of the American colonists; his wife Bathsheba, daughter of an English general, was equally supportive of King George III. To say that their views were incompatible would have been putting it mildly, and so it was not surprising that Bathsheba looked elsewhere for more congenial company. She found it in Ezra Ross, a young man with whom she soon commenced a torrid affair. And whether inspired by feelings of patriotism, or the overwhelming wish to marry Ezra, Bathsheba decided that her husband had to die. The means whereby that might be achieved came in the unexpected shape of two English soldiers who, in February 1778, sought sanctuary at her house, without Joshua's knowledge, of course.

The soldiers had deserted from the English forces which were then under the command of General Lord Cornwallis; that gallant officer was captured by the 'enemy' some months later and, as a prisoner of war, was exchanged in 1781 for Henry Laurens, the wealthy vice-president of South Carolina. Laurens had been captured on the high seas by English warships while en route to Holland, where he had hoped to persuade the Dutch to enter the conflict on the side of the Americans. Accused of high treason, he was imprisoned in the Tower of London where, on arrival, he was greeted by the Yeoman Warders (the 'Beefeaters') on duty whistling *Yankee Doodle Dandy*! Ironically, four years later, General Lord Cornwallis was appointed Constable of the Tower of London by George III!

But back to Bathsheba. Who better, she decided, to rid her of Joshua, than the two deserters? Trained to kill and decidedly bribeable, they were the obvious choice, and she also cajoled her lover to join in. However, all three, lacking any finesse, simply attacked Joshua and, after beating him up, threw his body down a well. Unfortunately for the murderers, the cadaver was later discovered by locals while drawing water. The authorities were notified and the soldiers were caught spending their ill-gotten gains: the game was up.

All four stood trial on the date most befitting to their maladroit method of committing murder, 1 April 1778. In court Bathsheba claimed to be pregnant, and had she been in England and in that condition her execution would have been postponed until after the birth. However, the reverse procedure was applied; she was hanged first and then examined, the doctors discovering that she was carrying a foetus barely six months old.

 Nuremberg executioner Franz Schmidt reported how, in 1604, Elizabeth Puffin, a maid, attacked her employer's brother-in-law, striking his head eleven blows and nearly severing one of his arms. Then, stealing some money, she escaped, only to be arrested soon afterwards. In prison she pleaded a respite of 32 weeks because she said she was pregnant, and the committee of sworn women visited her no fewer than 18 times. They must have finally discovered that she was lying, for Franz wrote: 'I beheaded her with the sword – she behaved in a Christian way.'

Sullivan, Mary (Australia)

If you had to be hanged at all, it was much better to have a professional doing it rather than a convict who had volunteered for the job in order to avoid quarrying rocks or building roads. But, unfortunately, Mary Sullivan didn't have that choice.

Mary had been transported to the penal colony in Tasmania for committing a trivial offence in England, and was employed, as so many of the convicted women were, as a servant in a house owned by one of the more permanent settlers.

In 1852, for some unaccountable reason, she strangled one of the small children of the family, and threw the little corpse into a water butt before absconding. When caught, she showed not the slightest emotion, nor were there any psychological symptoms that could account for her crime. With hindsight and the present knowledge of what life was like for those transported thousands of miles away from their families, treated more like animals than human beings, with no prospect of ever returning home, it can only be assumed that hers were the actions of someone totally without hope.

Little time was wasted in sentencing her to death, and even on the scaffold she evinced no signs of fear. Worse was to come, however, for her executioner was Solomon Blay, a felon transported from England in 1837 for counterfeiting. During his new career as chief hangman in the colony he had never shown any indication that he intended to advance the art of hanging a condemned person by reducing the amount of pain they were experiencing, and obviously had no intention of starting with Mary Sullivan. He had previously dispatched Henry Jackson, whose struggles were reported as being 'prolonged beyond the usual period of suffering', and in 1844 he allowed Thomas Marshall to writhe on the rope for many minutes, so he saw no reason why he should modify his technique just because his victim was female. Even those in the huge crowd hissed and booed his deliberate tardiness as he left her standing on the trapdoors, hooded and noosed, for an unusually long time, then added insult to injury by 'chucking' (tugging) the rope to see that it was tight enough around her throat before finally operating the drop.

In 1787 the first batch of convicts, 736 in number, were shipped out to the penal colony in Australia. Elizabeth Beckford was the second oldest woman among them; seventy years of age, she had been sentenced to transportation for seven years for stealing 12 lb of cheese. Another Elizabeth among the human cargo was

Elizabeth Powley, who not only stole some bacon and flour, but also 24 ounces of butter, valued at 12 pence. She was originally sentenced to hang but this was commuted to transportation. She never ate butter again.

T

Thompson, Ellen (Australia)

Yet another case of a dominant woman and a weak-willed man – and yet more bungled executions. Ellen, calculatingly ruthless yet with motherly affection for her children, fell in love with John Harrison, simple, selfish and, the cause of his downfall, madly in love with Ellen. The third member of the ill-fated triangle, the first of the three to die, was Ellen's husband Billie. Billie was a man of integrity, hard-working and fair, albeit uncompromising and mean-minded. By labouring all hours on his farm he had become wealthy and prosperous, the only failure in his life being that of his marriage. He and Ellen quarrelled incessantly, the atmosphere becoming so heated that, unable to stand each other's company, Billie built and lived in a cottage about a hundred yards away from the main farmhouse, where Ellen lived. Regardless of his attitude towards her, Billie still had his principles, especially in respect of his family, and so in 1885 he made a will in which he left the farm and all his property to his wife and children. Not a sensible thing to do under the fraught circumstances – but how was he to know?

On learning of the will, Ellen, aware that Billie was much older than her and so was likely to die first, worked even harder on the farm, determined to increase its ultimate value when she took over, but a woman could do only so much heavy work, and when, in 1886, harvesting time came round, extra hands had to be employed. One of the labourers was John Harrison, a demobbed soldier of the British Army looking for work. Scything and reaping together in the fields, Ellen got to know John and he became utterly infatuated with her, the affinity between them resulting in Ellen's lonely nights in the farmhouse becoming a thing of the past. And it was then that Ellen realised where her future lay – and with whom – and exactly how to achieve it.

The first step was to circulate rumours that Billie had business troubles, cash-flow problems that were causing him to be severely depressed, to the point that he was even contemplating suicide. And the next step was to kill him.

On the night of 2 October of that year, a neighbouring farmer was wakened by Ellen who was hysterically shouting that Billie was dead, that he had blown the top of his head off with a shotgun. The police were sent for, the detectives quickly coming to the conclusion that suicide could be ruled out, and that murder had been committed. This decision was probably based on the fact that the murderers had placed the gun next to the body, whereas had Billie pointed the weapon at his own head and fired it, the recoil would have propelled it across the room, to land on the floor.

The lovers were arrested and in May 1887 appeared in the Supreme Court in Townsville, North Queensland. The trial was repeatedly interrupted by Ellen who, desperate to throw all the blame on her partner, shouted wildly, 'This is no court of justice – all the world is working against me!' and constantly hurled abuse at the prosecution witnesses. When the jury returned with a verdict of guilty, her furious protests reached a crescendo; when asked by the judge whether she had anything to say, she exclaimed:

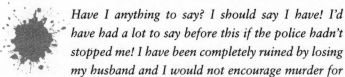

Have I anything to say? I should say I have! I'd have had a lot to say before this if the police hadn't stopped me! I have been completely ruined by losing my husband and I would not encourage murder for £1,000. Since early life I have struggled hard with Old Billie Thompson. I am a brick – every inch of me. But Old Billie was not a suitable husband, he was so jealous of everything that I could hardly live. He made a will and left me everything, but I would not disgrace him by having a fancy man. Old Billie often said that he would commit suicide, and all the evidence here is horrid lying. If it was murder at all, the Chinaman here did it, because he and Old Billie had a row over some land. Here am I in this dreadful North, disgraced and found guilty of murder; I have not got a shilling, and when I am gone you will find that I did not murder Old Billie Thompson.

Her frenzied protests went on for three-quarters of an hour, only stopping when the judge placed the black cap on his head and sentenced both the lovers to death. 'Oh my God!' Ellen cried, and slumped against John Harrison sitting next to her in the dock, then fought the guards as they took her away.

Some days later Ellen and John were taken by ship to Brisbane, where they were imprisoned in the Boggo Road Gaol. The case attracted wide public attention, the newspapers reporting that in one of her outbursts Ellen had declared that she would never die at a hangman's hands, that she would appeal to the State Governor for clemency. In one letter to him she wrote:

I have already made one appeal to you for the life of John Harrison, whom I believe is innocent. I have three demands to make: firstly, in the event of my innocence being proved, my children are to receive

£500 [presumably as compensation]. Secondly, that all my statements will be returned to me so that I can destroy them, and thirdly that Pope Cooper [the trial judge] may be never allowed to sentence another woman in Queensland. If these demands are not granted, I will stick out for my rights at the foot of the gallows, but if they are allowed, I will die on the gallows like an angel.

This somewhat illogically reasoned appeal was rejected, and the execution was set to take place on 13 June 1887. Thousands of applications to witness the dual event were received from the public but only one was granted, that of a professor of phrenology who was to be permitted to measure the contours and dimensions of the corpses' heads, and perhaps even take plaster casts of them after their bodies had been cut down.

At 8 a.m. on the fateful day, Ellen, wearing a black dress and a little black bonnet, carrying a crucifix in her hands, was escorted by two prison guards to the execution chamber. At first she seemed resigned to her fate, but on seeing the gallows her calm deserted her. 'Ah, soon I'll be in a land where people won't be able to tell lies about me!' she shouted, and as she set her foot on the scaffold steps she exclaimed, 'I will die like an angel!'

At the top stood the extremely hirsute executioner, 'Blackbeard' (at that time, that nickname was given to all Australian hangmen, in the same way as English ones were dubbed 'Jack Ketch'). Positioning her on the trapdoors, Blackbeard proceeded to bind her arms, although allowed her to retain the crucifix. Then came the white hood and the noose, her prayers being audible through the material. Then, as described by an eyewitness, 'the hangman sprang back and pulled the lever. A dull and dreadful thud shattered the brooding stillness as the trapdoors flew open and the woman hurtled to her doom. But Blackbeard had made a frightful mistake!

The drop had been too long and the woman's skin was broken. She bled profusely.'

Harrison's execution followed, with the same ghastly results, his throat also being torn open. Such horrific miscalculations resulted in that particular executioner declaring afterwards that he would never officiate at another hanging.

Editors of the local papers were later presented with the findings and subsequent character assessments diagnosed by the learned phrenologist, Professor Blumenthal. In Ellen Thompson, he said that he found combativeness and destructiveness in very large proportions. Domestic affections were fairly full, while selfish and animal propensities were large. In Harrison he found that combativeness was excessively large, and destructiveness was also full. From these observations, he declared, it would seem that the woman was the moving spirit in the plot, and her passion for Harrison probably inspired her. These scientific conclusions no doubt resulted in the newspaper readers anxiously feeling their own – and their spouses' – heads for similar homicidal characteristics.

John Nicol, a seaman on one of the convict ships bound for Australia in the eighteenth century, married one of the convicts, a Sarah Whitlam. He wrote in his book, The Life and Adventures of John Nicol, Mariner, *published in 1822: 'She was as true and kind a creature as ever lived. I courted her for a week and upwards, and would have married her, had a clergyman been on board. I fixed my fancy on her from the moment I knocked the rivet out of her leg irons upon the anvil [on being brought on board] and am firmly resolved to bring her back to England when her time is up, as my wife.' Sadly, however, he had to return alone, leaving her and their young son behind in Australia.*

Ticquet, Angelique (France)

In seventeenth-century Paris the focus of masculine attention was directed towards the ravishingly attractive Angelique Cartier, daughter of a rich printer and bookbinder. Yet despite every advance made by the young and wealthy noblemen who flocked around her, she surprised local aristocracy by marrying M. Ticquet, a magistrate and councillor of Parliament. But the union turned out to be a fiasco; her none too well-off husband soon realised that his income was totally inadequate to provide Angelique with the wherewithal needed to maintain her personal servants, her carriages, her lavish soirees and receptions, to which only the elite were invited. Among the latter was a certain M. de Montgeorges, a captain in the French Guards Regiment, and an affair soon commenced; indeed very far from discreet, for Angelique made no secret of it, with the result that her cuckolded husband became the laughing stock of the City.

Domestic matters went from bad to worse, and Angelique's contempt for her husband degenerated into cold hatred, to the extent that she planned to have him murdered. Accordingly she induced her porter, Jacques Moura, to enlist some underworld hitmen who would be prepared to eliminate the unfortunate man. However, she later abandoned that idea and instead decided to add poison to his nightly cup of broth. Unfortunately for her, although fortunate for her husband, the manservant whose task it was to take the drink up to his master suspected her motives and 'accidentally' dropped the cup, spilling its contents. Thwarted, Angelique revived her original plan, and the hired killers went into action, with the result that a few nights later, as M. Ticquet was returning home, he was attacked and shot five times, but none of the wounds proved fatal.

MARTYRS, MURDERESSES AND MADWOMEN

Although the subsequent police investigations failed to identify the would-be murderers, Angelique and Moura were arrested and put on trial. On 3 June 1699 the judge pronounced sentence; the porter was to be hanged and Angelique Cartier to be decapitated in the Place de Grève; her property was to be confiscated for the benefit of the King, except for 100,000 livres, which would go to her husband.

As it was customary that those condemned to death should first confirm the court's verdict by confessing to their crimes, Angelique was led by one of her former admirers, Criminal Lieutenant Deffits, to the torture chamber, where the sentence was then read out to her. A confession not being forthcoming, she was subjected to the dreaded Water Torture. Strapped down on a bench, a cow horn was inserted in her mouth, jugs of water then being poured in. Angelique needed little of such appalling persuasion, and soon admitted her part in the attempt on her husband's life.

Some days later she was escorted to the scaffold where the executioner, Charles Sanson, awaited. As she arrived, a heavy thunderstorm broke over the city, scattering the enormous crowd that had gathered to watch and gloat over the execution of such a figure of high society. Sanson, not daring to proceed with the beheading – for to attempt to swing the heavy two-handed sword while standing on slippery wet boards could end in catastrophe – led his victim to shelter, a nerve-racking half an hour passing before she mounted the steps of the scaffold. After praying, she said, 'Sir, will you be good enough to show me the position I am to take?' Charles replied, 'Kneel down with your head up; lift your hair away from your neck, so that it falls forward over your face.' As she did so, he stepped back and swung the sword round in order to gain the necessary momentum before actually aiming it – only to lose all concentration as she suddenly exclaimed, 'Be sure not to disfigure me!' Too late to stop, Charles sought to direct the razor-edged weapon to its target, but only succeeded in slashing the side of his victim's neck! Again he tried, the crescendo of violent abuse coming from the crowd only serving to distract him further, and it was not until he had delivered a third, more accurate stroke, was the woman's head finally severed from her body. Justice had been done.

Mme Roland, mentioned elsewhere, faced death by the guillotine with dignity, and even felt compassion for the other doomed aristocrats accompanying her in the tumbril. As they arrived at the scaffold she noticed that one of them, M. Lamarche, was on the point of collapse and had to be helped down by an assistant executioner. Although women were usually allowed to be guillotined first, she said pityingly, 'I can only spare you the sight of blood – go first, poor man!'

Turner, Anne (England)

Although it was Anne who was hanged, the real instigator of the murder plot was a poisonous woman who actually got away with it. Even at the age of fifteen, Frances Howard was a seductive young woman in the Court of James I, and the man who willingly walked into her spider's web was Robert Carr, a fair-haired, ginger-bearded page whose very intimate friendship with the boy-favouring King was so much appreciated by His Majesty that he ennobled Carr, who then took the title of Viscount Rochester, and gave him a important position in court in which he dealt with State affairs. (James I's generosity to those he favoured led one court critic to say, behind his hand of course, that 'James hunted everything that ran, and knighted everything that crawled!')

MARTYRS, MURDERESSES AND MADWOMEN

But pandering to James' sexual tastes did not prejudice Rochester against women as gorgeous as Frances, and when he fell madly in love with her, his only problem was that he was not overly well-educated. In 1611 he persuaded a highly intelligent though penniless courtier, Sir Thomas Overbury, to help him deal with the official documents – and also to write passionate love letters to Frances on his behalf, even though at the time she was the wife of the equally youthful Earl of Essex. Overbury was quite satisfied to perform this task as long as he shared in the bountiful gifts and money lavished on Carr by the King.

Problems arose when Essex, having been abroad, returned, forcing Frances to forego any further clandestine meetings with Rochester. Determined to rid herself of her boring husband, she contacted a doctor's widow, Anne Turner, reputedly a witch and, rumoured by some, to be the keeper of a bagnio, a brothel. Anne introduced her to a Dr Simon Forman who, at a price, sold her a potion designed to render her husband impotent, and another to enhance the passions of Rochester, should it be needed! By now King James had become aware of the intrigue, but as it didn't conflict with his relationship with Rochester, he wasn't concerned – indeed, on the contrary, he promoted Rochester to the posts of Lord High Treasurer of Scotland, Knight of the Garter and First Secretary of State. Furthermore, to keep his favourite happy, he agreed that Frances' marriage to Essex should be annulled and that she should marry Rochester.

So everyone was happy, except Essex and Overbury. Essex was soon to become single again, against his will, but he didn't matter; however, Overbury realised that he would be written out of the frame; Rochester, on having the manipulative and unscrupulous Frances at his side, would have no further need of his services and so would no longer continue to subsidise Overbury's expensive way of life. Desperately Overbury warned his friend that the woman would only spell trouble if he married her; he made disparaging remarks, even calling her a whore, a fatal step, for Rochester told his mistress. Livid that anyone should dare to refer to her in such scurrilous terms, and determined to remove Overbury permanently from her future husband's orbit, she swore vengeance. Together, she and Rochester manoeuvred Overbury into incurring the disfavour of the King, with the result that she consequently had Overbury exactly where she wanted him – in the Bloody Tower, within the Tower of London!

Frances then employed a Dr James Franklin, an expert in such toxic substances as rose algar, cantharides, lapis constitis and, naturally, arsenic, together with such specialities as 'great spiders', which had to be crushed first, of course, and diamonds, similarly treated. Such was Frances' influence that she had the Lieutenant of the Tower replaced by another knight, Sir Gervase Elwys, over whom she had complete control, and he in turn employed reputed sorcerer Richard Weston, who served up some of Frances' own tasty dishes to the prisoner Overbury, tarts so potent that once, when Weston lifted the pastry lid from one of them, he nearly had the tip of his finger burned off, and it was not the heat of the contents that was to blame! Demanding speedy results, Frances proceeded to reinforce her kitchen staff by recruiting Anne Turner again. Anne also contributed to the Overbury diet sheet, preparing such delicious repasts as roast partridge seasoned with cantharides instead of pepper, and sugared delicacies containing arsenic and sublimate of mercury.

The months went by and somehow, despite exuding appalling rashes of suppurating boils and abscesses all over his body, Overbury stubbornly refused to die. Eventually Frances lost her patience with him, and on 14 September 1613, she engaged a French physician, Dr De Lobell, to supply some sublimate of mercury, and this was injected directly into Overbury's bowels by a chemist's assistant. Obligingly, Overbury died in agony at 6 a.m. the next morning, his demise being accelerated, reportedly, by Weston, who smothered him at the last minute. And lest anyone in authority should see the hideous eruptions that covered the corpse's skin, it was wrapped in a sheet and, uncoffined, buried immediately and without ceremony in the Royal Chapel of St Peter ad Vincula within the Tower of London.

Then it was time for all to rejoice. Within days the marriage of Frances and Essex was annulled and she married Rochester; with magnificent effrontery she was married 'in her hair', the symbol of a virgin bride (probably wearing her hair loose). To celebrate the occasion James promoted Rochester even further up the social ladder by creating him Earl of Somerset, which naturally delighted Frances, as Countess of Somerset.

But then the hammer blow fell. The insignificant apprentice, wielder of the deadly syringe, had been removed from the scene to maintain secrecy, and sent to live in Holland. Unfortunately for all concerned he contracted a fatal illness, and on his deathbed, desirous of cleansing his conscience, he confessed absolutely everything. For the Somersets, Richard Weston and Anne Turner, the game was up. Weston also talked, spilling chapter and verse, but it availed him naught, for on 23 October 1615 he was hanged at Tyburn. Sir Gervase Elwys met the same death on Tower Hill, though was allowed the favour of having his servant pull on his legs in order to expedite his strangulation, and Dr James Franklin met his death at St Thomas' Waterings.

For some unaccountable reason, perhaps because the king feared what might be disclosed by his favourite in any final speech delivered on the scaffold, Robert and Frances, Earl and Countess of Somerset, escaped execution, James graciously commuting their sentence to one of being imprisoned in the Tower. There they were incarcerated in the very room in the Bloody Tower in which their victim had lived – and died. On being led there, Frances shrieked in terror, convinced that she would be haunted by Overbury's ghost, and eventually the couple were moved elsewhere, to die ignored and forgotten.

And Anne Turner? On 9 November 1615 she was taken to Tyburn, the cynosure of thousands of eyes as, pale and dishevelled, she stood trembling on the drop while Hangman Derrick executed the sentence of the court by opening the trapdoors on which she stood.

Imitation might well be the sincerest form of flattery, but not when the hangman is deliberately wearing something similar! As described above, Anne Turner was hanged on 9 November 1615, a later historian reporting that 'Mistress Turner, the first inventress of yellow starch, was executed wearing a gown with Frills and a Cobweb Lawn Ruff of that colour at Tyburn, and with her death I believe that yellow starch, which so much disfigured our Nation and rendered them so ridiculous and fantastic, will receive its Funeral.' The hangman added a touch of colour to his usual funereal garb by also wearing yellow cuffs; whether in sympathy with his victim or to mock her, is not known. Suffice it to say that the fashionable ladies of the day wasted no time in reverting to the whiter brand.

V

Voglin, Apollonia (Germany)

The Carolina Criminal Code of the Emperor Charles V decreed that a woman guilty of infanticide was to be buried alive or impaled, and the penalty of death by drowning was to be inflicted 'only where water for that purpose was conveniently at hand'. Unfortunately for Apollonia, some was at hand, so they drowned her.

While working on a farm, she gave birth to an infant and, having no one to turn to or to help her, she killed it. For that she was sentenced to death, and on 6 March 1578 she was taken to where a wooden stage had been built protruding over the river. Standing at its end, she was placed in a large sack, the top of which was then securely tied. Almost immediately she was pushed into the water and held below the surface by the Löwe, the assistant executioner, wielding a long pole until the bubbles ceased to rise.

Such executions were far from efficient; it was reported that on one occasion 'the poor wretch managed to free herself from the sack, but was not reprieved, though her death struggles lasted almost a full hour'.

Executioner Franz Schmidt, in charge of such proceedings, was a rarity in his trade. Educated and, to a certain extent, possessing a flair for scientific subjects, the latter talent even resulted in him dissecting some of his victims. Never one to inflict unnecessary suffering, it was mainly due to his efforts that, in 1580, the authorities finally agreed that instead of drowning women guilty of infanticide, he could behead them with the sword, although it was pointed out to him that such a method might easily damage his professional reputation 'since those females, through timidity, might fall to the ground and thus hinder the executioner, who might then be obliged to finish them off as they lay prone on the earth.' There were no reports of that happening, and so renowned was his prowess with the sword that such women died almost instantly, their heads then being nailed above the gallows.

 We might not know who 'Juanita' was or even her second name; what is known is that in 1851 she killed a would-be burglar in self-defence and was unjustly sentenced to death for murder. There being

no gallows available, she was taken to a bridge outside town, a rope was thrown over a crossbeam and the noose positioned around her neck. But before the delegated executioner could push her off, she exclaimed, 'Adios, señores!' and with a smile threw herself into the gorge below.

W

Warriston, Lady Jean (Scotland)

This is a story of two Scottish maidens: one, the instigator of the crime; the other, the justice-dealing device. Jean Warriston, wife of the Laird of Warriston, lived in a grand manor house situated a mile outside Edinburgh. A young woman – she was only 20 – she was renowned for her beauty. Whether that was a factor in the crime she committed, whether her affections lay in another direction, or whether she found the relationship with her husband totally unsustainable, is not known; what is known is that she induced some members of her staff to assist her in murdering him.

On the evening of 1 July 1600, her plan was put into operation. Robert Weir, one of the estate's grooms, came to the house and hid himself in the cellar, and later that night Lady Warriston joined him. Together they went upstairs to where the Laird lay asleep. Once in the room, Weir attacked his master, first stunning him with his fists, then dragging him out of bed, where he proceeded to strangle him. And all this time Jean Warriston stood and watched.

Notified, probably by neighbours, the police arrived on the following morning. Jean, together with others who had plotted the murder, namely her nurse Janet Murdo and two maidservants, were arrested – but not Robert Weir who, wisely, had taken to his heels after his dire deed. Within days the suspects appeared before the Edinburgh magistrates; Jean, the nurse, and one of the servants being found guilty. All were sentenced to be tied to the stake, strangled, then burned to ashes.

In the condemned cell in the Tollbooth, the city gaol, Jean refused to accept her fate. Indeed, the minister who was attempting to give her spiritual solace later complained that:

> *I found her raging in an insensate fury, disdainfully taunting every word of grace that was uttered to her, impatiently tearing her hair out, sometimes running up and down like one possessed, throwing herself on the bed and refusing all the comfort of my words, and when the Bible was brought to her, she flung it against the walls twice or thrice most irreverently. And having been brought something to drink, she supped, then threw the cup on the floor and turned her back to me!*

The minister, however, was determined to save, or at least prepare, her soul during the few hours that were left to her, and kept up a constant barrage of prayers and pronouncements, not even allowing her to sleep, until she eventually showed some signs of penitence.

It was about then that some good news, if it can be thus described, was brought to her. Instead of being strangled and burned, she was to be decapitated by the guillotine-like Scottish maiden. And at 4 a.m. on the morning of 5 July 1600, Lady Jean Warriston was taken by tumbril to the Girth Cross at the end of Canongate, where the fearsome machine stood. There, after prayers had been said, she knelt; a brief moment passed, and then the executioner released the heavily weighted blade – and as the sound of the impact reverberated around the walls of the ancient buildings surrounding the Cross, her head rolled on to the sawdust-strewn boards.

Her accomplices fared much worse. Janet Murdo, her nurse, together with the maidservant, were taken to Castle Hill where they were strangled and then burned. The actual murderer, Robert Weir, escaped justice for four years, but when finally captured he was broken on the wheel; spread-eagled on it, his limbs were methodically shattered by the executioner's iron bar, the last blow being aimed at his heart.

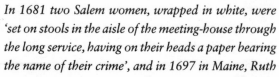 *In 1681 two Salem women, wrapped in white, were 'set on stools in the aisle of the meeting-house through the long service, having on their heads a paper bearing the name of their crime', and in 1697 in Maine, Ruth Gouch, being found guilty of a hateful crime, was ordered 'to stand in a white sheet publickly in the Congregation, two several Sabbath days, and likewise one day in the General Court'.*

Webster, Catherine (England)

If you covet someone's belongings, how do you gain possession of them? If you steal them, you run the risk of being caught with them by the police; the risk is even greater if you first murder the owner. Even if you effectively dispose of the body, how do you claim ownership of the belongings afterwards? Catherine Webster thought she knew the answer – but her ultimate appearance in the company of hangman William Marwood on the scaffold proved just how wrong she was.

Kate, as she was generally known, already had a criminal record. Born in Ireland, a thief and a pickpocket when young, she stole sufficient money to buy a boat ticket to Liverpool and then moved to the south of the country. By the age of thirty she'd had various jobs, invariably leaving after having stolen minor items of value, and in 1879 she was employed in Richmond as a maid by a Mrs Julia Martha Thomas, a rather strict woman who believed that her staff, when given time off, should return on time. On occasions, though, Kate would remain drinking in the local public house until closing time, and for this she was rebuked by her employer. On 2 March 1879, however, things were different. Kate was late, Mrs Thomas furious, and a bitter row ensued. Kate's ungovernable temper got the better of her and, going out to the garden shed, she returned with an axe which she proceeded to bury in Mrs Thomas' skull. She then went to bed.

Next morning she got up, washed and dressed, had breakfast, then calmly set about dismembering her mistress' body with the axe, dumping the large pieces of flesh and bone in the copper. Filling it up with water, she lighted the fire beneath it, and passed the time by scrubbing the bloodstains from the floor and walls. The remains, being by then easier to handle, she allowed to cool down before putting them in an assortment of bags. Taking them one at a time, she then threw them over the bridge into the River Thames. Having got rid of them all, she returned and, assuming the identity of her dead employer, promptly advertised the house and its contents for sale.

Unfortunately, the parapet of the bridge being rather high, not all the packages fell into the river; one landed close to the bank, where it was later found by an angler. His shocked reaction can well be imagined when, on opening it, he found the contents to be chunks of boiled flesh. The police were informed and, the remains being discovered to be those of Mrs Thomas, they hastened round to her address, only to find that the bird had flown – Kate, having made a quick though profitable sale of just about everything, had sailed for Ireland.

Catherine Webster was arrested at her home in Killane by the Royal Irish Constabulary, where she was found to have some of Mrs Thomas' valuables in her possession. Brought back to England, she appeared in court in the Old Bailey on 2 July 1879, charged with murder. Despite vehemently claiming to be innocent of the crime, and blaming everyone else, including some of those who had bought the household effects, she was found guilty.

On 29 July hangman William Marwood, having earlier lingered near her cell and covertly assessed her weight and average fitness in order to calculate the length of drop he should give her, greeted her on Wandsworth Prison scaffold. Ignoring her abusive though muffled outbursts, he expertly hooded and noosed her, then mentally congratulated himself on the accuracy of his mathematics as she dropped like a stone and died within seconds.

It was said that at the very end she had confessed to the murder – but never revealed the whereabouts of the bag containing Mrs Thomas' head. And as for the rumours that jars of human dripping were sold to local innkeepers at the time, only Kate – and the cooks involved – could say yea or nay!

Whether or not 'the prisoner ate a hearty meal' always fascinated the public and in the case of Barbara Graham, mentioned elsewhere, the media supplied the details, reporting that it consisted of a hot fudge sundae and a milkshake which she drank while listening to jazz records.

The Execution of Catherine Webster

White, Mary (England)

Following an execution, vendors of broadsheets containing descriptions of the condemned person and his or her crime, together with a picture of the felon on the gallows (usually the same picture at every execution!), and sometimes a tear-jerking poem, would ply their wares around the streets. One of the leading printers of these was James Catnatch who had offices in the Seven Dials district of London in the early 1800s. As a typical example of the melodramatic Victorian phraseology employed in such leaflets, his actual broadsheet recounting the "Orrible Scene' at Mary's execution is quoted here in full. And even if you've felt no compassion for any of the women so far, please shed a tear for Mary as you read this – for she was innocent!

The Life, Trial and Execution of MARY WHITE. Aged 19, she was executed at Exeter on Saturday last, for the murder of her Master and Mistress; giving an account of HER INNOCENCE BEING PROVED AND THE REAL MURDERER DISCOVERED.

The master and mistress of the above female were most inhumanly butchered by having their throats cut from ear to ear. This young woman had lived servant with these aged and unfortunate people upwards of seven years, and was much esteemed by all who knew her; and by her general good conduct had gained the confidence of those with whom she lived, who entrusted her with the management of their affairs and placed the greatest reliance on her honesty. They had kept the large Inn at Exeter for a number of years, but had a short time retired to a small pot-house, to pass the remainder of their days in greater quietude than the bustle of an inn permitted.

The Life, Trial, and Execution of

MARY WHITE.

Aged 19, who was executed at Exeter, on Saturday last, for the murder of her Master and Mistress; giving an account of

Her Innocence being Proved, and the Real Murderer Discovered.

THE master and mistress of the above female was most inhumanly butchered by having their throats cut from ear to ear. This young woman had lived servant with these aged and unfortunate people upwards of seven years, and was much esteemed by all who knew her; and by her general good conduct had gained the confidence of those with whom she lived, who entrusted her with the management of their affairs, and placed the greatest reliance on her honesty. They had kept the large Inn at Exeter for a number of years, but had a short time since retired to a small pot-house, to pass the remainder of their days in greater quietude than the bustle of an Inn permitted. It was the practice of the old couple to retire to rest about nine o'clock at night, and rise about the same hour in the morning, leaving every thing to the servant's care, not having any child of their own, it was generally believed that her master would behave handsomely to her, providing she married according to his wishes. This brought the girl a number of lovers and among them a young man the name of Smith was most assiduous in his attention towards her, who, behaving always with the greatest propriety, became a great favourite with the old couple.

On Saturday, Smith went as usual to the house, and when the company had left, and the old couple retired to rest, the servant sat with him by the kitchen fire. She had occasion to leave the kitchen a short time, and on her return she missed him. On hearing a noise, she ran up stairs to her mistress's room, where to her great terror, she found the drawers plundered, and her master and mistress lying with their throats cut, and the blood gushing in torrents from the wounds. She immediately threw up a front window and gave the alarm, and the neighbours entering no one being found in the house besides her, suspicion fell upon her, and from constancy to her lover, she permitted herself to be fully committed to trial. At the late assizes she was arraigned, convicted, and sentenced to be hung and dissected.

At the place of execution she addressed the numerous by-standers as follows:—

'Good People.---You ere now come to see the latter end of a poor unfortunate young woman, 19 years of age, who is brought to an ignominious death for murder; I say there is a just God that sitteth in the judgment seat of Heaven, before whom I must shortly appear to answer for all my sins. I most solemnly declare before God and the world, that I am innocent of the murder as the child unborn'. She burst into tears.

After this she prayed with the Minister, and sung a penitential psalm, she went down upon her knees, and prayed that the Almighty would convince the multitude assembled of her innocency or guilty by showing them the following miracles---that if she was guilty it might be one of the finest days that could come from heaven; but if she were innocent that the darkness might overspread the town during the time she was suspended. Her supplication reached the throne of grace for immediately on her being turned off, a dark thick cloud covered the country for many miles, attended with thunder, lightning, and rain. Smith, who was a spectator, stung with guilt and horror, rushed through the crowd, exclaiming ' I AM THE MURDERER" and delivered himself into the hands of justice. He fully confessed his guilt, but declared that the deed was not premediated, but he was struck with a desire to gain their riches, and he intended to have murdered his sweetheart also. He is fully committed for trial at the next Assizes.

A Copy of Verses.

OH! you that have not hearts of stone,
 Attend to what I say,
For Death has real'd my early doom,
 And summon'd me away;
Alas! this dreadful fate of mine,
 That I should die in scorn,
Although as guiltless of the crime
 As is the babe unborn.

To atone for blood I never shed,
 In midst of youth and bloom;
I to the fatal scaffold led,
 Must meet a Murderer's doom,
And while I stand exposed there,
 Before the knot is tied,
My innocence I will declare,
 To all the world wide.

Farewell my aged Mother dear,
 Your tender heart is broke,
Alas! you'll never live I fear,
 To bear this cruel stroke;
What would your tender bosom feel,
 To see your darling child,
That she had noursh'd at her breast,
 Brought to an end so vile.

Before my eyes are clos'd I pray,
 And Heav'n my prayers hear,
My innocence may be reveal'd,
 And be as noon-day clear;
And bring the red hand to light,
 Who did the horrid deed,
That all may know poor Mary White,
 Was innocent indeed.

She met her ignominious death,
 Resign'd to her hard fate,
But scarce had yielded up her breath,
 When awful to relate,
A man confess'd unto the crime,
 For which the maiden died;
And now in irons is confin'd,
 His Trial to abide.

J. Catnach, Printer, 2, & 3, Monmouth-court, 7 Dials.

Broadsheet of Mary White's Execution

It was the practice of the old couple to retire to rest about nine o'clock at night and rise about the same time in the morning, leaving everything to the servant's care; not having any child of their own, it was generally believed that her master would behave handsomely to her, providing she married according to his wishes. This brought the girl a number of lovers and among them a young man, the name of Smith, was most assiduous in his attention towards her, who, behaved always with the greatest propriety, became a great favourite with the old couple.

On Saturday, Smith went as usual to the house, and when the company had left, and the old couple retired to rest, the servant sat with him by the kitchen fire. She had occasion to leave the kitchen a short time, and on her return she missed him. On hearing a noise, she ran upstairs, where to her great terror she found the drawers plundered and her master and mistress lying with their throats cut, and the blood gushing in torrents from the wounds. She immediately threw up a front window and gave the alarm, and the neighbours entering, no one being found in the house besides her, suspicion fell upon her, and from constancy to her lover, she permitted herself to be fully committed to trial. At the last Assizes she was arraigned, convicted and sentenced to be hung and dissected.

At the place of execution she addressed the numerous bystanders as follows: 'Good People – You are now come to see the latter end of a poor unfortunate young woman, 19 years of age, who is brought to an ignominious death for murder; I say that there is a just God that sitteth in the judgment seat of Heaven, before whom I must shortly appear to answer for all my sins. I most solemnly declare before God and the world, that I am innocent of the murder as the child unborn.' She burst into tears.

After this she prayed with the Minister and sung a penitential psalm; she went down upon her knees, and prayed that the

Almighty would convince the multitude assembled of her innocence or guilty, by shewing the following miracles; that if she was guilty it might be one of the finest days that could come from heaven; but if she were innocent then the darkness might overspread the town during the time she was suspended. Her supplication reached the throne of grace for immediately on her being turned off, a dark thick cloud covered the country for many miles, attending with thunder, lightning and rain.

Smith, who was a spectator, stung with guilt and horror, rushed through the crowd exclaiming, 'I AM THE MURDERER!' and delivered himself into the hands of justice. He fully confessed his guilt, but declared that the deed was not premeditated, but he was struck with desire to gain their riches, and he intended to murder his sweetheart also. He is fully committed for trial at the next Assizes.

COPY OF VERSES:
Oh, you that hath not hearts of stone, Attend to what I say,
For Death has seal'd my early doom, and summon'd me away;
Alas! This dreadful fate of mine, that I should die in scorn,
Although as guiltless of the crime, as is the babe unborn.

To atone for blood I never shed, in midst of youth and bloom,
I to the fatal scaffold led, must meet a Murderer's doom,
And while I stand exposed there, before the knot is tied,
My innocence I will declare, to all the world wide.

Farewell my aged Mother dear, your tender heart is broke,
Alas! You'll never live, I fear, to bear this cruel stroke
What would your tender bosom feel, to see your darling child,
That she had nourish'd at her breast, brought to an end so vile.

Before my eyes are clos'd I pray, and Heav'n my prayers hear,
My innocence may be reveal'd and be as noon-day clear;
And bring the real hand to light, who did the horrid deed,
That all may know poor Mary White, was innocent indeed.

She met her ignominious death, resign'd to her hard fate,
But scarce had yielded up her breath, when awful to relate,
A man confess'd unto the crime, for which the maiden died,
And now in irons is confined, his Trial to abide.

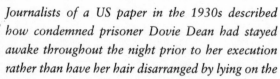

Journalists of a US paper in the 1930s described how condemned prisoner Dovie Dean had stayed awake throughout the night prior to her execution rather than have her hair disarranged by lying on the pillows. Bonnie Brown Heady, awaiting execution in 1953 for kidnapping and murder, complained bitterly that as well as being unable to varnish her nails, she was not even allowed to set her hair the way she wanted.

Williams, Anne (England)

Another bossy woman, another meek man – and yet more poison. Called a 'fiend' by the *Newgate Calendar*, it went on to describe how, for the purpose of killing her husband, Anne arranged for their manservant to buy some white mercury, which she mixed with the gruel she intended to give him, thereby adding insult to injury, because she knew very well that he hated that particular food. Interestingly, Anne must have had some scientific knowledge, in that she knew what effect a liquid would have on the chemical she had just administered to him, for she then told him to get a glass of ale for her, and one for himself, the result being that he was immediately seized with appalling stomach cramps and vomiting. In his agonies he called her a wicked woman and exclaimed that he knew he was dying, but Anne was entirely unrepentant. It would certainly seem that the purchaser of the poison was rather more than merely a servant, for the *Calendar* stated that 'she told the man, whom she meant afterwards to share her bed, that she had given her husband the stuff he had bought, and that it was operated purely'.

Despite medical aid, her husband's prophecy was correct, for he died the following morning. Such a crime being impossible to conceal, Anne was put on trial and found guilty. And as killing one's husband was not just murder, for which one was hanged, but was petit treason (killing the head of the family), on 13 April 1753 she was taken to the marketplace in Gloucester, where she was tied to the stake and burnt to ashes, the hundreds of spectators showing little pity for her fate.

Anne Williams Burning at the Stake

Margery Watson, a notorious scold who lived in Whitby, Yorkshire, was sentenced to be ducked by the constable – unless she publicly asked pardon of James Wilkinson's wife in Whitby Church or at the Market Cross.

Wilson, Catherine (England)

A poison case again, but this time not arsenic or even white mercury! Catherine Wilson was the lady who administered it, and had ample opportunity, when, in 1853, she was employed as housekeeper to a Mr Peter Mawer, an elderly gentleman who lived in Boston, Lincolnshire. He suffered severely from gout, and when the pain became unbearable, she would give him his medicine, a remedy named colchicum, which was derived from the dried seeds of the autumn crocus. Catherine discovered that colchicum, if taken in small doses, brought relief, but was highly toxic if taken in large quantities. And when Mr Mawer showed his appreciation of her abilities as a personal nurse by promising to make her sole legatee in his will, she wasted no time in showing her appreciation by increasing the dosage!

In the October of the following year, poor Mr Mawer died. The doctor who had prescribed the colchicum decided that his patient must have been in so much pain that he had taken a larger dose than was safe, and the resultant verdict was one of accidental death. Catherine, shedding tears worthy of any crocodile, cashed in on the property and belongings due to her under the will, then headed for pastures new in London. There she joined the high-spending, heavy-drinking circuit, in one club happening to meet a man named Dixon, to whom she became so attached that together they moved into an apartment at 27 Alfred Place, Bedford Square, just off Tottenham Court Road.

They introduced themselves to Mrs Soames, the landlady, as Mr and Mrs Wilson, and continued to enjoy the London nightlife, but Dixon started to reveal his true colours, savagely beating Catherine when drunk. She, however, had an antidote for such behaviour, and gave him a large dose of the colchicum in her possession. The result was that he started to feel unwell, very unwell, in fact. Their landlady sympathised, especially when Catherine explained that her 'husband' had had attacks like that for years and, in fact, was not expected to live for much longer. Nor did he. The local physician, Dr Whitburn, when asked to sign the death certificate, demurred on the grounds that he was not their usual physician, and, despite the widow's tearful plea not to cut her dear husband up 'because he had always been horrified at the thought of his body being mutilated', he stipulated that a post-mortem should be performed. But Catherine got away with it, nothing suspicious being discovered, and the death certificate was accordingly signed.

Mrs Soames proved such a comfort to the grieving widow that they became close friends, but little did the landlady realise that she was to be the next victim of a cold-blooded serial killer. Before twelve months had passed, Catherine opened her little box containing colchicum again, and ill health unaccountably overtook Mrs Soames.

Catherine then assumed her role as nurse, mixed more of her special brand of medicine, and five days afterwards her patient died. Dr Whitburn attended again and another post-mortem took place. Death by natural causes being assumed, another death certificate was issued. Catherine must have felt intoxicated with power as it became obvious to her that there was obviously nothing to prevent her from doing it again – and again.

Soon afterwards, in 1860, while shopping in London, she made the acquaintance of a Mrs Atkinson, and while in her company, Catherine sympathised with her new friend for losing her purse, an item which she herself had managed to acquire. Some weeks later Mrs Atkinson wrote to her from the millinery shop she and her husband owned, in Kirkby Lonsdale, Cumberland (now Cumbria), to say that she was coming to London again to purchase a large amount of stock for the shop. The prospect of increasing her bank balance was not to be missed, so Catherine promptly suggested that her friend should come and stay with her. Mrs Atkinson was delighted to renew her friendship with Catherine, so joined her at her house in Loughborough Road, Brixton. Mr Atkinson was of course only too pleased that his wife would have company whilst going round the wholesale dealers, but his shocked reaction can only be imagined when he received a telegram informing him that his wife was seriously ill and that he should come at once. By the time he arrived, his wife was already dead.

Catherine had already realised that any local doctor, having no knowledge of Mrs Atkinson's medical history, would refuse to issue a death certificate, so she prepared for that eventuality by telling the devastated husband that on her deathbed his wife had implored her not to let anyone cut up her body. Accordingly, Mr Atkinson refused to give the doctor his permission. And when he later enquired about the hundreds of pounds that Mrs Atkinson had brought with her to buy the new stock, Catherine expressed her surprise that his wife had not written and told him that en route to London she had felt unwell, left the train at Rugby and, while resting in the waiting room there, the money had been stolen. As for the diamond ring Catherine was wearing, well, that had been given to her by his wife for looking after her.

It will never be known just how many more women fell victim to Catherine's deadly poison, but the end came in February 1862, nine years after her first murder. She had obtained the post of nurse to an elderly and frail lady, Mrs Sarah Carnell who lived in Marylebone. Once again she tended her charge so devotedly that again she was promised a large legacy, but unfortunately she had used up all the colchicum. Undaunted, and really believing that she was invulnerable, she simply changed her recipe. When asked by her patient to collect some of her usual medicine from the chemist, Catherine did so, and also brought what she said was a 'soothing draught' which would make her employer feel better. As it was not yet time for the usual medicine, she poured some of the emollient fluid into a tumbler and handed it to Mrs Carnell who, on holding the glass, exclaimed that it felt warm. Nevertheless she took a mouthful – then spat it out again, only to stare in horror as the drops which had landed on the top sheet started to burn holes in it! Realising her error, Catherine Wilson ran from the room and fled from the house, but a detailed description of her was circulated and six weeks later, in April 1862, she was arrested, charged at Marylebone Police Court with attempted murder, and put on trial.

In court she was accused of administering oil of vitriol (sulphuric acid) to Mrs Carnell. Her lawyer suggested that it was accidental and no fault of his client's; the chemist's inexperienced assistant must have given it to her by mistake. The judge scornfully rejected that theory, pointing out that had the lad given a glass bottle of sulphuric acid to the prisoner in the dock, it would have become red-hot and burst while she was carrying it back to the house, and therefore she must have had it in her possession in its own container!

The jury was sent out to consider their verdict, and while they were doing so, the counsel for the defence was approached by a man who identified himself as a detective of the Lincoln police force, the officer then informing the lawyer that in the event of the prisoner being found not guilty, he had warrants for her arrest on no fewer than seven murder charges. Eventually the jurors filed back into the courtroom and for some reason known only to themselves, perhaps giving her the benefit of the doubt, the foreman delivered the result of their deliberations – not guilty! Catherine Wilson, surprised and delighted at having been found innocent, stepped from the dock – and was immediately arrested by the Lincoln police officer.

She was held in prison while investigations into the deaths of Messrs Mawer and Dixon, Mrs Atkinson and Mrs Soames were carried out. Corpses were exhumed and post-mortems conducted. The results were beyond doubt, the doctors agreeing that the colchicum seeds had been infused and probably administered to her patients and partners in such 'health restoring' drinks as brandy, wine, or tea. This damning evidence was given to the court at her subsequent trial at the Old Bailey, Catherine Wilson listening apparently unconcerned; not a flicker of emotion betrayed her feelings, even when the judge donned the black cap and sentenced her to death.

On execution day, 20 October 1862, 20,000 spectators crowded the area around Newgate to watch a woman who had committed so many horrific crimes receive the justice she so richly deserved, but she ignored the jeers and catcalls as hangman William Calcraft placed the noose around her slim neck. Catherine Wilson had needed several drops of colchicum to dispatch her victims – the executioner required only one drop to dispatch his.

Hangmen were usually the target of public abuse and even their wives were reviled by spectators and neighbours, one being Ann Cheshire, wife of executioner Thomas Cheshire. So infuriated was she in August 1829 when four small children shouted 'Jack Ketch!' after her, that she promptly picked them up and dropped them

into a cellar area ten feet deep, fortunately without hurting
them to any great extent. Although in court she claimed that it
was all an accident, nevertheless she was bound over to be of
good behaviour in future.

Wood, Margaret (Scotland)

One way of making a witch confess her association with the Devil
was to torture her with the boots, of which several types were
in existence (see Appendix 1). These were sometimes known in
Scotland, where she lived, as 'bootikins', 'caspilaws', 'cashielaws'
or 'brodequins'. Regardless of which name or variety, the end
result of their application to one's legs was sheer and unrelieved
agony, as Margaret found out on 2 February 1631, after the
seventeen members of the Privy Council, meeting the previous day,
had ordered that 'Margaret Wod to be putt to the tortour of the
bootes, the morn, at ten of the clocke, in the Laich Councell Hous
of Edinburgh; and that the whole councell be present when the
tortour is given.'

The last clause was included because not everyone in authority
wanted to watch a victim suffering in the boots. One exception, a
royal one at that, was James II, when he was Duke of York. Bishop
Burnet, in his book *History of His Own Times*, related that:

> *When any are to be stuck in the boots, it is done in*
> *the presence of the council, and upon that happening,*
> *almost all offer [attempt] to run away. The sight is*
> *so dreadful that without an order restraining such a*
> *number to stay as a quorum, the press-boards [between which*
> *the legs are crushed] would remain unused. But the Duke of*

York, while he was in Scotland, was so far from running away, that he looked on all the while with an unmoved indifference, and with an attention as if he were watching a curious experiment. This gave a terrible impression of him to all that observed it, as a man that had no bowels of mercy in him.

Scolds' bridles, the scourge of nagging women, were not imported into the American Colonies by early settlers, for they discovered that a stick, partially split and pinched on the tongue, was just as efficacious! The sentence imposed in 1651 on Goody Edwards, a resident of Southampton, Long Island, declared that: 'She is ordered to pay £3 or have her tongue in a cleft stick for contempt of court warrant.'

Z

Zelle, Margarete Gertrud (Holland)

Margarete Zelle was not only an exotic dancer, she was also a spy, more familiarly known as Mata Hari (Eye of the Morning). Born in Holland in August 1876 to an affluent family, she grew up to be a well-educated young woman, and she fell in love with a Dutch officer, Captain Rudolf McLeod, whom she married in 1895. The Captain was posted to the Dutch East Indies, Margaret accompanying him, but the dissolute social life led to her womanising and hard-drinking husband treating her with violence and even inducing her to play the 'badger game', in which she encouraged other men to make love to her, then be caught in a compromising position by her 'outraged' husband who would henceforth blackmail the blackguard!

By 1902 their marriage had failed disastrously and they returned to Holland where they were divorced. To earn a living Margarete exercised strenuously and took ballet lessons, then put them to good use by elaborating on the erotic dances she had seen in the Far East. Moving to Paris, she soon became much sought after by nightclubs, although at times she descended into prostitution to make a living. Returning to her home country, she was fortunate enough to meet an ex-lover, Karl Breitenstein, who loaned her some money. With that she went back to Paris and set herself up in the high class Hotel Crillon, where she audaciously created for herself a new identity – she was now Mata Hari, born in the East, trained to dance by her stepmother, the chief priestess of mystic and holy ceremonies.

Such was the lure of the lasciviousness of her nude dances, the erotic writhing of her slim limbs, the sinuous gestures of her slender hands as, with provocative slowness, she discarded the red veils loosely swathed around her, that across the Continent, princes and public alike worshipped her every performance. Among those who were captivated by her charms was the chief of Berlin's police force, von Jagow, and it was through him that she was recruited as a spy for the Germans during the First World War, her intimacy with so many statesmen and military commanders allowing her to extract vital information from them on a seemingly casual and admiring basis.

As the war progressed, suspicions arose about her activities, especially by the French government, and the blow fell in 1917 when an incriminating payment of 15,000 pesetas from von Jagow to agent H21 was intercepted but allowed to be delivered. A follow-up search of her hotel room revealed the cheque – and agent H21, Mata Hari, was taken into custody.

FEMALE EXECUTIONS

On 24 July of that year she was interrogated by a military court, intelligence agencies presenting overwhelming evidence of her complicity. The verdict was guilty, and she was sentenced to be shot by firing squad.

At 4 a.m. on 15 October 1917 she was told that her last appeal had failed. Rising from her bed in the condemned cell, she donned a smart tailormade outfit and was taken to Vincennes, the place of execution. There she faced the firing squad of twelve soldiers, positioned twelve paces in front of her. Proudly she waved away the offer of a blindfold; the officer in charge gave the orders to load, take aim and fire, and Mata Hari dropped to the ground. The officer then approached and delivered the *coup de grâce*, firing one round from his revolver into her head behind the ear.

Her body was taken away, the doctors then discovering that only four rifle bullets had struck her body; even aware that a spy had been responsible for betraying hundreds of one's countrymen, it was still difficult to shoot at a woman, especially one so elegant and beautiful, who just stood there and looked at you.

The last Christmas Day in the lives of President Nicolae Ceausescu and his wife Elena was 25 December 1989. Following revolution in Romania, their power base was overthrown and they were interrogated by a military tribunal, after which they were taken to a nearby area and shot, the firing squad consisting of one officer and two soldiers armed with machine guns. It was subsequently reported that the soldiers opened fire before being ordered, emptying their magazines and aiming so wildly that others standing nearby were also hit and wounded.

APPENDIX 1:
TYPES OF TORTURE

Boots

The boots ranked high among those tortures available to some courts; indeed, some called it 'the most severe and cruell paine in the whole worlde'. Whichever variety of this device was used, the victim, even if not subsequently executed, was almost invariably crippled for life. In the sixteenth and seventeenth centuries this particular method of persuasion was popular in France and Scotland (where it had the deceptively whimsical-sounding names of 'bootikins', 'brodequins', or 'cashilaws').

There were several variations of the device; one consisted of an upright board placed on either side of each leg of a seated victim, splinting them from knee to ankle, the boards being held together by ropes or iron rings within a frame. Wooden wedges would then be driven in slowly between the two inner boards, and then between the outer ones and the surrounding frame, lacerating the flesh and crushing the bone, incriminating questions being asked following each blow with the mallet. Another version was a single boot made of iron, large enough to encase both legs up to the knees. Wedges would then be driven downwards a little at a time, betwixt leg and metal, the injuries inflicted being as described above.

There was also a version known as the 'Spanish Boot', an iron legging which was tightened by a screw mechanism; additional incentives to confess were available, the device being heated until red-hot either before being clamped on the legs or while being tightened.

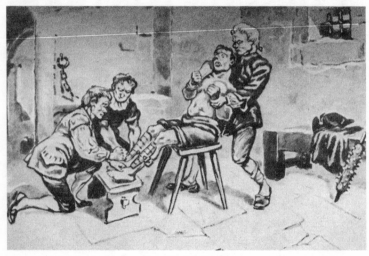

Torture by the Boots

Bridles, or Branks

Intended mainly to be worn by witches, scolding or nagging wives, or argumentative neighbours, its basic design consisted of an iron framework in the form of a helmet-shaped cage which fitted tightly over the head, with eye-holes and an aperture for the mouth. At the

APPENDIX 1: TYPES OF TORTURE

front, protruding inwards, was a small flat plate which rested on the woman's tongue, the bridle then being locked about her neck. Other versions existed, some more painful than others. One type, used in prisons in the Tasmanian penal colony, was constructed of wood and leather and covered the mouth entirely except for a very small hole to permit the wearer to breathe. John West wrote, in his book *The History of Tasmania*, published in 1852, 'When the whole was secured with the various straps and buckles, a more complete bridle in resemblance could not well be witnessed.'

Bridles for Scolds and Witches

Another type, widely used in England and Scotland, had large tongue plates studded with sharp pins, or a small spiked wheel, a rowel, which lacerated the tongue should the victim try to protest, or a witch attempt to chant the magic spells by which she could summon the Devil, or change herself into a small animal and thus escape. As well as having to wear a bridle, witches were deprived of sleep, relays of guards being constantly on duty to deny them even a catnap.

Many versions had a chain attached to the front by which the scold or witch could be led through the streets, much to the derisory delight of her neighbours, their attention having been attracted by the sound of the spring-mounted bell on top.

Peine forte et dure

Until abolished by a statute in 1827, it was lawful to subject a prisoner to *Peine forte et dure*, severe and hard punishment, if he or she refused to plead guilty or not guilty when charged. Several versions of the sentence existed, but in general the sentence was:

To be remanded to prison and put into a low dark chamber, and there laid on his or her back on the bare floor naked, unless where decency forbade; that there should be placed [on a board] on his or her body as great a weight of iron as they could bear, and more; that they should have no sustenance save only on the first day three morsels of the worst bread, and on the second day three draughts of water that should be nearest the prison door; and that in this situation, such be alternatively the daily ration, till he or she died – or pleaded to the charge.

Sometimes heavy stones were used as weights, others being placed under the back to break the spine.

Rack

The Rack, Tower of London

As with other instruments of torture, many different types existed, but the basic design of the rack consisted of an open rectangular frame having four legs, over six feet in length and raised about three feet from the floor. The victim was laid on their back on the ground beneath it, their wrists and ankles being tied by ropes to a windlass, an axle, at each end of the frame. These were turned in opposite directions, each manned by two of the rack master's assistants. One man, by inserting a pole into one of the sockets in the shaft, would turn the windlass, tightening the ropes a fraction of an inch at a time; the other would insert his pole in similar fashion but keep it still, in order to maintain the pressure on the victim's joints while his companion transferred his pole to the next socket in the windlass.

The first stage of the torture was the hoisting of the victim until they were almost level with the frame, this initial strain, that of being lifted against his or her own weight, being sufficient to impose severe stresses on the joints of the wrists, elbows, hips, shoulders and knees, and to give some indication of the excruciating agony to come. The stretching, the gradual dislocation, and the questions would continue until the interrogator had been finally satisfied.

A later version incorporated a ratchet mechanism which held the ropes taut all the time, the incessant and terrifying click, click, click of the cogs and the creaking of the slowly tightening ropes being the only sounds in the silence of the torture chamber, other than the shuddering gasps of the sufferer.

Thumbscrews

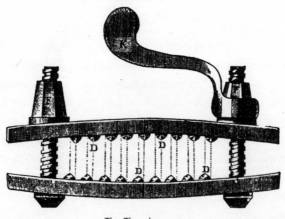

The Thumbscrews

Earlier resembling primitive nutcrackers, they soon developed into a deadly instrument consisting of two short iron bars of equal length, one having three small rods designed to fit into three matching holes in the other bar. The victim's thumbs or fingers were inserted between the bars on each side of the central rod, which had a screw thread on it. Once positioned over the quick of the nails, the wing nut on the central rod was tightened, forcing the upper bar downwards and so applying the requisite amount of pressure on the victim's nails. Pinioned in this fashion, the victim could be led anywhere as required, unable to resist. In some parts, Scotland in particular, thumbscrews were also known as pilliwinks, pilniwinks, penny-winks or pyrowinks; whatever their name, the result was pain.

Water Torture

The Water Torture

FEMALE EXECUTIONS

This method of persuasion required the prisoner to be bound to a bench, a cow horn then being inserted in his or her mouth. Following a refusal to answer an incriminating question to the satisfaction of the interrogators, a jug of water would be poured into the horn and the question repeated. Any reluctance to swallow would be overcome by the executioner pinching the victim's nose. This procedure would continue, swelling the victim's stomach to grotesque proportions and causing unbearable agony, either until all the required information had been extracted, or until the water, by eventually entering and filling the lungs, brought death by asphyxiation.

APPENDIX 2:
TYPES OF PUNISHMENT AND EXECUTION

Axe and Block

Being dispatched by cold steel rather than being hanged was granted as a privilege to those of royal or aristocratic birth, it being considered less ignoble to lose one's life as if slain in battle, rather than being suspended by the hempen rope. Such privilege, however, did not necessarily make death any less painful; on the contrary, for although being hanged brought a slow death by strangulation, the axe was little more than a crude unbalanced chopper. The target, the nape of the neck, was small; the wielder, cynosure of 10,000 or more eyes, nervous and clumsy; and even when delivered accurately it killed not by cutting or slicing but by brutally crushing its way through flesh and bone, muscle and sinew. It was, after all, a weapon for punishment, not for mercy.

FEMALE EXECUTIONS

Most English executions by the axe took place in London, the weapon being held ready for use in the Tower of London. The one currently on display therein is believed to be that which severed the heads of the three Scottish lords who led the Jacobite Rebellion in 1745, Lords Balmerino, Kilmarnock and Lovat. It measures nearly 36 inches in length and weighs almost eight pounds. The blade itself is rough and unpolished, the cutting edge ten and a half inches long. Its size and the fact that most of its weight is at the back of the blade means that when brought down rapidly, as of course it would be, the weapon would tend to twist slightly, throwing it off aim and so failing to strike the centre of the nape of the victim's neck.

Unlike hangings, executions by decapitation were comparatively rare events, the executioner thereby being deprived of the necessary practice. A further factor was that the axe's impact inevitably caused the block to bounce, and if the first stroke was inaccurate and so jolted the victim into a slightly different position, the executioner would need to readjust his point of aim for the next stroke, no mean task while being subjected to a hail of jeers, abuse and assorted missiles from the mob surrounding the scaffold.

The heading axe's vital partner, the block, was a large piece of wood of rectangular section, about two feet high so that the victim could kneel, its top being sculptured specifically for its gruesome purpose. Because it was essential that the victim's throat rested on a hard surface, the top had a hollow scooped out of the edges of each of the widest sides; at one side the hollow was wide, permitting the victim to push his – or her – shoulders as far forward as possible, the hollow on the opposite side being narrower to accommodate the chin. This positioned the victim's throat exactly where it was required, resting on the flat area between the two hollows.

Boiled to Death

This horrific penalty was carried out using a large cauldron filled with water, oil or tallow. Sometimes the victim was immersed, the liquid then being heated, or he or she was plunged into the already boiling contents, usually head first. In England an Act was passed specifically to execute one Richard Roose in that fashion, he having been found guilty of casting 'a certayne venym or poyson into the yeaste or barme wyth whych porrage or gruell was mayde for the famyly of the Byssopp of Rochester and others'. Seventeen members of the household fell ill, two of them dying, and when news of this un-English type of crime reached the Court, Henry VIII was 'inwardly abhorrying all such abhomynable offences, the sayde poysoning be adjudged high treason'. So he was condemned to be 'boyled to death without havynge any advautage of his clergie'. Margaret Davy, a maid who concocted a similar recipe to dispose of no fewer than three families, and another woman, a servant in a King's Lynn household who used the same toxic ingredients when preparing a meal for her employers, were dispatched in the same way.

An alternative method was to use a large shallow receptacle rather than a cauldron, oil, tallow or pitch being poured in. The victim was then partially immersed in the liquid and then fried to death.

Branding

Branding, from the Teutonic word 'brinnan', to burn, was used in many countries for centuries, and was applied by a hot iron which seared letters signifying the felon's particular crime into the fleshy part of the thumb, the forehead, cheeks or shoulders. In England the iron consisted of a long iron bolt with a wooden handle at one end and a raised letter at the other, a set of such instruments available in the courtroom or on the scaffold. The letters were 'SS' for sower of sedition, 'M' for malefactor, 'B' for blasphemer, 'R' for rogue, etc., so that everyone would know in future not only that someone was a criminal but also what particular type of crime the lawbreaker had committed, whether or not they had mended their ways. Women were also branded, a statute passed in 1624 declaring that:

Any woman being lawfully convicted by her confession or by the verdict of twelve men of the felonious taking of any money, goods or chattels above the value of twelve pence and under the value of ten shillings, or as an accessory to any such offence [...] shall for the first offence be branded and marked in the hand, upon the brawn of the thumb, with a hot burning iron, having a Roman letter 'T' [for Thief] upon the said iron; the said mark to be made by the gaoler openly in the Court, before the Judge.

Breaking on the Wheel

This was an agonising and prolonged way in which to die, and was used mainly on the Continent in the sixteenth to eighteenth centuries, although isolated cases reportedly took place in Scotland early in those years.

The felon was secured, spread-eagled, face upwards, on a large cartwheel mounted horizontally on an upright which passed through the hub, the wheel sometimes being slightly canted in order to give the spectators a better view of the brutal proceedings. The

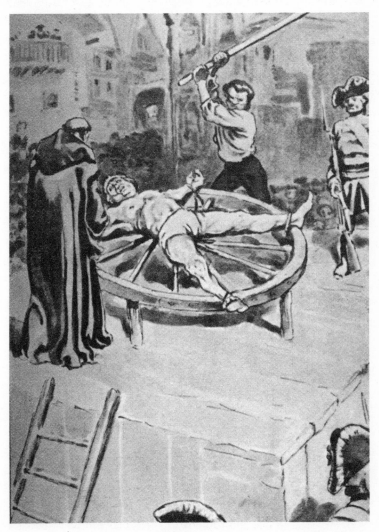

Breaking on the Wheel

wheel could be rotated in order to bring the particular part of the human target within reach of the executioner, thereby eliminating the need for him to walk round to the other side. Some versions of the device required the victim to be bound to the spokes, others to two lengths of timber in the form of a St Andrew's Cross nailed to the upper side of the wheel.

Death was meted out by the executioner wielding a heavy iron bar, three feet long by two inches square, or using a long-handled hammer. Slowly and methodically he would shatter the victim's limbs, the upper and forearms, the thighs and the lower legs; nor would other parts of the body escape being pulverised, until eventually the *coup de grâce*, known as the retentum, a final blow to the heart or the neck, would be delivered. Alternatively a cord around the throat would be pulled tight, depriving the victim of what little life was left in him. And on being removed from the wheel the corpse would resemble a rag doll, the various short sections of the shattered limbs being completely disconnected from each other.

The judges, in their mercy, might mitigate the sentence by permitting the death blow to be administered either following a certain number of strokes or after a certain length of time had elapsed. For example, one John Calas of Toulouse received a blow to the heart two hours after he had been strapped to the wheel.

Burned at the Stake

This was the dreaded sentence passed on heretics, sorcerers, witches and women found guilty of treasonable acts. Taken to a public site, usually the marketplace, they were either seated on a stool or made to stand in a tar barrel, secured to a stake by means of a rope or a chain attached to the hinged iron ring about their necks, and ropes or hoops around their bodies. Piles of wood would then be heaped waist-high around them and set alight. As the flames rose and the thick smoke billowed forth, the executioner would either speed their demise by removing the stool so that the ring strangled them, or pulled on the ring so that it choked them but, as occasionally happened, should the conflagration take too fierce a hold, he would be unable to get near, and it would be some hours before the fire abated, leaving just a pile of charred and smouldering ashes. Some victims were given the special privilege of having small bags of gunpowder fastened beneath their arms or between their legs, the eventual igniting of which brought death quicker than by the slow mounting of the flames.

Dissection

In 1832, the Anatomy Act was passed, which permitted surgeons to obtain corpses legally from institutions and hospitals for instructional purposes, if the bodies were unclaimed, or by agreement with the relatives. It also succeeded in stamping out overnight the ghastly practice whereby body-snatchers dug up literally thousands of newly buried corpses in cemeteries and sold them to surgical schools.

Prior to that date the old law stated briefly, 'that the Body of every Person convicted of Murder shall, after Execution, either be dissected or hung in Chains'. This had a dual purpose: to act as a deterrent to criminals who, not unnaturally, recoiled at the prospect of their cadavers being cut up, and also to provide specimens for the instruction of surgical students who would otherwise have to learn as they went along, on living patients.

Dissection of a Criminal

APPENDIX 2: TYPES OF PUNISHMENT AND EXECUTION

As a deterrent, that law had a certain effect on the criminal fraternity, chiefly because in those days hanging consisted of slow strangulation, and should they be cut down while still alive and then, as was usual, rushed to Surgeons' Hall, the prospect of watching the scalpel approaching their stomachs did not bear thinking about! This dread resulted in convicted criminals arranging for friends to pull their legs once the rope had tightened, or to rescue their 'corpses' from the hangman en route to the operating theatre.

Electric Chair

With the discovery and potentialities of electricity in the late 1800s, Americans started to adopt it for general use in their homes, but lacking the technical knowledge required to connect and earth devices such as lighting and heating appliances safely, many were electrocuted. It was therefore only a matter of time before some far-sighted and innovative individual realised that if the stuff could kill innocent people, why not use it to replace hanging? It was obviously quicker, much less distasteful a spectacle for official witnesses, and would prove to the world that once again the USA was more progressive than any other nation. And so the electric chair was born.

It consisted of a high-backed piece of oak furniture fitted with straps that secured the victim's head and chest, arms and legs. Two electrodes, metal plates each sandwiched between a rubber holder and a sponge pad moistened with salt solution, were attached to the felon's shaven head, and the base of the spine. After a black hood had been positioned over the face, the switch was operated, sending a current of 700 volts through the body for about seventeen seconds; after a brief respite a further charge of 1,030 volts was then delivered, with fatal results, although the body was badly burned.

Later experiments to improve conductivity were tried, some victims having their hands immersed in jars of saltwater to which electric wires were connected, but this was discontinued when it was ascertained that three electrodes, to the head and each ankle, were sufficient. Similarly a leather helmet lined with copper screening and damp sponging, wired to the circuitry, was designed, and the requisite voltage finally determined: two one-minute charges of 2,000 volts, with a ten-second interval would, it was estimated, bring about near-instantaneous death, although on occasions, more 'jolts' were needed.

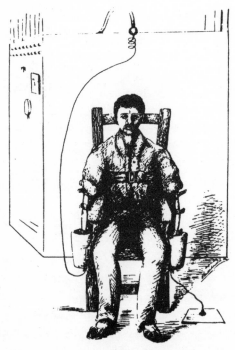

Early Electric Chair

APPENDIX 2: TYPES OF PUNISHMENT AND EXECUTION

Execution Sword

Although rarely used for judicial executions in England, the most notable being that of Queen Anne Boleyn, the sword was widely employed on the Continent for dispatching those condemned to death. Had it been adopted in England, much unimaginable suffering by the axe's victims could have been avoided, for, in contrast, the execution sword was a finely honed and superbly balanced instrument of death. About three feet or more in length, it weighed approximately four pounds; the blade, two inches wide, had parallel cutting edges and a broad, blunt tip, no point being necessary to achieve its purpose. A fuller, a wide groove, ran longitudinally along each side to allow the blood to flow towards the handle and not coagulate and so blunt the razor-sharp edges. The comparatively long handle, designed to be gripped with both hands, was covered with leather or fish-skin to provide a non-slip surface, the quillons, the guards, being wide and straight.

Contrary to popular belief the victim did not kneel over a block. Had he or she done so, the headsman himself would also have had to kneel and deliver a vertical blow inevitably lacking the force necessary to decapitate his victim. And if, instead of kneeling, he had stood erect, the blade would have struck the further edge of the block rather than the victim's neck. The procedure therefore was for the victim to kneel upright or to stand, the executioner swinging the blade horizontally round his head once or twice to gain the necessary momentum before delivering the fatal stroke. If undue suffering and horrific flesh wounds were to be avoided, cooperation by the victim was essential, for if he or she swayed or trembled too violently, more than one blow would be required.

Firing Squad

Depending on the country, firing squads vary in both size and armament, from one man with a pistol, two men with machine guns, to up to twelve men with rifles. Sometimes the target is the back of the victim's neck, the head or the heart. Generally, the firing squad is of eight to a dozen men, usually but not always soldiers, standing six yards or so from the victim, who is blindfolded and tied to a post, with a circular piece of white cloth over the heart as an aiming point. Rifles are collected at random by members of the firing squad, one weapon traditionally being loaded with a blank, reputedly to salve their consciences, enabling them to persuade themselves that they were not responsible for the victim's death, but with modern weaponry a blank-loaded rifle does not 'kick' as does one with a live round, nor is the cartridge ejected from the weapon.

The signal is given by the officer in charge by word of command, the hand, a wave of a cane or handkerchief, depending on the circumstances. The sergeant in charge of the squad is armed with a pistol and, should the victim show signs of life after the fusillade of shots, he has the responsibility of administering the *coup de grâce*, a shot to the temple.

Gas Chamber

This basically consists of a small airtight room made of steel, with two plate-glass observation windows – one for the benefit of the spectators, the other for officials to ensure that the execution is proceeding according to plan – and a chimney to vent the fumes afterwards. It is virtually a room within a room, resembling a space capsule just large enough to contain one or more chairs bolted to the floor, together with other essential equipment, one of the items being a container of sulphuric acid.

The victims are secured to the chairs by straps and after the officials have vacated the chamber, the door is closed tightly, hermetically sealing the room. The executioner, stationed in an adjoining room, operates a red-painted lever which, through linkwork, rotates a long rod extending into the gas chamber, thereby allowing it to lower a cloth sachet of sodium cyanide pellets into the acid, the resultant chemical reaction generating hydrogen cyanide, prussic acid (HCN). Exposure to three hundred parts of this toxic cocktail to one million parts of air is fatal, and even if the victim attempts to hold their breath, the longer they attempt to do so, the deeper the eventual breath – and the more rapid the death from asphyxiation.

This method of execution poses various hazards for those in the immediate vicinity. To ensure that only the victim dies by being gassed and not the officials and spectators as well, it is essential that the chamber is completely air-tight, that the seals around the chimney and operating rod, and in particular those around the door and the two windows, are totally effective. To further reduce the risk of a gas leakage, a pump to reduce the air pressure slightly inside the chamber is sometimes incorporated, so that a faulty seal would result in air being sucked in, rather than allowing the poisonous gas to leak out.

Nor do the risks end when the execution is over. For having to handle a victim after execution by the rope, electric chair, lethal injection or even broken on the wheel, might not be pleasant, but is at least safe and straightforward; picking up the component body parts after the sword, axe or guillotine had done their work must have been messy in the extreme, but was hardly dangerous to the individual involved; but carrying out the same tasks after a gas chamber execution is fraught with risks. Although powerful pumps extract the gas via the chimney before anyone re-enters the chamber, not only does the gas tend to condense on the walls and floor, but the clothes worn by the victim, even his or her very skin, become impregnated with the highly toxic prussic acid. All the surfaces within the room and the corpse itself have to be sprayed with neutralising bleach or ammonia, and the members of the prison staff detailed to remove the body have to wear protective clothing and oxygen masks.

Gibbet

This consisted of an upright with an arm at right-angles at the top resembling a signpost, on which was displayed a criminal's body as a deterrent. Where men and women conspired together to commit crimes, only the man faced being gibbeted, the woman being hanged; in the case of Catherine Hayes, described in this book, her two male accomplices, Wood and Billings, were gibbeted.

The corpse was initially enclosed in 'irons', a man-sized cage of narrow iron straps; the author Albert Hartshorne in his book *Hanging in Chains*, published in 1891, related that 'the irons were made to measure before the execution, and many a strong man who had stood fearless under the dread sentence of death, broke down when measured for his irons.' The procedure at Newgate Prison was to cut down the cadaver from the gallows and take it to the 'kitchen' where it was immersed in a cauldron of boiling tar or pitch, in order to preserve it for as long as possible against the ravages of birds and the weather. It was then placed in the irons, the ends of the iron straps being cold-riveted together tightly around the corpse by the prison blacksmith, after which it was suspended from the gibbet arm by a chain until it slowly rotted away, the smaller bones of the limbs first dropping out of the cage, followed later by the hips, shoulder blades, and finally by the skull. Gibbets, which were erected all over the country, usually on a hill or at crossroads, presented a macabre sight to passers-by, the creaking of the chains a terrifying sound at night.

The Gibbet

Guillotine

Introduced in France just in time for the multiple executions resultant upon the Revolution, the basic guillotine consisted of two six-inch thick oak uprights, ten feet high and secured by a crosspiece, mounted on a high wooden base. An inch-deep groove, cut vertically down the inner surfaces of each upright, provided the channels down which the triangular shaped blade travelled. This blade was six inches in depth and weighed fifteen pounds, with an iron block weighing 65 pounds mounted on top in order to maximise the speed of descent.

FEMALE EXECUTIONS

The blade was held in the raised position by a rope which passed through a ring on its top, each end passing through brass pulleys installed high up on each upright, the two lengths of rope then hanging down the outsides of the uprights and secured there. A block of wood, four inches wide and eight inches deep, scooped out to accommodate the victim's throat, was bolted to the base between the uprights. A transverse groove cut across its top allowed the falling blade to be brought to a shuddering halt after it had passed through the victim's neck, and attached to one side of this block was a hinged iron crescent, the lunette (so-called because it resembled a half-moon), which pressed the neck down, thereby holding the head immobile.

A narrow bench extended from the neck block at right-angles to the uprights, and at its free end was hinged a plank, the bascule, against which the victim was held facing the guillotine while his or her body and legs were quickly strapped to it. The plank was then rapidly pivoted into a horizontal position and slid forward, thereby placing the victim's neck between the two uprights. The iron crescent was instantly dropped into place, and on the release of the rope, the blade would descend, the severed head falling into the waiting basket. The torso was then rolled by the executioner's assistants into a full-length wicker basket positioned next to the guillotine, into which the head would also be transferred after having first been held high for the crowd's acclaim and abuse, the remains later being taken away for an ignominious burial.

So effective was the 'Widow Maker' that, after minor modifications had been incorporated, Monsieur de Paris, the executioner Charles-Henri Sanson, who had dedicated himself to dispatching his aristocratic victims as speedily and therefore as mercifully as possible, perfected his expertise to the extent that eventually he and his highly organised team of assistants were capable of executing 12 victims in 13 minutes, 20 in 42

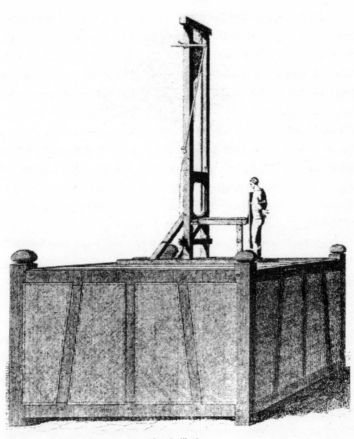

The Guillotine

minutes, 300 in three days and 1,300 in six weeks – a veritable production line of death. This was an incredible achievement when it is realised that these timings included not only the time taken by the actual decapitations, but also by Sanson having to go down the scaffold steps each time, call out the name of the next victim waiting patiently in line, shepherd them up the steps – not easy, their arms being bound behind them – and then manoeuvre them into position facing the bascule, to which they had to be secured.

Hanging

This is possibly the oldest method of execution. In twelfth-century England the gallows generally consisted of two uprights joined by a crossbeam capable of accommodating up to ten victims at a time. They would be forced to mount a ladder propped against the beam, the hangman's assistant, straddling the beam, would position the rough hempen rope with its primitive slip knot around their necks, and the hangman would twist the ladder, 'turning off ' the victim, death coming slowly and agonisingly by strangulation. As a concession the hangman would sometimes permit the victim's friends or servants to hasten the end by pulling the victim's legs or thumping the chest, the body then left for an hour before being cut down.

The general practice was to execute the criminal as near as possible to where he or she had committed the crime, but eventually more permanent sites were established in open areas rather than in the narrow streets and lanes, in order to accommodate the vast crowds that would inevitably gather. London's chief execution site was Tyburn, its name being derived from Ty-bourn, a small stream that once flowed there. The area was originally called 'The Elms', the stream being bordered by elm trees, a variety considered by the Normans to be the tree of justice, and being situated by the main road leading into the capital from the northwest, it was obvious that the spectacle of the scaffold and the corpses of those who had recently been hanged, swaying on the gibbets there, would have the greatest deterrent effect on visitors entering the City.

Its precise site is difficult to determine, but there is little doubt that the scaffold itself stood near the junction of Edgeware Road and Oxford Street (the latter once named 'Tyburn Way') and in fact, should one venture on to the small traffic island there, a plaque will be found, set in the cobbles. But in view of the fast-moving traffic, extreme caution should be exercised lest yet another tombstone should bear the inscription 'Died at Tyburn'!

Site of Tyburn Gallows

In 1571, in order to increase production – or rather, extermination – the Tyburn gallows were modified, a third upright and crossbar joining the other two, this triangular arrangement allowing a maximum of 24 felons to be hanged at the same time, eight from each arm. This device was christened the Triple Tree, and colloquially as the three-legged mare, the three-legged stool, and the deadly evergreen (because it bore fruit all the year round). The ladder method was also replaced, the victims being brought to the scaffold in a cart which halted beneath the gallows just long enough for the malefactors to be noosed; the horse would then receive a smart slap on the flanks, causing it to move away and take the cart, but not the passengers, with it.

The last execution took place there on 7 November 1783, after which, due to the expansion of the City's residential suburbs into the Tyburn area, the site was moved to Newgate Prison, executions still being carried out in public outside the walls of that gaol on a portable scaffold which, when required, was erected not unlike a flat-packed piece of furniture, albeit for much more sinister use, by twenty men who started the work at 10 p.m. the night before, completing it by 7 a.m. the following morning, for which each labourer received a pint of porter (a dark, sweet ale brewed from black malt) and the princely sum of 6s 8d.

Triple Tree, Tyburn

The platform was equipped with two parallel crossbeams positioned over the trapdoors: the 'drop'. These were eight feet wide and ten feet long, large enough to accommodate ten felons, and were designed to fall when a short lever was operated. After being hooded – to conceal their contorted features from the vast crowd of spectators – and noosed, the victims were allowed to fall a mere three or four feet, thereby dying a slow, lingering death by strangulation, watched by the sheriff and other officials who sat in the comfortable seats arranged at one side of the scaffold.

In England this inhumane 'short drop' method remained unaltered until late in the nineteenth century, when executioner

APPENDIX 2: TYPES OF PUNISHMENT AND EXECUTION

William Marwood introduced the more merciful 'long drop' method in which the distance the victim had to fall depended on his or her age, weight, build and general fitness – usually between six and ten feet – death coming almost instantly by the dislocation of the neck's vertebrae and severance of the spinal cord.

The last public execution in England took place on 26 May 1868. After that date all executions took place behind prison walls, a state of affairs deplored by the public at thus being deprived of what they considered to be their rightful – and free – entertainment, and equally deplored by those who supported the abolition of capital punishment altogether, claiming that being in private, without independent witnesses, executions would become even more brutal.

In the United States of America methods differed widely; most states employed the English method introduced by the early colonists, others diversified. In the 1920s in Connecticut, a diametrically opposite system was employed whereby, instead of falling, the victim was jerked rapidly upwards. It consisted of a noose formed at the end of a 50-foot long rope leading up through the ceiling of the execution chamber and down into an adjoining room, there to pass over a drum which incorporated a ratchet mechanism. At that end of the rope a weight equal to that of the victim was attached and was retained three feet above the floor, held there by linkwork controlled by a foot pedal. At the signal, pressure on the pedal released the weight, the abrupt jerk usually breaking the victim's neck instantly and propelling the body up to a height of about twelve feet. The drum mechanism would then allow the corpse to be lowered and released from the rope.

A method used earlier in that state involved the noosed and bound victim standing on a small hatch, their weight releasing a quantity of lead shot which rolled rapidly down a slope until its weight exceeded that of the victim and so operated the release of the hatch. Although this method thereby absolved any particular individual of self-induced blame for the death of the victim, it meant that the condemned person was virtually committing suicide and so was discontinued.

In New York State the traditional system was employed, but the drop lever was operated by an official screened from the victim's view; this anonymity method was also adopted by California, three cubicles being occupied by a guard, each pulling a lever, only one of which caused the trapdoors to open. Other American methods involved not a lever, but a hatchet, which fell, severing the rope. Those who had conspired in the assassination of President Lincoln were dispatched in an even more primitive way. On a platform twenty feet long and fifteen feet wide, the three men and one woman, bound and hooded, their nooses around their necks, stood on the long trapdoors beneath the beam positioned ten feet above the scaffold boards. The trapdoors were held level with the boards by vertical uprights beneath them, and when the officer in charge clapped his hands three times, the four soldiers beneath the scaffold kicked the blocks away, with the inevitable and fatal results.

Hanged, Drawn and Quartered

This was the penalty in England and Scotland for those who, by plotting to overthrow the sovereign by whatever means, were charged with having committed high treason. The method of execution was barbaric in the extreme, as exemplified by the death sentence passed in 1660 on the regicides who had signed the death warrant of Charles I in 1649:

Hanged, Drawn and Quartered

That you be led to the place from whence you came, and from there drawn upon a hurdle to the place of execution, and then you shall be hanged by the neck and, still being alive, shall be cut down, and your privy parts to be cut off, and your entrails be taken out of your body and, you being living, the same to be burned before your eyes, and your head to be cut off, and your body to be divided into four quarters, and head and shoulders to be disposed of at the pleasure of the King. And may the Lord have mercy on your soul.

Such appalling punishments were inflicted only on men; women were excused on grounds of modesty, the reason, as phrased by the contemporary chronicler Sir William Blackstone, being 'for the decency due to the sex forbids the exposure and publicly mangling their bodies'. They were publicly burned instead.

The 'cutting off of the privy parts' was a symbolic act to signify that, following such mutilation, the traitor would be unable to father children who might inherit his treasonable nature; hardly necessary in view of his imminent decapitation.

Heads on London Bridge

After the half-strangling, evisceration and dismembering of the victim, the severed body parts were displayed in public as deterrents to others who might attempt such foolhardy acts against the sovereign. The heads, after being boiled in saltwater with cumin seed to repel the attentions of scavenging birds, were exhibited in the marketplace or a similar venue in the cities in which the traitors had lived and plotted, the quarters being hung on the gates of those cities.

In the capital they were spiked on London Bridge, where they remained for months until thrown into the River Thames by the Bridge watchman, usually to make room for new arrivals. The Bridge was chosen as the most appropriate venue because for over six centuries it was the only river crossing in London and formed a continuation of Watling Street, the Roman road which traversed Kent from the Channel coast. As at Tyburn, the grisly exhibits were visible warnings to all entering the City of the awful retribution meted out to those who came with criminal intent, or sought to overthrow the realm.

Lethal Injection

More a hospital operation than an execution, except for the sinister overtones of the wide straps attached to the trolley, by which the 'patient' is then secured! The process commences with the condemned person initially receiving an injection of saline solution and a later one of antihistamine, the former to ease the passage of the drugs, the latter to counteract the coughing experienced following the injection of those drugs.

Some little time later the actual execution sequence begins. First an injection of sodium thiopentone, a rapid acting anaesthetic, is administered via a sixteen-gauge needle and catheter inserted into an appropriate vein. The victim next receives pancuronium bromide; this not only has the effect of relaxing the muscles, but also paralyses the respiration and brings about unconsciousness. One minute later, potassium chloride is injected, which stops the heart. This sequence results in the victim becoming unconscious within ten to fifteen seconds, death resulting from respiratory and cardiac arrest within two to four minutes – but only if the correct dosages and intervals between injections are strictly adhered to, otherwise the chemical make-up of the drugs changes adversely.

The risk of such mishaps were ever-present when the drugs were manually administered, but were eliminated to a great extent by a talented technician named Fred Leuchter who invented an automatic, computerised machine which, by controlling an intricate system of syringes and tubing, injects the correct amount of chemicals at precisely the right moment.

Fail-safe devices and a manual back-up arrangement are also incorporated in the system, and a doctor stationed behind a screen constantly monitors the victim's heart condition, thereby being able to confirm the moment of death.

Just as in a Californian execution by hanging, where a conscience-salving let-out is provided by having three guards in separate cubicles, each pulling a lever, only one of which actually opens the trapdoors, so in an execution by lethal injection two identical systems are used, neither operator knowing which one is functioning.

Apart from problems brought about either by human error or the malfunctioning of components of the system, difficulties also arise in inserting the syringes into the correct vein, especially where it is narrow or unattainable due to prolonged drug taking by the criminal. It is frequently necessary to make an incision in the flesh and lift the vein out in order to insert the needle.

Pillory

The Pillory, Whipping Post and Stocks

Specifically designed to publicly humiliate offenders, the town or village pillory was usually sited in the market square for the purpose of punishing those who committed 'community' crimes: 'if the culprit be a witch, a purveyor of putrid meat, stinking fish, innkeepers whose spirit measures contained a layer of pitch at the base, and coalmen whose sacks were narrower or shorter than the regulation size.'

Although various designs existed, the pillory usually consisted of a wooden post set firmly in the ground or on a platform, having at its top two horizontal boards mounted edge to edge, the uppermost one being hinged at one end to the lower one. Each had three semi-circular holes cut in it which matched up when the upper board was lowered. The victim stood immediately behind the post, his or her head being positioned in the central semi-circular aperture, the wrists similarly placed in the outer cut-outs; the upper board was then lowered and locked into place. The outer holes were strategically positioned far enough from the central hole to prevent the culprit from protecting his or her face from any missiles thrown, such as eggs, rotten fruit, or even dead cats. This shaming device, its name derived from the Greek meaning 'to look through a doorway', was considered so important by the government of the day that villages lacking one risked losing their right to hold a market, a vital asset to local traders.

Of widespread use in England until it was abolished in 1837, many people suffered in the 'Stretchneck', among them being a procuress who, in 1556, was found guilty 'of supplying harlots to citizens, apprentices and servants' and was pilloried (it seems that to supply gentlemen with such ladies of the night was permissible!). Four years later a maid who poisoned her mistress not only stood in the pillory but was also branded and had both ears cropped. Inevitably, things got out of hand; in 1731 Mother Needham, a notorious procuress with a ten-year criminal record, was pilloried, the crowd wreaking its own form of social justice by stoning her to death.

German women also suffered that form of public disgrace, as Marie Kurschnerin, described elsewhere in this book, found out before being hanged. She was secured in the pillory by the executioner's assistant, the Löwe, so named because he roared like a lion as he dragged his victim along to the scaffold.

Scottish Maiden

Its name was perhaps derived from the Celtic mod-dun, the place where justice was administered. Made of oak, the maiden consisted

The Scottish Maiden

of a five-foot-long horizontal beam to which were fixed two ten-foot-long posts mounted vertically, these being four inches wide by three and a half inches thick, bevelled at their corners. These were sited twelve inches apart and braced by two further lengths of timber attached to the horizontal beam, being secured to the uprights at a height of four feet from the ground. A further brace at the rear held the machine in the upright position, it being attached to a cross rail which joined the two posts together. The axe blade, an iron plate faced with steel, thirteen inches in length and ten and a half inches in breadth, its upper side weighted with a 75-pound block of lead, travelled in the copper-lined grooves cut in the inner surfaces of the posts and was retained at the top by a peg attached to a long cord which, when pulled by means of a lever, allowed the blade to descend at ever-increasing speed.

Three and a quarter feet from the ground a further crossbar joined the two posts, serving as a support for the victim's neck. This beam, eight inches broad and four and a half inches thick, had a wide groove cut in its upper surface filled with lead to resist the impact of the falling blade after it had passed through the flesh, muscle and spinal column. To prevent the victim withdrawing his or her head, an iron bar, hinged to one upright, was lowered and secured to the other upright before the peg was withdrawn and sentence carried out.

FOR THE RECORD

1298 – First witchcraft trial in England

1450 – First recorded use of the Tower rack

1547 – Abolition of boiling to death in England

1640 – Use of torture discontinued in England, except by royal prerogative

1649 – Greatest number hanged at one time in England: Tyburn, London,
23 men, 1 woman

1686 – Last hanging for witchcraft in England: Alice Molland

1690 – Last recorded torture in Scotland

1697 – Last burning alive for heresy in England

1708 – Abolition of torture in Scotland

1712 – Last trial for witchcraft in England: Jane Wenham, reprieved

1722 – Last witch believed to be burned in Scotland

1789 – Last woman burned in England: Christian Murphy, coiner

1790 – Abolition of burning in England of women for husband-murder

1791 – Abolition of death penalty for witchcraft in England

1798 – Abolition of torture in France

1809 – Last recorded ducking of scolds in England: Jenny Pipes

1814 – Abolition of beheading in England

1817 – Last person sentenced to ducking stool in England: Sarah Leeke
(reprieved, water too shallow, so no Leeke in the pond!)

1817 – Last recorded public flogging of a woman in England

FEMALE EXECUTIONS

1820 – Abolition of whipping of women in United Kingdom

1827 – Abolition of peine forte et dure in England

1829 – Abolition of branding in England, other than under military law

1832 – Abolition of dissection after hanging in England

1834 – Abolition of gibbeting in England

1837 – Abolition of the pillory in England

1879 – Total abolition of branding in England

1955 – Last woman hanged in United Kingdom: Ruth Ellis for murder

1955 – First woman hanged in new Republic of India, Rattan Bai Jain, for murder

SELECT BIBLIOGRAPHY

Abbott, G. *Family of Death* (Hale, 1995)

Abbott, G. *Rack, Rope and Red-Hot Pincers* (Headline,1993/Dobby 2002)

Abbott, G. *The Book of Execution* (Headline, 1994)

Andrews, W. *England in Days of Old* (Andrews, 1897)

Andrews, W. *Old Time Punishments* (Andrews, 1890)

Anon *The Record of Crimes, Judgements, Providences & Calamities* (London, 1825)

Barington, S. *Errors and Executioners* (David & Layton, 1909)

Berry, J. *My Experiences as an Executioner* (Percy Lund, 1892)

Bleakley, H. *Hangmen of England* (Chapman & Hall, 1929)

Brendon, M. *Loose Women and Tight Nooses* (Finkle Press, 1922)

Bryan, G. *Off with His Head!* (Hutchinson, 1934)

Calcraft, W. *The Life & Recollections of William Calcraft* (1870)

Camm, Dom. *Forgotten Shrines* (Macdonald, Evans, 1910)

Carment, J. *Glimpses of the Olden Times* (Jackson, 1893)

Christeson, R. *Treatise on Poisons* (A & C Black, 1836)

Croker, J. W. *History of the Guillotine* (Murray, 1853)

Davey, R. *The Tower of London* (1910)

Duff, C. *A Handbook on Hanging* (Freedom Press, 1948)

Eaton, H. *Famous Poison Trials* (Collins 1932)

FEMALE EXECUTIONS

Elliott, R. G. *Agent of Death* (John Long, 1941)

Evelyn, J. *Evelyn's Diary* (Bickers, Bush, 1879)

Ferrier, J. *Crooks and Crime* (Seeley, Service, 1928)

Glueck, S. & E. *500 Delinquent Women* (Knopf, 1934)

Gordon, C. *The Old Bailey and Newgate* (Fisher Unwin, 1902)

Holinshed, *R. Chronicles* (1586)

Howard, J. *State of the Prisons* (Dent, 1929)

Jackson, W. *The New & Complete Newgate Calendar* (London, 1818)

Johnson, W. B. *The Age of Arsenic* (Chapman, Hall, 1931)

Lacroix, P. *Manners, Customs and Dress in the Middle Ages* (1874)

Lawes, L. E. *Twenty Thousand Years in Sing Sing* (Constable, 1932)

Lenotre, G. *The Guillotine and Its Servants* (Hutchinson, 1929)

Machyn, H. *Diary of a London Resident* (Camden Society, 1848)

Marks, A. *Tyburn Tree* (Brown, Langham, 1908)

Milburn, J. B. *A Martyr of Old York* (Burns & Oates, 1900)

Oldfield, J. *The Penalty of Death* (1901)

Quinby, I. *Murder for Love* (Covici-Friede, 1931)

Schmidt, F. *A Hangman's Diary* (Philip Allan, 1928)

Sanson, H. *Memoirs of the Sansons* (Chatto & Windus, 1876)

Stow, J. *A Survey of London* (1720)

Swain, J. *Pleasures of the Torture Chamber* (Douglas, 1931)

Timbs, J. *Curiosities of London* (1855)

Verdène, G. *La Torture* (French edition) (R. Dorn, Paris, 1906)

Younghusband, Sir G. *The Tower of London from Within* (Jenkins, 1918)

Saturday Magazine series, 1833

Tyburn Gallows, London County Council, 1909

Calendar of State Papers, Domestic Series

Tower of London Records

Police Gazette series

INDEX

FEMALE EXECUTIONS

INDEX

FEMALE EXECUTIONS

EXECUTION
A Guide to The Ultimate Penalty

Geoffrey Abbott

£9.99
Paperback
ISBN: 978-1-84953-255-6

Execution is a gruesomely fascinating account of methods of judicial execution from around the world and through the ages, and includes such hair-raising categories as death by cannibalism, being sewn into an animal's belly and a thousand cuts.

In his own darkly humorous style, Geoffrey Abbott describes the instruments used and their effectiveness, and reveals the macabre origins of familiar phrases such as 'gone west' or 'drawn a blank', as well as the jargon of the underworld.

From the preparation of the victim to the disposal of the body, this book combines genuine historical detail and gory descriptions of both ancient and modern forms of execution and answers all the questions you are ever likely to ask, and some you would never want to imagine.

'A valuable and first-class book.'
        John J. Eddleston, author of *The Encyclopaedia of Executions*

Have you enjoyed this book?
If so, why not write a review on your favourite website?

If you're interested in finding out more about our books, find us
on Facebook at **Summersdale Publishers** and
follow us on Twitter at **@Summersdale**.

Thanks very much for buying this Summersdale book.

www.summersdale.com